BROKEN
SILENCE

A Triumphant Journey of a Human Trafficking Victim
to an Inspirational Advocate

BROKEN SILENCE

A Triumphant Journey of a Human Trafficking Victim
to an Inspirational Advocate

CHONG KIM

CK Publishing

BROKEN SILENCE: A Triumphant Journey of a Human Trafficking Victim to an Inspirational Advocate

ISBN: 978-0-615-96737-0

Editing: Get Write LLC

Cover Design: Erica Niwa

Printed in the United States of America.

"How can I feel empowered, when my brothers and sisters are still oppressed?"

- C. Kim

Disclaimer:

Names, places, and circumstances have been changed for confidentiality reasons and to protect the innocent. This book does contain some use of profanity along with sexual, rape and violent contents, please read with caution. Thank you.

- C. Kim

PRAISE FOR BROKEN SILENCE

"When hearing of the despair and inhuman posture Chong was subjected to, our hearts were filled with compassion. We applaud Chong for using her heart-wrenching pain for a greater purpose of educating on the topic of human trafficking. The lives of women will be touched and we pray they find freedom in breaking the silence."

Tim and Sherice Brown
Professional Football Hall of Fame

"As Chong Kim writes, *Broken Silence* is not an easy read, but let me tell you, it is a book you will not be able to put down. It is the story of a young girl's degradation, ruin, and subjugation beginning with a most difficult family and segueing into years of imprisonment and sexual slavery. But Chong Kim rises, above the exquisite pain—emotional and physical—and emerges on the other side, an example of the ability of the human spirit to heal itself and to then bring healing to others."

Sheila Isenberg
Author, *Muriel's War*
Director of Media Relations,
Woodstock Comedy Festival (Comedy for a Cause)

In the darkness of untold stories, Chong Kim shines a light into the world of capture in the world of human trafficking and what it took to survive. We must know this story, so bravely and determinately told.

Tantoo Cardinal
Actress
Dances with Wolves, Legends of the Fall and *Eden*

"Chong's story is a testimony of how even in the darkest moments of our lives, a ray of hope can shine. She has been through hell on earth through her trafficking ordeal, but it was incredible to hear God how healed her and set her free, not just physically but spiritually and for all eternity. Her life is a miracle and it is beautiful to see how she now provides hope, strength, and healing to others who have been down that same road. I amazed every time I talk with her because she is filled with so much joy, love, and laughter. She has been transformed and it is a blessing to see how her life is now transforming others."

Rev. Dr. Eddie Byun
Lead Pastor, Crossway Mission Church
Professor of Practical Theology,
Torch Trinity Graduate University
Author of *Justice Awakening* and *Praying for Your Pastor*

"*Broken Silence*" is riveting and, at times, filled with such pain, that the reader needs to step away and take a breath. Excellently written! Ms. Kim's life story gently takes her readers by the hand and leads them into her world. There, they are held captive as silent witnesses to abuses and trauma as seen through the eyes of both a child and an adult. The reader quickly comes to understand the vulnerabilities which are thus created and lead to further abuse, risk, abduction, addiction, and the hidden-in-plain-sight reality that is human trafficking. Those who suffer in silence, are trapped in an ongoing cycle of abuse well into adulthood, who fall asleep and wake up to another day of addiction, find themselves misunderstood, homeless, unspoken for, suicidal, hurting, afraid, lonely, oppressed and suppressed, who've lost their identities, and even their sense of self entirely... this is also a story for them. Heart-wrenching, eye-opening, a "must-read" for anyone, particularly those working with at-risk populations, her story will leave you breathless and with an entirely different view of not only the world, but your own neighborhood and community as well.

Sandi M. Heikkinen
B.S.W.

But now,
this is what the Lord says…
"Do not fear,
for I have redeemed you;
I have summoned you by name;
you are mine."

- Isaiah 43:1 (NIV)

Broken Silence

Sojourning through life in a quest for love,
longing acceptance in a world full of sorrow...
Rejected by loved ones in a domestic nightmare;
A vision of solitude in a quarry of tears...

Care to the wind in an unknown world;
into the arms of a savior, at last...
A soul is weighed in a perilous balance,
gasps for life were drowned by such fury.

Days became months in a hell of "why's"
released by a neighbor after desperate cries...
Wandering the streets, rejected by shelters;
Identities burned, existence was silenced...

One, so sincere, witnessed the needs,
approaching lovingly, benevolent kindness...
The words seemed so honest, a hand stretched forth:
Grasping it with faith, true life was at hand...

The months went by being trafficked and sold;
the endless nightmare of clients and slavery.
Greeted by hopelessness at every turn;
a dungeon of horrors, threats, and death.

From city to city a traveling brothel;
the souls of the lost in a tapestry of darkness.
Fleeing a client who knew all the ropes:
Eyes blinded by the god of money...

The song of revenge birthed a glamorous Madame;
total control of a deceptive kingdom...
Creating an empire once loathed through despair;
flashback's reality launched the escape.

Giving possessions to people in need;
lights from a distance with its riches and emptiness.
From church to church in various states,
pleading for help in a plight for freedom.

Broken and battered eluding fierce captors,
a book of Numbers became a good friend.
Destiny led to the "Breaking Away;"
perceiving a victim, embracing a being.

Frightened and lonely, they consoled out of love;
tears of healing, a spirit of joy...
Years have gone by with the will to survive;
enduring the pain, reaching out to others.

Telling this story to shine forth the light,
freeing the captives to live once again.
Breaking the shackles of those still bound;
finding true love in the rescue of others...

11-26-05

This book is dedicated to my children:

Angelica & AJ

Because of you,
Your existence alone inspired me
To be the fighter I am today.
Without you,
I would not be the mother
I fought so hard to be.

Love,
Mom

ACKNOWLEDGEMENTS

First and foremost, I want to thank God for loving me unconditionally, showing me my path, and giving me strength to overcome anything. I thank You so much for loving me above all else.

Mrs. McKenzie, my 3rd grade teacher who did everything she could to prove that I could make it on the honor roll. Because of you, I was encouraged to do better.

Ms. Carolyn, your humming brought me sunshine. Because of you, I have now become a fan of Eric Clapton. Thank you for being my advocate.

Nancy Miller, you took a chance on me and a risk you felt was worthwhile. You showed me that I am worth love, redemption, and respect. I can't thank you enough for believing in me.

Carl, Brian, Tim and Nancy Spain, thank you for encouraging me, challenging me and loving me even when I was difficult to love back. You are still family to me.

Dillon Burroughs, thank you for encouraging me to share my testimony, no matter how ugly the truth is.

Dan Schneider, thank you for being more than my advocate, but also a friend, encouraging me and always being there for me.

Sheila Isenberg, thank you for your ongoing encouragement, support, and endorsement. I am in awe of you from one writer to another.

Christina MacKenzie, thank you so much for having ears to hear, eyes to see my worth, and being my friend when things got real tough. You are definitely my sister-in-Christ. I appreciate and love all that you do.

Marla, Scott, and Joy, thank you for all you have contributed, shared, and for all the encouragement you brought to the table as I wrote this book.

All of the Survivors from Abuse to Exploitation: This book is definitely an acknowledgement to you and you have also encouraged me to fight on.

Pastor Foster Arne Allen (RIP). You were not just a pastor to me, but my brother-in-Christ. You always reminded me to "keep thriving" and so that I will do, my brother. You are surely missed.

Eboni, even though you are not here, I guarantee that your name will not be in silence, nor your existence, and how you have impacted my life. We will always be sisters.

Amaya Allen, you continue to encourage me with your insights, your humor, and your smile. I am so honored to see you grow and learn and thankful you have welcomed me in your life.

Willie, Angela, and Monica; my mother, my two amazing sisters (in Christ), since the beginning of our friendship, no matter what has gone on around us, you all continually keep me lifted in prayer and love. Thank you so much.

To my father, you have taught me so much even in circumstances I didn't understand. I miss your lectures and history lessons. Your humbleness and stepping out of the box encouraged me to be like you. You are my hero.

My last acknowledgement goes to the rest of my family; every one of you influenced me and shaped my life in different ways. The challenges that we have all faced; the ups and downs and so forth is a life lesson. I love you all.

Overall, I want to thank all my followers and change makers on social media and those who believe my worth, my testimony and my voice. I can't thank you enough. Without your encouragement, I wouldn't have gotten this book done. I appreciate you all and I hope those who read my book will find encouragement, inspiration and some life lessons. Thank you.

TABLE OF CONTENTS

PREFACE

As I begin to share the in-depth details of my story, please bear with me. The narrative will jump at times from one moment in time into a flashback mode. I apologize for this confusion, but I believe this may actually convey some of the damage that was done to my memory and bring you deeper into how it feels to be me. Even today, I often have memory lapses, and my recollections do not always flow in chronological order.

As I sit here putting pen to paper and move through the process of countless rewrites of this memoir, it has been a long journey for me to make sense of what I remember. I'm learning to write more proficiently and eloquently and in artistic detail that will fully capture my recovery from abuse to survival and eventual transformation into a butterfly. It isn't easy writing about trauma, especially when you have to force your mind to recount the abuse you worked so hard to eliminate from your memory. Many times, I'd wished for amnesia so that I couldn't remember the painful memories at all.

Spoken word and writing poetry have been passions of mine since I can remember; it was the outlet for my anger and my pain. I would write little journals here and there since I was a young girl. I always admired the thought of a girl owning her own diary with a lock in the front.

My mother never liked the idea of having a diary. She said keeping secrets were poisonous in a relationship and I believe she was right. Perhaps she didn't quite follow her own advice since she held many secrets that I later discovered throughout my journey of personal discovery. I still strive for the sort of honesty she preached even as she might have failed in its execution. Journals, however, are more about catharsis, and their magic appeals to me to this day. As such, I fully embrace poetic descriptions, and I have crafted the dialogue in my narrative to convey the emotional impact I remember having in each given moment.

There have been many times when I have contemplated the idea of publishing an autobiography, only to turn away from it before completion. My reasons for turning away were not because it wasn't good enough, but because of the cultural stigma I felt from my family, from other Asian communities and from other individuals who were close to my family. As I now move past those restrictions, I want to make it clear that I'm not here to exploit my family at all. My reason to share is to empower others, including ethnic groups who suffer from the same cultural stigma of which I'm speaking. It is to empower those who are given reasons not to speak, especially among Asian-American women who confront the exotic negative stereotypes that are transmitted through media and reinforced by their upbringing to obey the status quo and avoid causing disruption.

After my personal experience of being the "China Doll," I became exhausted with this self-imposed racism that is glamorized within the Asian community, along with some other ethnic groups. I refuse to sit by and pretend it's okay, especially when it serves to cloak the actions of others who continue to make victims of those very ethnic groups. If that means I have to be the one to speak out about it, then that is what I will do.

I was never trained for such writing. My mother was a homemaker, and this was considered the accepted norm. My father was a workaholic. Most Asian families that I personally knew were the same: the women worked at home, remained silent and were told what to do and what was expected of her. Most of my first lessons in my childhood reflected the intention that I would become the same.

I don't know where I learned to be outspoken, but it was not welcomed or praised. If I spoke out about something that I felt was wrong, I was constantly "shushed." This is one of the many reasons why I'm sharing today. As such, when it comes to writing a memoir or autobiography, I'm learning the steps as I go. As a first-time author, we shall go on this roller coaster ride together.

I am constantly reminded that sharing my story is a good thing. Along with transparency comes enduring the criticism of readers and critics, the judgment of my past, and having to put myself through the humility of complete honesty. This is all to let my readers know what I was thinking, feeling, how I expressed my anger, and how I chose to survive. That includes what methods I had to embrace and what moral values I had to sacrifice in order to do what I felt was right at the time. I can only hope that I have managed to craft this book well enough so that it can do its job of getting this message across to all who need to hear it.

If you want to know what truly inspired me to write my story, it was a movie that triggered my passion for music. The movie was called "Unleashed," starring Jet Li and my all-time favorite actor, Morgan Freeman. The movie itself is compelling, yet inspiring in many ways. This was not because the victim could "kick ass" in the movie, but the dynamic of how an adult male could be brainwashed to submission by his master, while at the same time having the ability to reach out to someone who could teach him love and humbleness.

We are very well aware that in reality, the healing process is not completed in 90 minutes. Nevertheless, this film captivated me more than any human trafficking film I have ever seen. It was a reflection of my own situation. I was abused at home. Through my journey of personal discovery, I've encountered people who not only shared their homes with me but also their love and compassion.

I found even more inspiration to write this story through the friends and acquaintances that I have developed over the years. My connection to people has always been deeper when they have the passion to speak out about injustice, civil rights activism, and truly believe in equality for all. However, that is only half of the equation.

I have another entourage of people that I continue to associate with: thugs, prostitutes, and outcasts. They continue to remind me where I have been and it's a constant reminder of where I came from. I choose not to ignore them.

It is with the hope that this work might somehow help in shedding light on their way of life that I find further inspiration to speak of my time among their ranks. When I was among them, I always felt that we were misunderstood, taken advantage of and underestimated in our intelligence and our perseverance. Truthfully, there's only so much that a survivor can do. Eventually, the trying becomes too difficult and inevitably, we repeat the cycle. I hope that what I have written might provoke just a little extra kindness and justice being given to those who live such hard lives.

The struggle to write this document has not been a smooth one. There comes a point in your life where you begin to feel tired of trying and then all of your hopes and dreams collapse beneath you. Many times, I could've gone that route as well. In every instance, there were people that I encountered, whether by chance or by design, who set me back on my course. I may not have realized it at that moment, but over time, a person comes to remember those breaking points and how this affects them today.

I want to say "thank you" for all the people that have come in and out of my life, whether for good or for bad. Because of you, I am who I am today. I am now able to put these thoughts into words on a page. I even include those who underestimated me or betrayed me, for it was your very lack of confidence in me which made me fight for my dreams that much more. Those people I call my "Challengers," because they provoked me to fight through until the end.

My friends who are still left behind and unheard of, know that I do remember you and I have you in my heart and prayers. My rescue didn't come from some brave police officer or some evangelist that hoped to get rewarded in heaven, but people with whom Jesus Christ Himself would've surrounded Himself. Yes—thieves, prostitutes, gang members, and drug dealers gave me a place to stay, protected me like a watchdog and became my family. They inspired me in some pivotal way. If there is any definition of true Christians, they were the ones, along with a group of college students in Texas that welcomed me into their home, befriended me and saw past the flaws conjured by my own enslavement. They didn't judge me. They loved me. Because of them, I now see Christianity in a whole different light than I used to. I am very blessed by the people I had the opportunity to know and who have challenged me as well.

In writing this story, I have also challenged myself. The most difficult part about survival is the continuum; it's hard work that you have to apply in your life every single day. What I mean is this: As an addict, the urges to get high will never end as long as I'm alive, breathing, and surviving. I'm always going to run into triggers, flashbacks, or cravings, but I have to continue reminding myself that getting high "one more time" isn't going to be just one, two or three times; it will bring me back to hell.

No one could have ever told me how much being a survivor is an ongoing effort, but it is. It can also be very frightening. It makes you want to run and hide.

Even through the darkest hours of my life, I still saw a light at the end of the tunnel. I would spend my moments of silence envisioning myself being free and at peace. It's like getting that promotion or that gold medal in the Olympics. It's so close that you can almost taste it, yet it feels so far away. Even so, you know in your heart it was destined just for you. That is what I felt when I wrote this book. Every time I felt withdrawn from the courage to share my experience, I pictured the many lives I'd inspired just through my words and then I continued writing. That is what allowed me to finish the work, and present it to you today.

INTRODUCTION

This is my personal recollection of my life; it's compelling but it's raw. I have contemplated on the graphic details of what I went through, and whether it was a healthy desire to describe in such detail how I endured the trauma, survived it, and found my own path to being free from my own enslavement, which lasted far longer than the enslavement imposed upon me. It's my way to voice what I have experienced—one who overcame this adversity and found ways to stay above water. I don't want to say that I feel obligated to share my story, but at the same time, I want to inspire hope to my fellow survivors out there who have yet to speak.

I want to share how I was able to gain back my life and shift the gears of empowerment to benefit not only myself but many other victims out there. This is definitely a memoir of my harrowing experience with the childhood trauma of sexual abuse and my life as a sex-slave in the trafficking underground in the United States. You may have read about me in articles in other places, but if you want to know the truth of everything about my life, then look no further. In previous articles that you may have read about me, certain details were changed due to editorial standards and also because I was not ready to tell the whole story in full. Now I have the chance to bring my voice to life.

This book is not your ordinary survival story of family abuse but also enters into exploring the way we extend trust in our society and involves corruption of certain officials who have earned that trust. The story opens a new door of realization on a part of our domestic economy in which I was forced to be involved. This is my detailed story of how I obtained my legal residency as a Naturalized Citizen in the United States in 1984-1985, even though my family and I immigrated here legally in 1977. I fell victim to enslavement not even 10 years later, aided by the people who were responsible for keeping American citizens safe from harm. I found no relief from the local authorities or the Immigration and Naturalization Services (INS) which had the power to save me. Instead, I was shuffled into a bureaucratic nightmare, treated like an undocumented person, and made into a vulnerable target of the trafficking world.

This work may also shake your preconceived notions of who traffickers are and the level of support they enjoy. My traffickers weren't ordinary hoodlums from the rough area of New York or some low-life pimp in the urban areas of any random city. These men and women were extremely powerful and very well established.

What makes this story so difficult for some to accept is that we refuse to face the truth. We have put our faith in some people to ensure our justice system functions well, and some of them are controlling the revolving door of the Human Market. This book's narrative will help you understand this reality using my experiences in hopes of becoming the ultimate threat to this highly-organized crime network.

My descriptions and recollections will also correlate how family dynamics of child abuse or domestic violence play a huge part in how a victim can be "chosen" to be enslaved into Domestic Trafficking, along with how these experiences create many of the types of "vulnerabilities" that traffickers see in their potential "prey." When hearing the term "Human Trafficking," many readers will be familiar with the concept but believe it to be a primarily international issue that does not exist on American soil. It might be thought that those who are abducted are only brought here from overseas on the "rare" occasion when it does happen here. The truth is about to shock you.

I would like to extend a particular warning to those who are faith-based readers. This is NOT a Christian book, although I do share my relationship with God, what faith means to me and how I found it. This is a book which covers all aspects of my life, and I'll be sharing with you my perspectives on sex, politics, and religion as well. Allow me to take you on a journey into my world. Most of it may shock you and may even disgust you, but at least you will know the truth. I hope you will enjoy reading this book as I have enjoyed sharing it with you.

Thank you,
C. K.

CHAPTER 1

SUMMER OF '89

I remember the achingly beautiful summer day. The cool creek beckoned me to quench the oncoming summer heat of the mid-morning sun. It was late summer, and school had just commenced. It was a weekend and weekends were always precious. My dog, Cookie, yapped at my feet as I trotted off to lose myself in a day of idleness.

Then came her voice. "Song Ja! Come here!" It was Mother's voice. Cold and demanding. It was the voice of authority that my sisters and I were trained to obey instantly.

Despite her tone, I didn't yet fear that my idle day would evaporate. My mother was strict and used that tone at the least provocation. This could easily be a minor chore or a warning to return home before a certain hour.

I cannot say the events that followed would transpire any differently had I known that the conversation would become so very pivotal to the rest of my life. So dramatically was obedience a part of my life. I entertained no thought of ignoring my mother, running on to the creek and leaving this conversation behind. Would I have had the courage to face what lingered inside my mind, or would it have done more damage for those long-buried memories to stay hidden even longer? Was I fortunate that day, or was that the beginning of the darkest part of my life's journey?

All I know for sure is that if I had to pick a point where the intersection of my deepest nightmares and everyday reality had become intertwined, that was it. Not because my suffering began at that time, but it became a part of my living memory in that moment. Before this, the sweet shield of youth had partly protected me. So many people look back at the youngest years of their lives and recall only shreds and fragments of those carefree years. To them, it can be inconsequential, while to others it is unfortunate or even frustrating to have lost those years which made up the first decade or so of life. For me, it was sweet relief that was about to come to a crashing end.

The unknown part of my brain that tried to suppress what could not be endured was slipping, and it was during the Summer of 1989 when those leaks would finally cause the conversation that would break open the floodgates.

So, I will begin with the dreams. They bubbled up out of my past to infect my nights with terror that I could not understand. As sure as I would heed the call of my mother, those terrible dreams always found me in the dark of the night.

$$* \qquad * \qquad *$$

The day was warm. There was no breeze. The heat soaked into everyone and doing nothing came easy, but the air was still and could smother a person if she sat without moving. It was only 8:30 in the morning and the heat would get far worse before it got any better.

Fortunately, I was three years old, and sitting still never comes naturally to the very young. I felt bad for my infant sister, stuck in her crib all day. I never knew how she managed to survive that. Moving around and playing was what kept me sane in those days. I had a few toys, but my imagination took over well enough to forget some of the claustrophobia of our small upstairs apartment, wedged in the heart of an urban complex.

My game was broken by my father shouting from the front door. "Time to go!"

It hardly mattered where, though I recalled he had mentioned something about going to the sitter's that day. I couldn't recall who was looking after us, nor why our father was leaving us for the day. He worked all the time. I was too young to know what demands were placed on him. Why would it matter? It would be more open air, at least for the car ride!

I bolted past him, not really paying attention to the fine quality of his polo shirt, black slacks, and well-shined shoes. He looked like he was on the way to make some business deal. Maybe he was just being polite to the sitter. He had me dressed in my best denim overalls and a pink t-shirt. The outfit was durable enough to handle my rough-housing, while nice enough to give a good impression. My hair was back in pig tails, bangs trimmed, and everything carefully tied back. I liked the look because it kept my hair from getting in my eyes all the time.

The drive was not long, but longer than normal. I really had no idea where we were by the time we got there. I didn't recognize the normal sitter, but that wasn't too strange. So many people seemed to move around back then. When one sitter moved on, my parents found someone new.

Even in Elmore City, the Korean population was not huge, so it was a bit of a surprise to find a short, Korean lady waiting behind the white-metal, screen door of the house where we went. She tried to smile at me as I came closer. It wasn't an easy smile, and I didn't smile back. She opened the door, and I went in.

The house didn't stink, but something felt wrong. I didn't know what to think and looked back at my father. I wanted to say something, but I knew he would simply fix me with a glare and demand that I not embarrass him.

I was sure he could feel it too. He didn't look at ease but he wasn't upset either. He was talking quickly and in low tones to the sitter lady in rapid Korean.

Shrugging, I turned my attention back to the interior. It was sparsely decorated with only the smallest things you needed to live in a place.

I turned around again, and my father was already pushing at the door. He headed out and didn't turn back. It hurt a little, and I intended to give him a good pout when he came back to get me for not saying goodbye.

The Korean lady gave me that hard smile again and waved at me to go into the living room. Something about her face looked disturbed, and it was clear she didn't intend to follow. Trying to be obedient, I moved over to the archway into the living room beyond.

There was a worn-out recliner there. It was faded yellow, like old straw, and that suited the ragged man sitting in it. He was the right age to be the Korean lady's husband. He didn't talk to me at all. All he did was look at me, and his mouth bent into a thing I would call a smile, but it was so squashed and ugly.

I didn't like him, but he was the sitter, and you obeyed the sitter. Those were the rules, or you got punished. So, I tried my best to smile at him.

He got up from his seat. He came right at me and held out his hands. I extended mine back, as he obviously wanted to pick me up. I hadn't expected that sort of immediate tenderness from anyone who looked so ragged. His puffed, white hair framed his balding head in a strange halo against the room's sparse light. He was huge. As he got near me, I realize how huge he was. His stomach was round, and I might have decided he was Santa Clause if it were not for the absence of any beard, except a pattern of rough stubble.

He stooped down just enough to sweep me up and carried me out of the room. I figured he would head for the kitchen where the Korean lady had gone. Instead, he took me further into the house, and into the back room. The bed there was not fully made. From the bent look of the wood, I guessed it was his. The poor mattress had been putting up with his weight.

He stomped over to the bed, and I clung on tight with my little arms, somehow feeling it wouldn't be exactly safe to let go. The dingy yellow drapes which matched that recliner were tightly shut, and the only light was from a dimly glowing, bedside lamp.

The man leaned down and I couldn't hold on. I tumbled softly to the bed. He left me there and stealthily walked back over to shut the creaking door. I could suddenly feel my heart palpitating as he gave a deep sigh, looked my way, and then walked back over. He settled on the bed, making it groan terribly, and leaned in closer to me.

5

His breath made me gag…

*　　*　　*

"No!"

I sat up, screaming. My breath came in ragged bursts, and my eyes darted around as if trying to pierce this new reality, desperate that it be real even as I feared that I was still caught in the dream.

My nightshirt was wet, the top of it soaked in tears while the rest was soaked in sweat. I wondered why it was so hard to see until I realized it was not day, but night—*deep* in the night.

Slowly, the familiar shapes of my home became clear. I could see the silhouettes of the furniture and people in the room. I was in the bottom of my bunk bed, and the ladder leading up to the top of it was there. I could hear my sister Mary's quiet breathing above me. Down on the floor, I could make out the mattress, and Charlotte's sleeping form huddled down against the night's slight chill.

Neither of them had been stirred at all by my scream. Did I do it that often, that they didn't even wake up anymore? Or, had I just screamed in my dream? I took a long, deep breath. It didn't matter. The dreams were mine, not theirs. I had no wish to scare them.

I glanced at the clock and noticed it flashing 12 o'clock. I slowly crept out of the bedroom and made my way down into the living room to read the hanging wall clock instead… 3:24 a.m. Too much of the night remained not to go back to bed, though I hardly felt like sleeping. I poured myself a glass of water and then retraced my steps.

As I slid into bed, I tried to close my eyes, but sleep wouldn't come. My mind kept racing back to those dreams. Were they real dreams? Why did my thoughts keep racing back to such things? I remembered the sitter and her husband. I knew they were real. But had all that happened, or was it just my mind playing strange tricks on me? The details were always so hazy. Most of the time, I didn't even think I really wanted to remember.

I knew I needed some sleep, so I stared at the flashing clock and tried to let its constant blink lull me back to sleep. It began to work. I needed the sleep. School was the next day. The only reason to like school was that it filled the day.

I'll admit that I hated the country. I know some people see the magic in the rustic way of life, but I was a city girl. I was 13 at the time, and living away from the city amongst the cows, the ranches, and the countryside felt like prison. My last home had been Elmore City, and I had learned its ways with an eager need to explore. The shops. The pathways. Yes, even the small parks. Sure, some people embraced the countryside as one big park, but I wasn't in the mood to see things in any positive sort of way. The countryside near our new home of Tacoma, Oklahoma, was just one big emptiness. I didn't have the desire nor the inspiration to go spelunking down the creek or navigating the wide stretch of wheat fields. I just wanted my city back.

It wasn't like I even lived close to any friends my age. My sisters were all younger. Charlotte was 11, Mary was 9, and then there was Melissa who was 2. Charlotte could follow along well enough in those days, but they were still my sisters. I loved them. But, that didn't erase the fact that you had to walk until your feet hurt just to go see one of the neighbors! Again, I just wanted my city back.

School was one of the biggest reasons for my rather harsh judgment of all things rural. It was something to pass the time, but it was also a terrible reminder of what I had lost. Back in Elmore City, there were so many people like me. It was wonderful. When so many people are different, everyone just ends up being treated the same. Some people came. Others left each year. It just meant there were new friends to make.

Not there. Not in Tacoma. When I was younger, we had lived in Tacoma before. My father's company made him move, and we stayed near Tacoma several years earlier. As a result, I had cause to hate the idea of coming back. I attended Turtle Creek School then and I hated it. I despised it then, and I didn't see that opinion changing any time soon. The full reasons for my virulent dislike were still not clear to me but would soon come back to life.

I had only been in school for a few days, and I was already lost in dismay. I knew that it would take at least two years before my father was moved again. In Elmore City, I didn't ever hear the curses that made my toes curl and fingers clench. "Chink." "Gook." 'Spic." Where did children even hear that sort of thing? I had heard a couple kids whisper this one spiteful word to a couple of black kids in Elmore City, but then a group of their friends had gone over and beat up the ones who had used it. I never understood that. I really didn't understand the concept of a racial slur until I arrived at Turtle Creek.

Suddenly, I knew all about it. There, I felt alone. I was the only Asian or student of color in the whole school, which made me the outsider.

My sister and I had been in the same grade ever since elementary school, back when I had first gone to Eagle Crest Elementary. They viewed my blended Korean and English as a speech impediment. The teachers simply had no idea how to deal with that, and I had been held back twice.

I shudder to think where I would be had we not returned to Elmore City. I owe much to the teachers there who had recognized the true issue and allowed me to catch up a little. I don't recall if I ever gained equality with students my own age, but at least I didn't feel like I was being treated like I could not accomplish a task because of my intelligence. I didn't excel at some things, including the manipulation of numbers, which would factor so greatly in my coming life.

Afterward, I returned to Tacoma. While I was better armed against the prejudices, my limited comprehension of the English language proved to be a stumbling block. I was still not educated enough in their opinion. I was unable to prevent them from holding me back again. I felt so alone.

Both of my parents were Korean. I had no idea if they were treated the same, especially my father at his place of employment. They worked so much. My father was always busy manufacturing whatever machines his company produced. My mother was a homemaker with four children and seemed to live in the laundry room and kitchen. I was on my own.

My father was not an option to solve the problem. He worked evening hours more often than not, and most of the time he was in bed when he was home. I found some small delight in hearing him come home. I was always a night owl, and listening for his arrival was comforting. My father's return home signaled the end of any attention I would get from my mother. She tended to him upon his late return and expected him to handle any discipline when he was around. His discipline took the form of disappointed frowns, occasional spankings, or ignoring us. Knowing that I didn't need to fear my mother discovering me awake was a sort of freedom I enjoyed.

Despite that tiny fond memory, my father and I were never close. His work schedule didn't allow him to be more than a passing presence in my younger life. Even more, he simply didn't connect with us. He wanted a son. This was not a guess, but a comment I overheard on several occasions—most often when he was bent over fixing some piece of failed household equipment. Repairing things took him away from his morning sleep or kept him up late at night. I would hear him grouch about how he could teach a son to keep the mechanics of the house in good condition.

It seems strange to say such things, but traditional Korean gender roles were as much a part of my young life as the racism I experienced in Tacoma. Having a son in the family would have brought credit upon us, whereas having four daughters was only a burden that my father had to endure. This was a truth I was taught by my mother, and we did not question such things. It was wrong to object or try and see reason in such teachings. This was Korean culture as presented by my mother, and whatever the truth might be, this was *my* truth at that age.

The same thing applied to my hip dysplasia, a condition I have dealt with my entire life. Simply put, one of my legs is an inch or so longer than the other, which causes me to limp when I walk. I had several surgeries, but the issue was never fully rectified. To me, it was an inconvenience. To my mother, I was the reason for the ill luck that befell our family whenever negative events came to pass.

Being different was tantamount to being evil to my mother. I recall the lengths she would go to in order to hide, minimize, or ignore that part of me. Perhaps one of my earliest, unwitting victories was to arrive at even that young age without a serious, psychological complex regarding that leg. To me, it was just part of being me. It always was.

This new experience of racism was not always there and was not always a part of me. There had been years of my life when I was not treated so poorly, so I dared to ask my mother about it once. I asked if there was something I could do to ease the pain or turn aside their torment. My mother was not cruel in that moment. She smiled in what she thought was a tender way and tried to help in the only way she knew how. She told me to ignore it. She told me not to cause waves. Our whole family was Catholic. Devout Catholics who attended weekly mass and tried to be good people. She reminded me of tolerance and the goodness of not wanting revenge and the righteousness of turning the other cheek. I was still young. I wondered why the "good people" way of life didn't seem to apply to the other kids. That was the last time I really asked her about it for a while.

Along with my mother, my sisters and I had to learn to recognize the warning signs of when her willingness to humor our questions had come to an end. It was considered disrespectful to research what you were taught, to question it, or even wonder if conflicting beliefs were true. Rationality had very little to do with it. Obedience did. That was the real point. She wanted our obedience to be instinctive.

For me, it never was. Did I have a naturally precocious nature or naturally inquisitive mind? I was the eldest, and so I was also the example for my sisters. Disciplining me would have a trickle-down effect. When I gave in, my sisters would give in more easily. I was also the focal point for the bad luck because of my disability. Perhaps my mother saw punishing me as striking at the symbol of bad fortune in our family.

Whatever the reasons, I was what my mother would call "difficult to train." I mentioned that I was a night owl. This conflicted directly with the hard line of an 8:30 p.m. bedtime that was set for us. My sisters had no problem passing out. Maybe they learned quickly from watching what happened to me. All I know is that when 9:00 p.m. came and mother checked on us once more, I dreaded the lashing that would follow. If I so much as twitched as she flipped on the lights, even if I was trying my hardest to sleep, the belt would be laid into me regardless. She didn't want me *trying* to obey. She wanted me *to* obey. The fact that my body was not sleeping when she wanted it to was abhorrent to her.

I can also trace some of my difficulties with language back to the strange variations in my mother's disciplinary tactics. When we first emigrated from Korea in the spring of 1977, I was little more than an infant. Both of my parents wanted to give me some hope of integration and agreed to have me stay at my uncle's place in Dallas over the summer. Since he was listed as my guardian to assist me and my family with getting passports and documents to remain in the country, it made sense that he became a part of my upbringing. I moved back and forth between his place and my parents' place for those first years until I started kindergarten. Then, the exchange became more formalized. I would live at his place during the summer, and with my parents during the school year.

For many children, this would have been a boon. Both languages would have come naturally to children exposed to them and encouraged fluency in both. For me, it was a study in two worlds which were toxic to each other.

When I was with my uncle, there was very little opportunity to speak Korean. He was American military personnel and had married my aunt while over in Korea. He didn't understand any of the Korean tongues beside some basics. He always seemed like a kind, respectable sort of man, and I always regretted that my time with him came to an end in those early years after my aunt divorced him.

My aunt never loved him, she used him to enter the United States. He deserved to be treated better. We stayed in touch since we were close to our cousins, but the divorce and the constant separation of custody took a toll on everyone and our communications began to fade.

When I returned home, my mother was determined to have my sisters and I learn Korean. I was actively beaten for failures in recalling my lessons in Korean. When I misspoke and mispronounced words I had not used in months, I would be chastised in the harshest of ways. I was treated like I was failing my culture. More and more, my mother would speak increasingly basic Korean to me. She could not speak English and refused to acknowledge when I used less than perfect diction in my Korean.

Despite this strange mix, she never gave up on the expectation that my sisters and I would somehow regain our native tongue. At parties, she would speak to house guests in rapid Korean—so quickly that I could barely understand it—of her supreme disappointment in me. Nevertheless, her efforts to home school me in Korean never fully vanished.

I wished every day that she would give up on me. The lessons we received were not pleasant. Corporal punishment was as regular in our language lessons as they were in our piano lessons, and the joy was siphoned out of both.

During that particular summer, not long before the commencement of the school year, my mother made one last, powerful effort to remind us of our Korean. With all of the explanations I had to hate my return to Turtle Creek, here at least was a wonderful reason for the summer to end: It marked the end of those lessons.

They began with my mother buying us spiral notebooks with numbered pages from 1 to 77, front to back. She glared at us each in turn and made herself rather clear. "This notebook is to learn *Korean*. Do not draw or play on the paper, okay?" She warned us, using simple words that we could not have misunderstood.

Of course, we all replied immediately. "Yes, Ma'am."

I honestly remember intending to do as she asked. I was not yet thirteen, and promises lasted as long as my memory did, which was never long at all. I started to sketch various pictures in my notebook on one idle afternoon. By the time that I realized what I had done, I started to panic. I tore out the pages and stuffed them in the trash can of my sister's room. I am not proud that I tried to deflect the blame that way, but I was scared out of my mind.

Later that evening, my mother asked us for our notebooks so she could check our lessons. I slowly handed her my notebook and bit my lip, knowing she would notice the jump in page numbers.

Sure enough, the accusation came. "What is this page?" She slipped through the book as if it must be lying to her, for certainly one of *her* daughters would not have disobeyed her so blatantly.

"I… dunno." I slowly shrugged my shoulders. It was a foolish deception that could not have lasted.

It was over more quickly than I feared. Charlotte spoke up, "Momma, they're in here." She pulled out my wad of crumpled, marked-up pages from the trash can.

My mother set them on the coffee table, and slowly counted the pages from front to back. She glared over at me, counting with solemn weight. I knew that each page she counted would add to the number of lashes I would receive.

My sisters all ducked their heads, trying not to draw attention to themselves. I recall forgiving Charlotte immediately. What right did I have to expect her to disobey my mother's demand? I would be angry later, but right then I couldn't blame them for not speaking out or trying to help.

My attention was fully on my mother in that moment. I started to cry, wordless and uncertain what to say.

She would have none of it. "What did I say?"

I flinched, covering my face, afraid she would strike me.

My posture only seemed to anger her further. "What did *I say*?"

"I don't know," I responded softly, not knowing what she wanted to hear—not knowing what to say to make this pain pass me by.

I remember the snap of her shoes on the floor as she came at me, slapping me on the side of my face. Her hand clapped on my ear, making them ring. I tried to pull away, scooting back until my back was against the wall. She continued to hit me with one fist after another. When that had too little of an effect, she grabbed my hair from the top and slammed my head back against the wall. I began to scream uncontrollably.

"*Shut up!*" she screamed at me, looming over me still.

I fell to the floor and began to crawl away. She followed me down the hall, kicking me in the stomach. I couldn't stop crying even as she demanded that I do so. It was impossible, but that didn't matter to her. I didn't obey instinctively. My tears didn't stop at her command, and she just saw this as further betrayal.

Inside, thoughts of self-blame clawed around inside my head. I berated myself inside as my mother shouted at me outside. "You are so stupid! Why did you do that? Why are you crying? She'll just hurt you more! Listen to her, and shut up! This is totally your fault!" But it was too late, and such thoughts couldn't save me.

I devolved into simple prayer, begging God to stop my mother. I was on the floor with her kicking at me. I simply held my hands in front of my face and tried to protect myself.

Suddenly, inspiration came to me. I don't know from where. Even as the blows rained down on me, I dragged myself up to a kneeling posture. Slowly, I rubbed my hands together as if washing them, remembering the way my mother taught me that Koreans properly apologized to authority figures.

I saw nothing but hate in her eyes. Her hand rose again, ready to strike. She didn't believe me. She didn't believe my penitence. I lowered my eyes. I wanted to see the blow coming, to help make it hurt less, but that would make me seem less sorry.

The blow never came. The phone rang.

I was sure that blow would have come. I gave everything to her. After all the hurt she had delivered to me, after all of that, I had begged her to stop. I had turned the other cheek as she had always told me to do and asked for her forgiveness. I had debased myself completely in front of her.

It was the phone that stopped her. Not me.

She broke off from her torment and shuffled over to the phone. It was impolite to leave the caller waiting. She hustled over and answered. Her voice was normal. In a heartbeat, she transformed. All was normal. All was quiet. She was out of breath and explained that away with a small laugh. "I was outside and had to run."

A blind call from an outsider had saved me where my own pleas had not. Even my sisters had been sobbing, begging her to stop, and nothing had worked. Why? What did she find so abhorrent in me? How was I so flawed?

I sat there for what felt like hours. I folded my legs in front of me and counted the cuts and bruises on my body. I was numb and simply didn't know how to move on.

I remember my sister lingering nearby with tears in her eyes, too. She slipped up to me and cried as she fell to her knees beside me, "I'm sorry!"

I was so angry that I couldn't hear that sort of thing. I slammed my door in her face and cried myself to sleep. There were times I would remain in my room for days after such sessions, even if it happened mid-afternoon and it meant starving until the next day. I couldn't face my family after that. It made it hard to ever face them.

It felt like a mockery of life—like a play being acted out. No one ever admitted the ugly reality lurking behind all the carefully staged sets. We played our parts of the happy family. Whenever there were guests or phone calls, they were welcomed with kind smiles and open arms. My father smiled and acted like he was the head of a fine clan while my mother took credit for running a solid household. We children held our tongues and said only clever things to make the adults laugh.

Is it any surprise, then, that despite all the trouble I expected at school, I could not wait for the summer to end? During those long and heated days, my only partial refuge came at the creek. My dachshund, Cookie, would join me on those walks. I could retreat to my special place to cry, vent, and argue with a God I didn't even know truly existed. I would throw pebbles into the water and watch circles grow. I would make wishes on those ripples in the stream, and then know those wishes would vanish unheard just as the ripples faded against the edges of the water.

What hope did I have that things could change? I had heard that American children were taught to speak out, and aggressively demanded to be heard. It wasn't the same in my family, and they told me that that was not the way of the Korean people. I was taught that crying was weakness, that complaining was the sign of a weak mind, and to be seen but not heard—except to speak well of my parents. With such teachings, what hope had I to change what seemed to be my reality?

So, that was my reality. I was shunned by both cultures. At home, I was the disabled child and what my mother would call illiterate, despite my decently functional ability in Korean. At school, I was either assessed as having a speech disability or dismissed as a "geek," an "ugly duckling," or as undesirable.

School held more hope, for school was my way to the outside world. That is where I invested most of my effort. There was simply no way I could change my mother. So, I lost all interest in my own culture and began to rebel against my lessons whenever I could. I didn't want to be Korean anymore.

Oddly enough, I actually became more and more at peace with my disability in this way. In a strange reversal, if I was going to abandon my Korean culture, then all of its restraints went with it. I was growing tired of the constant surgeries that surrounded the rare circumstances of my condition. I had ultimately decided to let go of the constant hope that my "disfigurement" would be washed away. It ceased to matter that I might then be the perfect, eldest daughter my mother always wanted.

I focused on school. But, the path to the future is never that easy. The more I focused on school, the more those dreams came. Those damn dreams that seemed to speak to me, demanding I hear them.

I didn't want to hear them. Maybe I needed to, but I didn't want to know.

In the end, I had no choice. What they had to say was the truth, and truth has a powerful way of finding its way to the surface.

*　　　*　　　*

There were four or five of us. I knew them, of course. We were there together sometimes. Sometimes it was just one of us. It changed from day-to-day. I didn't know if it was just because some parents were busy some days, or if we all had scheduled days to be there.

All of us shivered against the cold in the basement. It was chilled, and the pavement on the unfinished floor felt clammy against my feet. I didn't know where my clothes had gone. I felt so small and frail. It wasn't the cold that made me wrap my arms around myself, quivering and shaking.

My eyes trailed after the frizzy haired man. Our eyes were locked on him, watching him like rabbits watch a wolf ranging near them. I was clueless about so much of what happened to me then, but I knew this was wrong. I knew I shouldn't be naked. I knew HE shouldn't be naked, walking around us with that camera in his hands and fondling himself with the other.

I found my tongue, blurting out, "I want my momma!"

His face twisted in a horrid mockery of tenderness and leaned down to caress my face with his hand. I tried to turn my head, but he grabbed hold of my chin. He kept me looking at him,"But you're so pretty."

A cold chill ran down my spine. I cried silent tears as I closed my eyes, willing myself to be away from that dark room. I felt him trying to press his lips to mine, and press his tongue into my mouth, and nothing would make it go away.

I felt fingers crawling down me, touching me, and his voice whispering at me, trying to reach me through my denial, "Sssshhhh, everything's going to be okay."

*　　　*　　　*

"Stop it! I hate you! I *hate* you!" I screamed it back, all of my anger exploding outwards in a sudden rush.

15

Hands were on me, but not his. Hands that shook me awake. "Sis? Sis, what's wrong?"

I knew that voice! Mary! I knew the concern within it. I dragged myself out of the nightmare and opened my eyes. Sobbing, every response stuck in my throat. I couldn't even begin to explain. Why would these dreams not stop coming for me? My thoughts kept racing with fear and rejection that this could have ever happened? I would remember it, wouldn't I? Right now, wouldn't I remember it?

Slowly, I found my own words. I whispered back, fast and low. "I keep… having this dream. I don't know what it is. I don't even know if it's true. But it feels so real!"

"It's just a dream, isn't it?"

"I know the man I keep seeing. I've seen him, I know it. He's a white man that was married to one of our sitters when I was younger. I… I keep dreaming of him touching me… where he isn't supposed to touch me." I laid there, holding my breath, waiting for a response from my sister.

"Oh." She replied softly, at a loss for what to say.

I felt a sudden wash of anger. I know I sounded foolish, but right then I was both angry and scared and didn't care if I sounded irrational. I fought to keep my voice low. I didn't want to wake up Charlotte. Despite that, my words carried a harshness that I was sure my sister could feel. She drew back from me with a worried look as I hissed, "If what I dreamt about is true, then when I grow up I'm going to get a shot gun and kill him for what he did to me!"

With that, I turned over to my side and fell asleep crying. Crying, and praying dreams wouldn't find me again that night.

The next morning was the morning my mother called for me.

My mind did not leap to any conclusion as to what she wanted. After all the discipline and fear, I should have known the lessons my sisters had already learned. I should have known Mary would have heard the commitment in my voice when I promised to find that man and kill him. Even in a 13-year-old girl, a serious death threat could shake the one who hears it uttered.

I had very little choice but to call back, "I'm coming!" I raced back to the house, not wanting to keep her waiting. She had the tone that said the longer I made her wait, the more I would regret it. This had been so close to being a good day, and it might still be salvaged if I could just avoid angering mother into a fit.

I entered just as Charlotte was walking out the door. Her eyes were downcast and apologetic. I tried to get some hint from her as to what mother might want, casting a silent plea her way.

She just whispered quickly back, "I heard. I was awake. Sorry, Sis, I had to tell Mom." Then, she darted out the door, leaving me even more confused than I was before. The whole confession to my other sister in the dead of night was like a lifetime ago, faded into the background pattern of a hundred sleepless nights filled with similar nightmares.

My mother had her legs folded into a lotus position and pointed at the ground in front of her. "Sit down," she commanded in a low monotone that betrayed nothing.

I coiled myself down in front of her with as much grace as I could manage. My palms started to sweat. This was bad. I understood her rage. This cold, serpentine confrontation was all wrong.

She leaned forward a little. "Why did you say you want to kill somebody?" she asked.

At that moment, it still didn't register what she was asking about. My confused look started to cause her brow to knit with anger as if I was hiding something. Then, it hit me. Mary was not the only one awake! My scream must have woken Charlotte. She had kept pretending to be asleep in case mother had walked in.

My mouth worked as if trying to find words, trying to stall mother from exploding into anger. I was trying to think of some way to explain this away. Then, something snapped. I was tired of keeping this secret inside of me. The emotional toll it was taking on me was simply too great.

Despite all of my thoughts, the words that came out first sounded almost pointless. I blurted out, "I keep having this dream about a man."

Now it was my mother's turn to show confusion on her face. "What man?"

"He's white, and I know he's real, mother. I remember it. There was a Korean lady who used to live in Elmore City. They would watch Charlotte and me, remember? Her husband and she would watch us when we were very small."

I saw my mother's face going white.

Her reaction gave me strength. She remembered! I knew it at that moment. "He would touch me! He would take naked pictures of us and take me to his room and do things with me. I keep dreaming it!" My tears were falling now, my calm shattering. I looked at my mother, hoping for sympathy. Always before, where there was none, I needed there to be sympathy now. I needed a mother *now*.

Instead, there was just shock. Shock, and the dull question, "Song Ja, you remember?"

I couldn't believe my ears. "Remember? What do you mean? Is it true? For sure? How can you know!" All my dread came crashing around me. It was true. All of it, true!

My mother just waved her hands vaguely. It was her turn to try and find a way to explain, and she had just as little success as I. "You were only a baby, Song Ja. You weren't supposed to remember. You shouldn't have remembered!"

I rose higher on my knees, anger starting to animate me. I forgot all about the lessons of respect as I started to shout back at her, "What are you talking about? What was I not supposed to know? How... how old was I? Did he go to jail? How do you know what he did to me?" Her reluctance to say anything was sounding like she was defending this creature of a man, and she couldn't stand to hear that.

"You were only three years old! You kept saying he was touching you, but your daddy and I didn't know what you were talking about! So, we said he thought you were just cute and so touched your arm or picked you up and played games with you. I told you it was OK if someone does that. We didn't know, Song Ja. Not... not right away."

"Not right away? You said it was OK so I would go back? How did you end up knowing, mother? *You knew!*"

"Not for sure, Song Ja. Calm down."

"I will *not!*"

"Another girl! It was another girl! She told her mom. When your daddy came to pick you up, he saw a police car. When he asked Ojum Ma... that's the Korean lady... what happened, she said it wasn't her husband's fault. She said he was slow."

"Slow? So that makes it ok for her to cover up what he has done? Are you defending her? I was... how old was I, mother? Three? Six? Do you know what he did to me? He hurt me!" I cried openly, and there was no shame in it this time. Only anger. Anger and disbelief.

That was the worst part. I couldn't believe my mother wanted to create an excuse for whoever that man had been. Why? Because to talk about this would bring shame on their family and ours? Because she would be a victim, and that would be even worse than having a disabled child? Was that it?

A hole opened in my heart, and I had never felt so alone. I was torn into emotional rags, and all I wanted was for my mother to finally reach out and draw me into her. To hold me and hold me until all of the pain went away.

Instead, she just sat there and cried.

Around us, my sisters filed into the room. They whispered behind me, but could not approach. They had heard my screams but had nothing else to say.

I had nothing to say either.

I couldn't understand why when she had been so strict with me, taken so many liberties with me, and literally sought to strike the evil from me to only now be less strict with the evil that had befallen me. Why would she not attack it? Why was she willing to let it be, and to have me ignore it and pretend it never happened? Why had it been another mother protecting *her* child that had ended the ordeal?

What might have been a bonding experience between us instead became the final moment when I knew she would never be there to protect me.

From that point forward, I gained something of a sense of purpose for the following years. I wanted to learn more about those like me. I wanted to educate myself. I was too young then to truly pursue it. I remember having a desire to be a cop or an attorney and make sure that those kinds of monsters rotted in jail. Such were the fantasies of a newly empowered teenager standing on the brink of early adulthood.

I was limited by my surroundings, but I was committed. I did what research I could on child abuse. I learned what it was, and learned what rights children had. It was during that particular summer I realized what I had endured. This led to other discoveries. I learned what domestic abuse meant, and it became a guiding star for me as I grew towards being an adult to remember this.

If nothing else, I had to remember this: If ever I was blessed with children, I could only think over and over that I would break the cycle, and never let it happen to them.

CHAPTER 2

CLASSROOM SECRETS

Memories long forgotten were shaken loose from the moment of that first confrontation. The fight with my mother truly was the beginning. Before that summer, I couldn't deal with what happened to me. I suppressed so much. Now that the admission had finally been made by my mother, I could no longer deny that I had experienced abuse.

I began to educate myself. I learned the terminology surrounding such abuses and learned what those terms meant. I was still little more than a child, and this process would take years, but I was determined. My teenage years were largely consumed with coming to terms with what happened to me in my youth.

That exploration proved more difficult than could have I ever imagined. Old memories resurfaced. New dreams led me to unlock and admit other experiences that were part of the cause of my simmering fury over how I had been treated. Perhaps it was the very discipline of my youth that had kept it buried so deep until that moment and never allowed me to explore it. I was taught not to question anything. Only my mother's betrayal really freed me from that restriction.

Perhaps I was also afraid. Who wouldn't be scared facing such terrors at that age? The heat of my anger finally found some release and rose above that fear. I had to face it, no matter what came of it.

What I discovered damaged me. I have no doubt about that. I lost so much faith in so many people who might have been available for me to reach out to in darker times to follow. Each new discovery stripped away another protection from me. Each new discovery eroded my ability to really evaluate others and learn how to trust. This *knowledge* placed barriers between my ability to know other people. It led to some loneliness during my high school years, but even worse, it restricted my involvement with others.

I never learned what was proper for others to do, and what was proper for them to do to me. I found some solace in that whatever damage was done, at least I knew the truth. Even with that small gift, I have come to accept that my view of the world was flawed from the very start.

It was hard enough to face the fact that my childhood was broken with dysfunctional parents, while living through flashbacks of childhood sexual abuse. I had hoped to find some sanctuary at school. It was away from my mother and I was finally past the point where I was considered "disabled" because of my language issues. This is not to say that I was an angelic child in school. Far from it. I think most people would understand after reading these accounts why I became increasingly irritable and something of a rascal in school.

While I would never call myself bad to the core, I reacted to protect myself in the way children often did. I lashed out at those who would come near me and try to befriend me. I was attacked by those who saw me as a weaker person, and I responded by doing the same. I played my own games, like asking other boys in my class if they were allowed to hit girls; when they answered "no," I would slap them, hit or kick them, and push the limits of their tolerance. I was taught about violence, and so I responded with violence.

I was always chastised for my behavior issues. Now, I had begun to learn why. I discovered that victims of child abuse were often known to misbehave, yearning for a place to act out and vent their unspoken troubles.

As I discovered more about myself, I attributed my previous difficulties in paying attention to the abuse I received at home. I wasn't a bad kid, but rather just a kid no one could understand. It took specific and dedicated research to learn more about what happened to me. Public awareness of things like "child abuse" and "domestic violence" were not in the mainstream. Teachers weren't yet being taught to care for children with traumatic issues.

Even to this day, I still question all that I think I know of my early years in school. I know that as I learned more later in life, I came to understand other abuses that I had experienced in school. It took time. I couldn't call anyone to corroborate what my memories were telling me. I never told any of my teachers or classmates about my family problems. I would never have confided in them about anything else that happened at school.

Even if all of my teachers and classmates were not involved in direct abuse, I experienced so much racism and hatred, especially in Tacoma, that the idea of trusting anyone at home or school was beyond my ability to comprehend. Anyone else who might have been in my corner, I drove away with my own errant, disrespectful behavior.

One of the pivotal events which clarified some of these scattered memories happened in June of 2006. I reconnected with an old classmate of mine named Skyler who had attended my elementary school. He also attended the same church as I did in those days. It was one of the few places I have never feared and one of the few places I never experienced abuse.

I might have often questioned God, and wondered how so wonderful a being could allow such terrible things to befall a person, but God's house was never a source of terror for me. We talked about our time in church and shared good memories of the times our families were together. The more we talked, the more that discussion shifted to the school we shared. The more we trusted each other, the more I was able to confirm that my flashbacks were as true as I had always believed them to be. His support was a key reason why I can speak about my difficult years in elementary. I thank him for giving me the strength to find the words to say what must be said, both for my own catharsis and to let others know that they too can find the strength to speak about events that have happened to them if they share similar torments.

These experiences did not all come back to me in chronological order. To make sense of it all, I must begin with what came first. What I speak of here does not represent all of what I endured, but these events are certainly moments which stand out most powerfully in my mind. They paint the best picture of the difficult times which set the stage for my future.

As I have implied before, I was something of an outcast during my elementary years. I was held back twice due to the wrongful assessment of my language issues being regarded as speech impediments. I repeated kindergarten. When I advanced from a special needs class, I was then held back in grades 2 and 3. I got used to being the older student in my classes. I was most often considered an outcast in my classes by both being older and from being Korean. I was desperate for someone to reach out to me and become a friend even though I pushed people away. To say I was a difficult child would be an understatement.

That led to the first instance of abuse I really remember. Miss Dempsey, was not only my first grade teacher, but she was also my Physical Education (PE) teacher. She was my home room teacher and would belittle or bully me in the classroom. Whenever I feared her strife, it caused me to wet myself, then she would torment me in front of the class. While in PE, she was aware of the limited mobility in my legs but refused my doctor's order to refrain me from extreme physical activities. This also opened my eyes, not just in the racism I endured, but to witness another student being bullied and abused by the same teacher. When the boy wet himself she would command him to take off his jeans and underwear, and run laps around the gym. The boy was black and I was the troublemaker who would listen even if I was speaking. Did I mention I was in the first grade?

My next incident came not from the faculty but from a classmate. It wasn't even one of the older students, but one of the younger ones in my own class. A boy in my class named Sean had what you might call "a crush" on me. If I had reason to think of excuses for his behavior, it is possible he simply had no idea how to react to the impulses his hormones were giving him. He was exploring his nature. I hate to think of what sort of monster he has become, considering how he began his sexual awakening.

Sean and I were both placed in the special needs classes together. I can't recall his reason for being there. In my mind, I do not believe it was for any lack of mental acuity. Teachers were quick to lump any behavioral problems together without separating them as to individual need. That was exceedingly common back then in most educational systems. Whatever they had identified in Sean, he was tossed into my class and left to fend for himself as much as I was.

My teachers within both my normal homeroom and special needs classes were ill-equipped to handle children like us. I had a young female teacher for my homeroom teacher who had just graduated from a university and she appeared inexperienced with children. I also had a more elderly teacher who resembled a witch in the "Wizard of Oz" to me, and her classroom tactics were just as medieval. I will get into her more a little later. For now, it simply needs to be said that the most expedient means of dealing with disciplinary problems were often taken first.

I remember us sitting in the special education classroom watching some random film. Sean sat next to me, trying to saddle up as close as he could. Without warning, I felt him take my hand and try to place it on his private area. When I jerked my hand away, it was more from him having snatched my hand in the first place, not really understanding anything deeper was at play.

The reaction to that startled me even worse. He screamed out the teacher's name and pretended to cry. When the teacher switched on the lights and looked our way, he was ready to jump in.

"She hit me!" he blurted.

I was in shock. I couldn't believe that he had lied. I didn't even really know *why* he had lied! I tried to defend myself, "No, I didn't!"

"Then what did you do, Miss Song?" The teacher's stern face demanded an answer.

"I didn't hit him! He tried to make me touch his pee-pee!" I exclaimed.

By the expression on her face, I knew she did not believe me. A note of desperation in her face made it clear she didn't *want* to deal with such complicated problems. It was far easier to decide I was lying. She pointed to the door, waited for me to storm out, and followed behind me. With a jab of her finger, she pointed at the floor, "You will sit here until the film is over, I will not tolerate liars."

I just did what she said without arguing. I felt so humiliated. My word had been rejected and I had been called a "liar" who then had to sit there with other students walking past. Everyone knew that anyone placed in the hall was in trouble.

This pattern continued over the first part of the school year. I was tricked by him several times, and each time carried with it Sean's apparent early fascination with sexuality and girls. He had an instinctive cunningness, setting traps for me against which I had no defense. For example, Sean stole a doll from one of the popular girl's desk and stuck it in mine. He walked by me, and whispered the threat, "I'm gonna tell the teacher you stole Janet's doll."

Naturally enough, I turned and glared at him, "Why would you do that? I didn't do it."

"Well, I won't tell anyone if you come sit with me in the closet at the back of the classroom."

I didn't understand the purpose behind his games, but I knew enough that I didn't like them. He played them on a weekly if not daily basis, and I hated his persistent fascination with me. I remember wishing he would find someone else to bother and then regretting that instantly when the strict lessons of my Catholic upbringing returned and realized I had just wished his foul behavior on another. It felt like such a trap! So, I did the only thing I could, and rejected him, hoping this time would be the last. "I won't go! Go away!"

Sean's hand was in the air before I was even finished, dealing the dirt to the homeroom teacher that I had the doll in my desk. I tried to jump in, explaining I hadn't done anything, but the doll was there. The teacher refused any more complicated answer than that I was an exceedingly brave but poor liar. The result was easy enough to guess. I was dragged to the principal's office, my parents were called, and I was spanked or worse upon my return home for being the disobedient child that could only seem to misbehave.

The terrible attention continued for most of the school year. What were already terrible grades, got even worse. The stress of that interaction and the injustice of continually being disbelieved were compounded in addition to my difficulties with language. My spirit broke a little, and eventually, I even stopped fighting Sean. Fighting him only led to beatings at home, so I just began to give in. I cried each time, but he really didn't seem to notice.

As often happens with such things, his attention turned away as I ceased to fight. It was my very objections that might have spurred him on, and as I became more and more pliant, his interest waned. He switched to another classmate named Shannon. She was one of my best friends, and we would often confide in each other about Sean's behavior on our walks home from school. It baffled us as to how it even made us feel filthy, but at least we had each other. That helped us survive a little, and gave me some hope that friends could be found even in dark places.

It would be reasonable to ask why neither of us thought to speak to other teachers about this or other incidents. Well, neglect was only one of the faults which had caused me to lose trust and faith in my teachers. I have already mentioned the racism I experienced at the hands of classmates. Be it subtle or be it overt, I certainly learned that being different was not easily accepted in that part of the country. I experienced equally negative treatment at the hands of many of my teachers. This stained any chance of finding trust for any in their ranks.

Some of the abuse was arguably not even focused solely on me because of my Korean heritage. Miss Ferris was the special education teacher of whom I have already spoken. She was somewhat older, perhaps in her early 50's in those days. I had to endure her mistreatment, but it stemmed from her being a holdover of less gentle teaching methods that were not quite as obsolete as they are today. One could picture her right at home with a ruler ready to rap your knuckles should your attention drift. I felt like she singled me out, and perhaps she did. I was a different face in the crowd, often distracted, angry, and not careful with the expressions on my face. From her, I was screamed at randomly, as if she meant to startle me. If I answered wrong, I would be called "stupid" or made to stand in front of the class while she swatted me. At bathroom breaks, I wouldn't be allowed to go with the rest of the students so I would end up wetting my pants. I will never know exactly what about me caused me to be a target of hers, but I had earned her hatred and it continued unceasingly for the year she had me in her class.

A more pointed example of abuse was my homeroom teacher for my repeated fifth grade year in 1987. Her name was Ms. Dresden and she was close friends with Mrs. Zerrick, who was my sister Charlotte's teacher. Charlotte had managed to continue on pace in her own schooling. She had managed her own language conversion better than I had so she had never been held back. No doubt she was a bit embarrassed to be in the same grade together, but we kept well separated, made our own friends, and did our best to pretend it wasn't part of our shared reality. I regret that now, thinking back, for I never really spoke to Charlotte about her own difficulties with Mrs. Zerrick. We might have helped each other and supported each other instead of ignoring each other. Then again, with my mother's strict discipline at home, I am not sure either of us could have admitted any such "weaknesses" to each other.

Both Ms. Dresden and Mrs. Zerrick had deep, racist trends inside them. I was so familiar with dealing with such things in other students that their own traits were instantly recognizable, even if I didn't know what to call them. Later, looking back on it, it was easy to classify them. Back then, they were simply two more bullies I had to endure. What hurt was that they were supposed to be among my protectors. What ended up hurting worst of all is that they ceased being available for me when something even worse happened. As it was, anytime Ms. Dresden sent me out in the hallway, she would call Mrs. Zerrick to partake in joint harassment. I felt humiliated that two teachers were yelling at me in tandem.

These instances took on the tone of bullying, not proper discipline procedures. Their mannerisms couldn't even be excused by being "old school" like Miss Jones, who was my kindergarten teacher. Most of their comments blended into one, long, horrible montage, but a single incident stands out in my memory. I recall Mrs. Zerrick leaning into my face, flecks of spittle hitting my cheeks and forehead as she castigated me with the poisonous phrase, "I'm gonna' cut off your Chinese tongue if you scream one more time." Of course, I was scared. Her persona resembled my mother enough to fear a real beating might be at hand. Mrs. Zerrick tended to wear severe, almost prison-guard style outfits, and she could be very imposing with her stocky frame. She was short for an adult, but that just meant she managed to get down to my level and right in my face all the better. The lack of their ability to distinguish Chinese from Korean heritage was the ignorant cap on their racist attacks. That confirmed that I had no hope of actually winning them over. They didn't even care about the truth, but just wanted someone to hate. I remember a time when Mrs. Zerrick brought nunchucks to school and swung them over her head and threaten to use them on a black student, shouting out obscene racial slurs. I was in fear of the abuse, so I ran and got the principal involved. By the time the students returned to the classrooms, the principal punished both me and the male student for tattling. The boy was the victim and he was being reprimanded, for what? How could I ever approach the principal with even the simplest of problems, much less what was to follow?

Despite all of that and the other torment, it was the school's assistant principal who would tear my life apart in those days. Every other torment faded to a background murmur next to what he did to me.

I remember it starting during a lunch period. Mr. Gable was a well-known sight, for he often acted as the cafeteria monitor. He was strolling up and down the aisles, straightening vacated chairs and ensuring that students were behaving. As he eased by me, I felt his attention fall on me a little more heavily. He found some reason to lean in close, and it was close enough that I just reacted. I couldn't believe he would have tried to kiss or touch me right out there in the open, but it felt like he was trying to do exactly that. A part of me recognized the way he imposed on my space and reacted as I wish I could have reacted when I was three years old and faced with that first man who had hurt me. I flung my fork right at him, my spaghetti staining his shirt and face, and I bolted for the door.

He didn't come after me. Not right away. I was scared of him, but it was not a rational fear. I had not yet had my confrontation with my mother, and the dreams of those earlier days with the sitter had not yet surfaced. Only my subconscious had known to react. I wasn't wrong. However, I spent the whole recess hour trembling, more out of fear of being spanked for attacking the assistant principal than anything else.

As such, when he showed up at my classroom door, my heart started palpitating with the nervous expectation of a thrashing. I knew from long experience with my mother that trying to avoid the beating only made it twice as bad later. I just followed him meekly down the hall to his office.

From my previous experience, there is no surprise that none of the office workers were shocked to see me. I was very well known for my visits to the head principal, and the fact Mr. Gable had found cause to chastise me was only a surprise because it had taken that long for him to notice me misbehaving. He guided me into his inner office and closed the door. This was long before such meetings required witnesses or similar-gender interviews or other such modern safety measures. He sank into his leather chair, crisping the white sleeves of his shirt and folding his legs neatly in his dark blue pants. I remembered he took a few calming breaths before peering at me intently through the darkly-colored frames of his glasses. He sat forward a little, his hands clasping together tightly as if trying to control his tension or his anger at me.

"Song Ja, listen to me. I'm going to call your parents in regards to your behavior at lunch."

"No! Please, I'll do anything," I cried out, and I meant it. To me, that meant extra homework, or cleaning chalkboards, or any of a dozen other tedious punishments. Certainly, any of that would have been preferable to the beatings I would receive at home. I didn't even have any real argument to offer. Why had I thrown my fork at him? He had scared me, but I was still young and didn't know where the fear inside me had come from. Even if I had known, when had my parents ever been supportive enough of me that I would credit them as likely to believe me? The potential spankings or beatings I would receive were real, whereas, the danger of Mr. Gable was indistinct and hazy, more of a fear born from my past.

"Then you'll have to stay after school for one hour with me every day until your punishment is completed."

In a twisted irony, I think I might have actually sighed in relief. "What do you want me to do?" I asked.

"That is up to me to decide at this point, but what I am going to do is call your parents so they know you'll be late."

I began to cry, my world crumbling once again. "But, I'm gonna' be in trouble anyway, 'cause they'll think I did something bad!" I was begging him for help. In further, terrible irony I was actually half-confessing the abuse I endured at home by my reaction to a simple phone call. I was obviously terrified.

Mr. Gable held up a hand to try and calm me down. He was so slick. So calm. "I'm going to tell them that you're going to help me out. How does that sound to you?"

My jaw dropped, but actually in a sort of thankful disbelief that anyone would do that for me. I nodded my head, even though I wasn't sure why he would do such a thing for me. Anything was better than me getting whipped at home.

He motioned for me to be quiet, and so I just sat there watching as he picked up the receiver and dialed the numbers on the keypad. "Hello, Mr. Kim? This is Mr. Gable, the assistant principal at your daughter's school. How are you doing?" He sat there and smiled, listening to the answer.

Once my father's initial greeting passed, he went on, "Oh, I am quite well. No, Song Ja is not in trouble. I am happy to not have to call you in the same way you've always heard from the school. Maybe, this will be the first step to turning her around."

He began to chuckle, "I know, I will try and be patient, but I really think she can be a help to us here. We have need of an after-school student assistant for a school project for while, and I think it would benefit her a great deal to put in an honest hour of extra work after school each day. What do you think?"

I sat there and heard my dad's voice, but it was so muffled I couldn't make out what was actually being said on the other end.

Then, Mr. Gable's smile grew even brighter. "Excellent! I am glad to hear that. I can have Song Ja give you a call when she is done so you can either come get her or at least you'll know when to expect her home if she walks. Oh no, thank *you*. She'll be a great help. You have a great day, too! Goodbye." He hung up the phone and smiled straight at me.

"Come back to my office after school, okay?" he said.

"Yes, sir. Can I go now?" I asked.

He responded with a nod and went back to his own work.

By the time I returned back to the classroom, the students were curious what happened. I saw no reason not to tell them, and in truth, I was even thinking of the whole thing with a bit of hope. Sure, I knew it wasn't a project, but whatever punishment Mr. Gable had in mind was almost certainly better than my mother's belt or my father's cold treatment. I told them that I was doing some project, and didn't think to tell even my teacher about the lie behind it. I didn't want anyone to know who might let that truth slip back to my parents.

Later that day, I went to his office and sat in one of the chairs in the lobby. Mr. Jameson, the head principal, saw me and asked me why I was in the office. Before I could say anything, Mr. Gable came out of his office and told him that I was there to see him. He gave the head principal the truth, as well as the lie that had been told. Pleased to see I was being both disciplined and yet also protected from an overreaction by my parents, Mr. Jameson left me in what he assumed was capable, trustworthy hands.

Mr. Gable summoned me forward, and I followed him out of the office. We walked down the hall into a locked room that I was unaware existed. The room was smaller and it appeared more private than his office. I had no idea what the purpose of that room was. I looked like a long-vacant office that no one used anymore.

He pulled the rolling chair out and pointed underneath the desk and told me to hide there.

I was hesitant at first. I wasn't sure why he wanted me to hide. Did anyone even go in that room anymore? I heard a noise, and he hustled me under the desk and told me to be silent. Then, the door opened and I heard the after-hours janitor come in.

Mr. Gable told him that he needed quiet for making some private calls, and had gone out-of-the-way so they could keep doing their work without disturbing him. He asked the maintenance person to do him the favor of not doing any noisy work for the next hour and leaving him undisturbed. The whole exchange was quite polite and friendly, and the janitor agreed easily enough and left.

The door closed, and Mr. Gable locked the door behind him. Then, he came around the desk, sat in the chair, and looked down at me. My eyes were wide, beginning to fear what this was all about.

When I saw him pulling the belt from the buckle I became sick to my stomach. I knew at that moment he had no intention of punishing me in any sort of normal way. I was still too young to connect this with it being his abhorrent behavior. I still thought it was simply what he had chosen as my punishment. "I'm sorry, I won't be a bad girl anymore," I pleaded through sobs.

"Ssshhhh, you're okay. You're not doing anything wrong. I've decided not to punish you at all." His voice was smooth and sickeningly gentle as he pulled his pants down.

Terrible regret at all my choices was thick in my mind. I was wrong. My mother's thrashings were not worse than this. "I don't wanna' do this!"

"Song Ja, I want you to listen to me carefully. This is going to happen. You promised me that if I helped you, you would help me. I came through for you. When I called your parents, I didn't tell them you were bad. I even said you were a good girl, didn't I?" he asked with a soft tone.

I just sat underneath the desk and nodded my head with tears flowing from my eyes.

"If we don't do this, I will have to go back to the office and call up your parents, but I can't tell them I lied, now can I? So I'll have to tell them you messed up the project, and that you embarrassed me after I tried to help you. You'll be in even more trouble then, wouldn't you? Do you want me to do that?"

"No! I'll be good, I promise!" I cried.

"Then you have to be quiet, okay?" he commanded, his voice became firm. He pulled his penis out of his pants, pulled my head closer to him and told me to open my mouth. I just tried to survive what came next, crying as he kept telling me to be quiet. I had no idea how long it lasted, but I couldn't wait to go home. After, I wanted to wash my mouth out. He pulled his pants up and adjusted himself, then finally let me go. I ran to the girl's restroom and cried in one of the stalls.

He had set himself up to repeat the whole thing, and he knew how to keep me afraid to reject him. I had nowhere to turn, anyway. Parents... Teachers... Classmates... They had all been stripped away. I can't remember how it ended or how long he managed to keep finding excuses for me to see him after school, but I never forgot the pain. I felt so disgusted and it was a secret that I alone was forced to keep. There were so many things to fear. I was so afraid that someone would think I was the perverted one. I was so afraid that my parents would beat me for what was going on. I was completely lost, and I find little wonder in why I buried this inside as thoroughly as I tried to suppress previous incidents of abuse until they came roaring back to the surface in later years.

That didn't mean those incidents didn't leave a mark. A wall was built between me and others. I think immediately of my own thoughtless rejection of a kind boy, not even a couple of years later. I was in Elmore City, just before my return to Tacoma and the events that would lead to my confrontation with my mother.

I guess the best description for what happened was that I had a crush. All sorts of unusual emotions were going through me, and they frightened me. Having endured abhorrent and illegal expressions of sexuality thus far, I certainly had no positive role model for how to approach my own first warm feelings for another. Jacob had blonde hair, blue eyes, and a funny way of making me laugh no matter what. Every time the two of us got together, we would create the most wonderful chaos. Teachers had to split us up in classrooms, and we still got into trouble. It was a glorious way to act out, and the best part was that he somehow melted away the concern over the chastisement I might receive from my parents or anyone else.

For a long time, there was nothing romantic or cute about our interactions. He would walk up to me and pull my hair, knock me down, or grab something of mine to make me chase him. I did the same back, and he laughed in turn. I didn't know what to call this feeling and I wasn't sure how to place it, but I knew that when there were moments where he was gone or not in the classroom, I felt empty. I thought this was oddly strange since I never felt anything like this for any boy.

Spring arrived and another random day dawned. On that day, for whatever reason, Jacob found some sort of courage and decided to take a step in letting me know he returned the crush I harbored inside. We were on our way to our special needs class. He had to take a reading lab while I finished my speech progression classes. He made an excuse to walk me over to my class, then got me to slow down with a fake trip, pretending he had hurt his leg. I look back now and see it as just a cute ploy by someone nervous about what he was about to do. With playfulness, he grabbed up my hand and tried to kiss me. It was totally innocent and had I not already been damaged, I like to think this would have been a wonderful first way to get a kiss.

That was not to be. I reacted instinctively. I was so scared that I slapped him. Hard. Then, I ran off, hiding behind the classroom and started to shake. Right then I couldn't understand why I became so afraid. He was a boy I knew I liked. I thought about it again, about him leaning into kiss me, and I had to clasp my hand around my mouth to keep from shrieking out and giving myself away.

I eventually calmed down and went to my speech class as usual. I wanted to go home. I didn't want him to stare at me and I was getting irritable and angry as he tried to catch my eye. Every time I looked up and I saw him looking straight at me, and I just wanted to punch him or scratch his face to make him stop looking at me. I couldn't comprehend the oddly mixed emotions.

When I got home I just started shaking. I didn't want to go to school again. Every time I thought about him, my subconscious mind wrestled my emotions out of my control, and I immediately couldn't help my thoughts from racing off, screaming at me, "Don't let him touch you! He's bad, he's bad!"

I became very frigid and scared at the same time. From that point on, I denied my feelings for him and completely pushed him away as if what I had felt for him never existed. After that school year, my family and I moved to Tacoma, Oklahoma. School ended and I never had a chance to work through those emotions, nor to connect with him on any other level. In truth, it would be years before I ever did.

CHAPTER 3

DANCING CLOWN

I have tried to be open and honest about each stage of my life within these pages, and now I will move into the years which followed my leaving home after the confrontation with my mother. That decision was not easy one. I am not proud of many of my actions in this era of my life, and my choices were not easy to explain. When articles were written about me or YouTube video interviews were conducted in years past, I was not ready to reveal this time of my life; both because of the choices, I had made and also the difficulty in rehashing a devastating emotional scar that cut me to the very core in my teenage years.

During a later interview with an amazing journalist who wanted to include my story in her documentary series, I had the chance to reunite with the person who had hurt me so terribly, and who was a central figure in my feelings of shame: a boy named James. After 16 years apart, I finally got the chance to try and speak with him and find some sort of answers, and perhaps some measure of peace regarding this chaotic period of my life of which he was a pivotal part.

In the aftermath of that conversation, it finally hit me. I found a way out of that trap of shame and sense of failure. I realized that it was not I that had failed in those moments. I had not lost him, but rather he had lost me. He had not had the bravery to face what was happening and turned his back on me. His betrayal sheared me even further away from any sort of healing process that would have kept me safe. I often wondered how my life would have changed had he not rejected me, but with this realization came a startling truth. It didn't matter. He was unable to face me when I staggered home to him that dark night, so how could I have relied on him to stand by me once I revealed the other hardships of my past? His fear and cowardice would have been revealed sooner or later. This was his weakness, not mine, and I had no reason to feel shame over talking about it. Of course, coming to this realization and then putting it all down in words are two completely different things, and it has been a difficult journey.

As well, what followed my first falling out with him led to a dark period in my life of which I am not proud. I know that poor choices can paint a person in a poor light. By unveiling these less than shining moments in my life, I feared it might cast a shadow of prejudice over all of the issues that I am trying to bring to life. It would be far easier to sympathize with me if I was an unsullied angel cast down by the evil around me. That would not be the truth, and what is more, that is also not even the normal way of things. The people who are the easiest to hurt and the easiest to take advantage of are often those who have already been hurt before, or who are a little lost and very exposed to the predators who hunt them. I will try and make clear the effect these events had on my life, and how they contributed to making me exposed and vulnerable to those very predators.

As such, when you read this chapter it may come to you as a shock. This is not just about actions done to me, but I went through a period where I chose to be a dancer and had a real fascination with the sex industry. I was so ashamed to reveal this, but without it, the picture of me is incomplete.

I had known James since early grade school. We grew up together. It would be wise to assume he wouldn't betray me, but he did. My feelings of love with James didn't occur until the school year of 1993 to 1994, but I will first begin by setting the stage, and for that, I must pick up where I left off following the confrontation with my mother. My trust in my family was completely shattered, and I reacted as poorly as one might expect from a betrayed 13-year-old who was cut adrift, yearning for answers and an understanding of how it all could have happened with no hope of finding any real catharsis. I threatened to run away from home, and the response from my parents was to make good on the threat and to kick me out of the house.

From there, I entered into the system of foster care, and it was not a pleasant experience. It was like the time in elementary school when violence visited me daily; and without coping skills or an outlet to vent my anger and depression, my behavior was misunderstood. I was filled with anger and a need to understand what had happened to me. To say I must have been difficult to deal with would be an understatement. That does not make the neglect I endured in those foster homes any less significant. I was not adopted but merely placed in the care of various families, and none of them ever felt like home. It was common for those families to use most of the money they were given for caring for me on other things. Hunger, privation and austere living became a normal state of affairs for me and the others who shared the same household with me and had the misfortune not to be biologically related to the owners.

Throughout my stay in the system, I befriended a young lady name Shamecka. We became inseparable and even the staff had to find ways to keep us apart. Shamecka and I were sisters in one particular home in which we both witnessed neglect of our foster baby brother and the parents even called him a racial slur, "*Jiggaboo*." Shamecka and I had heard the racial slur for the "N-word," but that one was foreign to us. When we asked the outreach staff, she reported the parents. What we received in return was more chores and punishment. No one heard our lamentation nor did anyone care. We were just viewed as two teens who didn't know how to appreciate an outsider taking us in. Due to the violence, I escaped from my family's home, only to be faced with another situation.

This led to one of the more difficult decisions in my life: the decision to not press charges against my parents. By 1991, the social work system got around to asking the hard questions that get asked when a child lives apart from their parents. This was my chance to raise the issues of abuse I had suffered at my mother's hands. There were several problems with that. First, the conditions under which I was living within the foster system hardly felt much better. I was still strapped with a belt, called racial slurs as my nickname, witnessed abuse towards the other foster kids who were not biologically theirs, and was otherwise neglected. I had a little added freedom, and the beatings didn't have the same, intensely personal feel that I suffered at the hands of my mother, and I definitely did not feel like I had found a true oasis from my troubles in any of the homes in which I was forced to live. Secondly, I had no indication from any of my time with my parents that my sisters were being ill-treated. I had always been the focal point. I was the one with the ill-luck disability and the one who had always misbehaved and drawn my mother's ire. If I pressed charges against my parents, it would certainly result in having my sisters torn away from them and cast into the same system I was enduring. Then, I could be certain they *would* be abused as I had been. I could not accept that, so I recanted my testimony. I continued on with school as best I could and left my family alone.

As the troubled teenager that I was, my time in school continued to be less than easy. I had added "foster child" to my list of reasons to be an outcast among my peers. I managed to eke out something of an education but spent just as much time being chastised by my teachers and railing against the racism I encountered on a daily basis. I was a kettle that was already steaming up, and with that pressure mounting, it was only a matter of time before I exploded. When a thoughtless

37

guidance counselor made the ridiculously bigoted comment that I should "return to China," I snapped. I punched her in the nose and dropped out of school in my junior year. Her insult was terrible, but there was a far larger reason why I was about to leave behind this part of my life in an almost violent way.

This then brings the story back to James and my first experience with "love." I was still very much naïve about sexuality and proper relationships. I might even call it worse than being naïve, for I was not just innocent, but rather my only encounters with sexuality up until this time had been situations of abuse. I was still a virgin, and I very much wanted to believe that those events had been abhorrent deviations to the way boys were supposed to act. I would watch classic movies of Cary Grant, Spencer Tracy, and Jimmy Stewart as they threw their coats down to help women across puddles and hold their arms with reassurances as they walked them home to safety. I saw examples of such wonderful male leads that would kiss your forehead and not rush to any greater intimacy without your consent. I convinced myself that this was the standard to which a man should persevere and that the fairytales of Sleeping Beauty and Snow White were the ideals of what to demand from boys who would court us. Somehow, despite the harm done to me, I had emerged as a hopeless romantic. I wanted the world as a whole to prove my previous encounters wrong. I wanted to awaken to the real world where good people existed, and I was convinced I had found the way up into that light.

That path lay through James. If you could say I had a high school sweetheart, he would be it. He was tall, skinny, and goofy-looking. He wasn't attractive in any conventional sense, but his eyes were transcendent to gaze into. He may not have carried the look of a football stud, but his humor, passion, and sincerity were what I fell for. He had been in my orbit for years and had gradually drawn closer to me as we entered the later school years. I would get into verbal arguments with my guardians about phone curfew nearly every night, so long did our conversations go on. It became so easy with him to leave the dark periods of the past behind, and even now as I write this, the feelings of young love flood back into my mind as if it was yesterday. I believed everything he said to me, and let myself get swept away on hope for the future.

He used to say all the right words. "I want to marry you after high school." Another of my favorites was when he would say, "You would be a wonderful mother." It was my dedicated wish not to become my mother, and to hear him grant me that would strike right to my core. Every time he would hint at the idea of us being together, my heart would skip a beat. There were times we were alone in his truck and he never made a move. He would trade nervous glances with me and we would both know that we wanted more, and yet I loved him for the innocent way he was trying to figure this all out with me. My world became his and I wanted to give him everything. I was so certain that he was my soul mate.

As part of the ongoing saga of my time spent in foster care, I would occasionally be sent home when the system decided it would no longer support me. This would last until I once again fled, was kicked out of the house, or otherwise had a falling out with my parents. At this point, I happened to be back at home in the late spring of 1994. It was then my family announced that we would be going to Korea to visit relatives for the summer. The thought of not seeing James for the summer nearly killed me. Out of desperation, I tore up my plane ticket and threw a violent tantrum at my father. As expected, my parents were livid but did not press the issue. I was old enough to look after myself, and I certainly was not their favorite child. They had little reason to fight to take me along.

In my mind, I was ready to take on the world. I was becoming increasingly independent from my parents due to my rebellion against their authority, and my feelings for James made me feel all the more invincible. Their leaving me only seemed to confirm my capability, and I was on top of the world. I had a whole summer of freedom! The possibilities felt endless, and I was eager to take advantage of them.

June came, and my parents had long since departed for their vacation. I thought that night would involve bringing James over to enjoy the empty house for the first time. Instead, it took a different turn when my best friend at the time Naomi called to convince me to take a different sort of adventure that night. We had both recently turned 18, and neither of us was overly fond of following the rules. She wanted to drive down to a small town south of Tacoma to find a club several of her friends were raving about. She was in a panic to get in on the action, and so I agreed.

We took my car and headed south. The very image of two teenaged girls who thought themselves much older and roaring to have a good time in a place we should never have been. Yes, there was an edge of rebellion in it all for going drinking while underage, but it went beyond that. I felt like I was an adult and ready to take control of my actions.

This was a statement to do something like this, and show I could handle anything.

We pulled into the gravel parking lot, strutted up to the door, and the bouncer seemed completely uninterested in checking our ID. We walked into the club and took stock of our new stomping ground. The room was dimly lit, fluorescent lights flashed everywhere, and the bass-heavy music thumped at a dangerous decibel level. It was thrilling at the start.

That thrill didn't last long. The base was so loud I could not tell the difference between my heart pounding away or the pulse of the bass. The strobe lights were making me feel nauseous and the stew of whatever I had eaten or drank over the last hours was not sitting well in my tummy being vibrated by the music. I went to look for my friend and told her that I would head back to the hotel we registered in for the night. She was concerned about how she was going to make it to the hotel without me, so I reassured her that I would call a cab. I didn't want her riding with some random stranger when it was her turn to go home, so I gave her keys to my car so that she wouldn't be stranded.

I called a cab, waited for it to pull up, and poured myself into the back seat. I wasn't drunk, but my head was pounding from the interior to the club that a headache was splitting me apart. I vaguely recall seeing the broad back of a white cabbie without a shirt on and telling him to take me to my hotel. He was the picture of disreputable, but I wasn't paying attention to his ragged denim shorts or uneven, mullet-shaped blonde hair and staggered farmer's tan. The hotel was only 3 miles away, and it didn't matter what he smelled like or if whatever. I wasn't there to make friends with him. I just wanted to be in the peace and solitude of my hotel room. I closed my eyes for a bit, wishing the headache would fade, and managed to drift off to sleep.

When I woke up, I knew something was wrong. The drive shouldn't have been that long. He had not shaken me awake to say we were there, but rather the driver was still focused out on the road. Worse, that road was now an empty highway well out of town heading into the wheat field.

This was a small town, and long before things like bulletproof glass was common in cabs even in big cities. I was able to reach over and tap him on the shoulder to summon him to turn around, saying, "Mister, you're going the wrong way."

The only answer I received was the lock clicking shut. I scooted over to one of the side doors to pull the handle but was jostled around by him pulling over suddenly to one side of the road. He came at me over the seat, and he punched me hard in the face. I collapsed, blacking out for some unknown time. Even when I came around, I was in such a daze that I couldn't process what was happening. I felt my body move back and forth. I could hear him breathing on me and I started to have a flashback of my child rape. I blacked out again, and mercifully I didn't awake again until I was alone.

I was so alone. I was also stranded in the middle of a wheat field in broad daylight, my buttoned-up shirt was torn, and with my bra missing and blood stains on the inside of my jeans. My body was so sore from the attack so that all I cared about was going home. I didn't want to think about it. All I wanted was James.

The walk was tortuously long to any sort of civilization, especially in that condition. I just kept thinking about being rescued and comforted. I wanted to be close to him and to have someone wash away what had just happened and tell me that it was going to be alright.

I don't remember how I found my way back to the motel, but by the time I walked up to my room, Naomi was beside herself with worry. The door was flung open and she rushed out to me. Her eyes widened in shock at the sight of bruises on my body.

"Oh my God! Are you okay? What happened?" she asked.

She was asking, and I knew she cared. I should have told her, but I could only keep this vision of my triumphant return to James's arms in my head. I wasn't sure I had the strength to admit more than once, and it had to be to him. Instead, I just shook my head, and said, "Can we just go home? I can't talk about this here."

During the two-hour car ride, neither one of us said anything to each other, I didn't know what to say and she was silent the whole time. I had her drive us to her home, and then I took over to somehow get myself to my parents' place alone. I still don't remember that drive. I just cried silently, saying nothing the whole way, and cherished the final moment I could be back with James.

I didn't even kick off my shoes before I was on the phone to him once I crossed my threshold. Thankfully, it was him that picked up his family's phone. "Hello?"

"James, it's me, Song Ja." I hated hearing my own voice trembling with fear and panic, but that didn't matter. I had a right to be losing my cool, and I had waited hours to finally do so for someone who could care.

"What's wrong?" he asked.

"James . . . I was raped." I had no other way to say it. I blurted it out and then waited for him to console me. A part of me felt so ashamed, but at the same time, I just needed him to say the words that would absolve me and soothe me and calm me.

"Did you go to the police?" he asked. His tone didn't sound affectionate. He sounded distant, even a little angry. Was he angry with me, on my behalf? I welcomed that a little, but right then I needed his sensitive side, not his vengeful one.

"No, I'm too scared."

"You should go."

The whole idea of telling my story scared the hell out of me. "Can you go with me?" I needed him to say "yes." With him at my side, I might be able to face this somehow.

His reply still didn't carry any warmth, but at least it was the answer I wanted to hear. "Yes, I'll go with you."

The first thrill of warmth ran through my cold frame for the first time that day. Some small dribble of hope came back into my life. I could get through this! "Okay, I'll come and pick you up." After I hung up the phone, I called another friend who I knew was a survivor of rape and told her what had happened. With James now on my side, I felt like I could assemble a group to see me through this. James had been the key, and I felt my own anger coming out, and my desire to do this right. I was still scared, but now I had momentum on my side. Trisha was her name, and she agreed to come with me.

I picked her up, and we were at James's house not long after. I remember wanting to be there when James opened the door to have his arms around me, but then there were his parents who might see me in my horrid state. I felt like a used creature and not myself at all. Not only that, but I had bruises all over my body and was starting to seriously feel the fatigue of the punishing day. So, instead, I asked Trisha to go and bring him out to the car so we could head on to the hospital.

Trisha went to the house and took far too long in returning. I caught sight of her arguing and talking to someone. When she returned to the car, I wasn't even yet disappointed. I was just confused.

Her first words made no sense. "Song Ja... James is not coming."

I had no answer. My mouth hung open. What she had said was blatantly impossible.

"He said you're not welcome here anymore." She gave me this sad look on her face. She had been through the awkward reactions that come from friends who can't cope with such tragic events, and she was watching me now endure the same thing.

I couldn't believe that he would abandon me like this; I had to hear it for myself. Despite Trisha's warnings, I jumped out of the car and walked over to the glass front-door. I saw his mother coming out and she pointed and waved at me to leave. I saw him inside sitting on the couch playing video games as if I didn't exist. I shouted out at him through the door, "What did I do? Why did you say you would come and support me if you were only going to *humiliate* me?"

His mother came to the door, pointing even more forcefully to leave, "Song Ja, you need to leave!"

I ignored her and kept trying to see past her to James. "Answer me, James! What did I do?" I cried. This strange, crushing rejection and his pretending to ignore me hurt more than the rape in that moment. The man I loved and to whom I was sure I was going to devote my heart and soul was trying to erase me from his existence.

When I proved inconsolable, he actually came to the door. I tried to see past his averted eyes and get some idea of what was going on, but he just kept staring at anything except me, standing close to his mother's side and not coming close to the door as if I was infected with something he had no wish to catch. "I don't love you and you need to leave."

None of it made sense. "Why are you doing this? Why?" My own voice was now shifting from pure confusion and pain and into the realm of anger. How dare he just cast me off like that? When I needed him most, he treated me like I was less than garbage, and didn't even bother to tell me why?

Trisha saw this was not going well, and knew I could only get into trouble. She came out of the car and encouraged me to back away. They were treating us like strangers, and I was the screaming lunatic on their lawn who was going to bring the authorities down on me at the very moment I needed to be looked after by those who cared. Her efforts probably saved me a lot of unnecessary pain, but I was hardly grateful in the moment. In time, I got back in the car and just cried my eyes out.

I couldn't believe what had happened to me. Despite all the horrid things that had happened, I had kept both my virginity and a certain awareness of what I wanted love to be like. I wasn't the teenager that ran around with different boys. I knew what I wanted and I saved myself for a boy. I wasn't looking for a bad boy or anything. I wanted my oddly goofy friend to become my lover and live together in peace. Now, he had simply tossed me aside because I was no longer worthy of him. I felt so betrayed. I had shared intimate thoughts with him and had every intention of giving him everything of who I was, and he turned around and emotionally raped my soul. The one person I never imagine hurting me destroyed me in ways I never imagined.

In the midst of that confusion and anger, Trisha took me by the hand and guided me through a process I barely recall happening. She convinced me to do what I could to take the cab driver to court. I knew that meant an examination, though I wasn't ready for the antiseptic feel to it all. We went to a rape crisis center, and I endured the humiliation of the examination in that cold, hospital room in a state of emotional isolation. The nurse hardly said a word to me, and I felt that her stare was one of pity and shame. All I could think about was James. No one was testing me for the scars and damage *he* did to me.

The scenario was playing over and over in my mind as if I had hit "repeat" the moment the video ended. What had happened? Why the change and why so cold? My mind was so enveloped in that quicksand of self-doubt, confusion, and anger, and questions of "why," that I didn't even remember my stay at the shelter. The few times I had to appear in court was a blur. The dull ache of hearing my own rapist say I jumped him and to hear my word placed against his as the sole real evidence washed over me, and I hardly noticed. Numbness set in, and I recall just nodding through a blank stare as my attorney told me we had lost the case. At that moment, I just didn't care.

Somewhere in that long process, I became completely disillusioned with school. If I had been a discipline problem before, now I was completely impossible. I withdrew into myself and was ready to be gone. When my guidance counselor made her insensitive and racist comment, it was all the excuse I needed to attack her and leave. That was how my last school year ended. Once the court case was concluded, I really had nothing to do but return home without any prospects for the future.

When I came home from my last day in the courtroom, the house was in disarray from my prolonged absence. My aunt had arrived to check up on me since I had not been answering the phone. She was in the process of starting to clean up and set things right. Of course, she was not in the best of moods having to clean up what seemed like my neglect. My memory was very hazy at that point, but I do remember arriving to see her standing on the front porch as I pulled up. When she saw the "hickey" marks on my neck, she backhanded me and called me a slut. I didn't care to explain myself. In a way, that is exactly how I felt. I jumped back in the car and drove off.

I didn't know where I was going or what I really intended at that point. Something inside me changed. I had always held some form of hope, but the last of it was dashed out on the floor. I wandered a bunch, and don't even really recall how I got by from day to day. It wasn't long before I started picking up bad habits, and began living from senseless moment to senseless moment. I started smoking cigarettes and weed as a way to dull the ache inside even further and learned every trick in the book to get my hands-on beer to wash away what memories I could.

Money became an issue quickly enough, and I was fortunate enough to find a bar owned by a Korean crew. The place was a strip club, and whatever anyone thinks of those types of establishments, the insanity brewing in my mind found it perfect to continue my trend of self-destruction. I started out as a cocktail waitress and learned the ropes of the business.

It wasn't long before I started to notice the other girls swinging around the poles. This was very foreign to me, but tempting in a way I can't explain. I had always fought against the loss of my innocence, thinking of myself as a good, Catholic girl even if I might have raised a little hell in my behavior at school now and again. I grew up with Catholic Koreans who were proper and well-behaved and followed traditional morals.

This new entourage of Koreans was not what I expected. One of the Korean ladies actually saw my interest and encouraged me to see what it felt like to work the tables and attract the attention of "white men who love Asian women." The ironic thing was, the Korean owners forbid me to be a dancer, just a drink hustler and a manipulative thief for the drunken customers who favored "yellow fever." I didn't give a shit about any sort of self-discovery. I just wanted to cast off the old life completely. What had it ever earned me, being the girl who had always followed the rules?

I gave the pole a shot. I remember my first time being on stage. I was so frigid and scared that I might have moved twice during the whole first song they had playing in the background. The others around me tried to shake me free of what they saw as stage fright. Part of me was struck by them, and I wanted to be like them. They were not just pretty. They seemed strong, powerful, and in control. They handled the men in the audience like the professionals they were, and I couldn't help but see a sort of power in that.

Two of them, in particular, embraced me as a new friend. One was Nancy who had blonde hair down past her buttocks and a curly set of bangs that matched her bouncy personality. She was responsible for finally making me feel a little more at ease.

Then, there was Kelli. She was a totally different sort. Where Nancy was charismatic and playful, Kelli was a firebrand. She would tell men off if she didn't like them, and her domineering personality took control of anyone in her orbit. I was one of them. She had an exotic element to her and used her Puerto Rican heritage to its maximum to stand out. She didn't apologize at all for her ethnicity, and that too became something I admired. It took me years to realize the men who desired me for my exotic look or ethnicity had nothing more than a racist interest. These men had no genuine interest in my dreams or ambitions of any sort except for the *oriental stereotype* that was fed to them through media and other sources. It didn't matter to me, I felt a sense of power. I felt wanted and desired and I believed they cared. I would even use my ethnicity to compete with the other dancers to gather more clients. Little did I realize I was allowing men who were non-Asian to abuse me.

Kelli took me under her wing and into her home. We became roommates and what I thought of as friends. In reality, she was older than me and I was a young, lost pup to her. In many ways, that is exactly what I was. She taught me to color my hair, put highlights in it to give me more of an "exotic" look, and filled in other aspects of my beauty education that had simply passed me by in my teenage life.

Whatever Kelli had us do, I never argued with her. She would introduce me as her sister, and I would go with the flow despite the ridiculous statement. The guys she said it to never really cared. I didn't argue or try to correct her and played her games right alongside her. I didn't know why, but all I remember is that I wanted to be just like her. I would see men falling at her feet and she would kick them to the curb. What strength she had, I would admire! Even as I admired her strength, I became more and more her lackey.

The stronger our friendship became, the more I lost control of my life. I focused fully on being the sidekick in *Kelli's* life. My lifestyle ceased to be important, and I was there to support and accent *her* lifestyle. As such, I fell into a vicious downward spiral. She was promiscuous and lived only for a good time. So, I started to act equally callous to those we met. I didn't care whose heart I was breaking or bruising. I didn't care about catching AIDS or HIV. Inside, I wouldn't hesitate to say there was some part of me that wanted to die. I would find men that were the sweetest guys you ever knew and hurt them to compensate for the pain that was in me, and Kelli was my instructor in how to play them.

I was being worn ragged by this style of life, and the reputation I earned for myself in the area grew. Kelli had no desire to let me actually learn from what I was doing. She wanted her sidekick, not a friend. So, she played me off of others, trading rumors to insulate me and keep me close. Anyone who might have helped me realize a little independence became enemies in Kelli's eyes, and she would warn me away from them under the guise of friendly advice that shouldn't be ignored.

After a while, no one wanted me to be near me. Those I had not hurt directly had been pushed away by Kelli's manipulation. Even the clubs wouldn't have me working there, and so I became completely dependent on Kelli as a roommate for a place to live. I became useless except for being what she wanted me to be. She was like the big sister I never had and I wanted to make her proud, so I did anything for her. I slept with men she brought over for me. If I ever saw a bright spark in any of those guys and had any warm feelings for any of them that even resembled a shadow of love, she would crush it immediately. She reminded me that they were like James. This brought up those dark emotions again, and inspired me to turn against them and shut them out.

Her tactics were effective. Even when I was not directly with her, she had stirred up the right emotions to make the fear and nerves at being with anyone else very real. In some part of me, I think I did recognize that our relationship was not a positive one. I would make excuses to arrange to stay at the place of another dancer under the guise of needing a change of scenery. The refreshing break from the alcohol abuse and emotional trials of being in Kelli's orbit were a double-edged sword. They helped me to survive, but I still had not broken free. Eventually, I would get pulled back in. Those breaks from her helped me last longer under her rough handling.

One example of the vicious cycle included the meeting of a former acquaintance. I had sought out the company of a dancer named Melanie recently and was staying at her place for a couple of days to get one of those breaks. We went for a drive to the lake to pass a few hours, and I ran into an old friend named Jordan. He had been engaged the last time we met, so while I recall some attraction to his slight build, blue eyes, and sweet personality, I had never really considered pursuing him. He was in the Army, and so I met his presence with some surprise as I figured he would be off on some military duties in another world other than rural Oklahoma.

More out of curiosity than anything, I went to him, "Jordan?"

He smiled in immediate recognition, "Song? Is that you?" He struggled to his feet with a limp.

Noting the difference from his formerly springy way of movement, I asked, "Are you okay?" I gave him a hand to help him up.

"I sprained my ankle. Nothing huge. Might make the rest of my week painful, though. I broke up with my fiancé, so I am cleaning up the trailer and getting my stuff before heading back to the barracks."

I hated the idea of him running off so soon. He was a fragment of my past that was a happier time. I was playing with hitting bottom, but this was one of my breaks from Kelli, and the idea of spending time with him felt even more refreshing. "I don't suppose you'd want some help?"

His smile made it clear he wouldn't turn me down, "Sure, if you're offering. I want to be out of there by the afternoon, so whenever you can come down to help would be great."

"Well then, I'll be there around 9 a.m." We traded smiles, hugged goodbye, and parted ways. I felt lighter than I had in a long time. It wasn't that I felt particularly warm about Jordan. We had been good friends, but he represented something more. We were hanging out. I had a value to him that went beyond my body. That felt great. No judgment. Just getting together to work on a task.

The next morning, I pulled up next to the trailer and saw him already working at dumping garbage and sorting out his things from the rest. I walked in, talked about what needed to be done, and got to work cleaning. I picked a section and dove into the honest-feeling work. We took breaks when it felt right, and as midday approached he went and got lunch. We both sat on lawn chairs and propped our feet on the closed ice chest. I was sweating from the heat of the sun and the trailer had no air conditioning, so I pulled my hair up with one hand and used the other hand to wave off the sweat. I noticed Jordan looking at me and I became immediately shy.

His warm tone didn't make it any better. So far, this had just been friends, but his change in demeanor suggested he was looking past that now. "You are so pretty."

My blush was full on now, and I smiled back not knowing what to say. Jordan was a friend I respected and saw him differently. Two sides of me were at war now. Kelli's hard lessons about how to play men and lead them on were at the front of my mind, but I had no wish to hurt him like that, he was a friend. I tried to let the moment pass and hoped he wouldn't pursue it. I was not sure I could trust myself. What side of me would he get? Kelli's femme fatale in the making, or the older romantic side of me that I had buried deep? The fact that he was more like James' kinder personality and less like the jerks I kicked to the curb with Kelli's help made the whole thing even more complicated. I didn't want another James at that moment, right?

We returned back to cleaning after our lunch break and got the rest finished off. I kept my distance but knew the end would come and we'd have to talk. Once the house was complete, we both stood outside awkwardly, wondering what to say.

He took my hand out of the blue, and told me seriously and directly, "Look, I've always liked you. I'm not engaged anymore and I'd like to see you again."

I felt flustered inside, but his gallantry and honest expression called me back to a time before I was hurt. The thought of James just melted away a little. Maybe the romantic side of me was not as dead as I had first thought. I agreed to see him again and so it began.

As I knew he would be, Jordan was very sweet. He was polite, generous, and romantic. He would bring me flowers, teddy bears and take me places to dine out even though there weren't very many fancy places to go except for steak houses or rib joints. At least it wasn't fast food. Every time we were in the car together, he would take me by the hand and kiss the back of my hand. Jordan never yelled at me, hit me or even made obscene comments. He was soft spoken, very gentle, and sweet.

Then, it began to scare me. My initial impulses wore off. I had too much time to think. He would take me to the movies, hold my hand, cuddle with me, and kiss me on the cheek—things that normal couples do on a typical date. The problem was, I didn't feel normal. There was no violence. No heartache. No pain. I wasn't playing games with him, and he showed no signs of betraying me. I wasn't playing any games with him, and that felt like a game in itself! Shouldn't I be looking for ways to break his heart like Kelli taught me? And what about him? I started to feel like I was just waiting for the other shoe to drop when he would take advantage of me if I didn't do the same thing to him first.

Then one night, he invited me to his place. It resembled an apartment even though it was a military barrack. I figured military living spaces were all like the rough, antiseptic dorm rooms in movies like "Full Metal Jacket" or other war movies that I watched in the past. This was small, but still an apartment all to his own. We started kissing, and one thing seemed like it would lead to another. He was cradling me in his arms, and his whispered words were as loving and sweet as I could have wanted.

This made me even more anxious. I tried to push aside those twisted thoughts trying to pop out of me. *"Isn't this what you wanted? Why am I freaking out?"* It stalled things, and so after a little more snuggling Jordan drifted off to sleep even as my own uneasy thoughts continued to roil inside me. I crept out of bed, put my clothes on, and closed myself in the bathroom. Escape was on my mind. I had to creep out of the apartment before morning, and I knew I couldn't explain why. It didn't make sense, not even to me, but I just knew I wasn't ready for this to go any further.

Then, he knocked on the door, and asked through the wood, "Are you okay?"

Startled, I realized I was crying without even really knowing it. All of that anxiety, fear, and anger were all surfacing at once, and I felt overwhelmed. Somehow, I choked out simply, "Yes, I'll be out in a moment." I started running the water, trying to wash away and hide the tears. I didn't want to scare him. When I opened the door, he was standing there with the blanket around him and a worried expression on his face.

He stepped forward and tried to kiss me, smiling from ear-to-ear.

I knew this wouldn't end well. The other side of me reached up and took control. I slammed the door and locked myself in the bathroom again. Even as the more innocent side of me scolded the other side for my actions, screaming at me in my own mind that *"He's a sweet guy! He's just like those men you watch on classic movies!"* I slid to the floor and started to cry. I felt the monster of rejection clawing its way up inside, yelling back just as powerfully, *"I don't want this! I don't want to be with him!"* I was torn in two and paralyzed from the internal debate. Looking back, this might indeed be the first point when that odd duality in me was born or at least conceived. I was so ripped in two, my practical side at war with my romantic one. It was not so well-defined back then, but it was part of me.

Outside, Jordan was understandably confused, and could only ask, "Are you okay, did I do something wrong?"

I didn't want to face him, it was almost as if I was in disgust. I reached up, wiped away my tears, and went out into the room in a rush. I did everything I could to avoid eye contact. "Look, it isn't you. It's me."

He tried to accept that, not quite sure what to think. He just nodded, and asked, "What do you want to do today, then? It's almost light."

I was searching for my belongings scattered around his room and still avoided looking his way. If I looked his way, I might cry again. "I can't stay. I have to do some things, sorry."

His confusion only grew. "Ok, can I call you later?"

That was the last thing I wanted in that moment, but I couldn't tell him that. "Yeah . . . sure if you want to." I stood up, smiled and walked out the door.

By the time I got into my car, he had managed to beat me there and was standing outside my car door with shorts and his white t-shirt on. I reacted as if he was an attacker stalking me, and gave a startled scream.

He had no idea what was going on, and I could see it on his face as he explained with a bewildered look, "What's wrong? I'm so sorry, I didn't mean to scare you, I wanted to give you a kiss goodbye."

Sweet as ever, and that just made it worse. "Like I said, it's not you, I just have to go. Bye!" I rushed into the car and drove off.

From then on, I avoided his calls deliberately. He would stop by and drop off flowers with notes saying how he missed me, and that made my issues worse. His pursuit started to cause triggers of fear and anxiety from others who had pursued me, and I thought he was finally showing his true colors. He was showing himself to be like all men who couldn't take "no" for an answer. Finally, I stormed back over to his place and gave back all the items he had given me, and told him I was done with him. I didn't love him, and we were at an end. I didn't feel any remorse, feeling vindicated and justified that my fears had been proven correct.

He was sad and disappointed, and tears were behind his eyes. I had grown up with the teachings of my family's version of Korean culture blended in with American values of those days, and those values told me that men weren't supposed to cry. I mocked him for it then, calling him a coward. I wanted to hurt him, and I succeeded.

"Why are you doing this, Song Ja?" The worst hurt I think was that he honestly had no idea.

"We aren't meant to be. That's it. I'm damaged. You don't want me." I flung that in his face and drove off. As I came home, I was so sure of myself. I was positive he would not have listened, and that there would be a message waiting on my answering machine. He would continue to pursue me, ignoring my wishes.

Instead, the answering machine was dark. He obeyed my request. I began to feel more frustrated than before. I sat in my room, crying, and not knowing what to do. What was wrong with me?

In that chaotic moment, Kelli called. She was both exactly the person I needed to speak with and the worst person I could possibly have chosen to speak with. She reminded me of how men were, about how troublesome and devious they were. She reminded me of all the reasons I had to hate them and brought my mind back to James for the first time in days or even weeks. She sank her claws back into me and asked me to come home. Right then, I needed the voice of someone who I felt understood me, and so I listened. That very day, I moved back in with Kelli, and the cycle with her continued. Still, Jordan lingered on my mind.

I like to think that it was his influence and kindness that finally allowed me to awaken to how toxic my relationship with Kelli had become. Where I found the courage to see the friendship for the domestic abuse scenario that it was, I will never know, but it might have been the memory of Jordan's kind smile which was part of it. He had never betrayed me. I was vulnerable. To me, all men were monsters. Maybe I just worked through enough of my anger at James to finally be done with it and needed something more. Perhaps, I just found myself in a place where the emptiness was no longer enough, and I had to find myself again. I had hit bottom, as the saying goes, and it was time to start climbing back up again.

I decided to leave. That took courage as well. I remember Kelli calling me like a desperate boyfriend, begging me to come back. It was not easy to say no. Whatever else she was, she had supported me, held me through terrible nights of crying, and had been there when no one else had been willing to do it. She would call and plead with me, "I love you, Song. Please come back, we are family, remember?" Walking away from her was beyond difficult.

Whatever her words, I knew I couldn't continue this lifestyle anymore. I wanted something different for myself. I packed up my stuff and left. I decided to clean myself up and return back to Oklahoma and start my life over again. I started to look for technical colleges to attend and pushed hard to put this chapter of my life behind me.

Still, I know this part of my life can never be truly erased. However hard I tried to forget my actions as a dancer, I can't ignore them. Even worse, no matter how hard I tried to bury the hurt James caused in me under the sins of my time with Kelli, the hurt never completely left me.

CHAPTER 4

BOYFRIEND

Having broken free of Kelli, I returned home in a peculiarly-fragile, yet dynamic state of mind. The effort of tearing free of her control had taken its toll on me, but I was now liberated and ready to regain some control of my life. I wanted more for myself, even as I wasn't sure what the future could possibly hold for me. I had hit bottom and was now trying to ascend again to something of a normal life.

I was still 18 and considering my options. There was no way I could see myself returning home. Even if my parents would forgive me, I couldn't face returning to my old life. I needed a change. I moved out with a friend to an apartment in Dallas and found a vocational-trade school to enroll in. I majored in Criminology and tried to forget my previous lifestyle that most would call disreputable.

Then there was the subject of love. Looking back and as I read this story I have assembled, it continues to be a wonder that I was not permanently poisoned against love and relationships. James' betrayal had strained me to the breaking point, but perhaps the good nature of Jordan had resurrected my inner feelings that good people could exist. There were interludes in my life where people like him existed that kept hope alive somewhere inside me even at the darkest of times. Unfortunately, it was not soon enough to save those first relationships. Now, months after, I was ready to open myself again to the possibility of finding someone special.

The problem with that is that my ability to separate those who were good for me and those who were not was still damaged. Just because my ideal of romantic love had persisted didn't mean I had suddenly acquired the ability to discern who were abusers from who were not. Kelli had further distorted my viewpoint and stopped me from acquiring a healthy viewpoint. She had tried to instill in me that all men were pigs. Jordan had proven that wrong, and I had left her. She had been my mentor, and now I was rejecting her teachings. I didn't want to see the world that way. However, I didn't know where the middle ground was. Not all men are terrible, but not all of them are saints either. I was still too innocent and naive to tell the difference. How many people at that age are truly conversant in the depths of real love and what it means to be committed to each other? I was swinging back and forth between extremes.

If you factor in my continued low self-esteem and the fact that normal warning signs of a violent personality passed right by me, I was frighteningly open to targeting by a predator of a different sort. That is precisely what happened.

Keith presented himself in a way that was eerily similar to Jordan. I don't think he knew specific details about Jordan or who he was until I told him, but predators like him know there are common factors for vulnerable personalities like me. Whatever the case, he was too much like Jordan, in a way. I still had a soft spot in my heart for Jordan and regretted the fact that my prejudices had forever driven him away. So, when Keith showed up on the scene in his military attire and handsome face, I was love-struck far too quickly. He would treat me to shows, buy me flowers, candy, and teddy bears, and all the things that proper boyfriends do for their young loves. This felt like a new chance to make something work after having spoiled it all with Jordan. I actually felt fortunate to have that chance. I fell for him hard and fast. I gave far too much trust without any forethought at all. He treated me like a queen, and any small cracks in his persona were washed away in the haze of happiness.

He said all the right things and played the gallant man well. He was affectionate and yet properly tentative about taking things too far. He would offer me his elbow as we walked, and open the passenger side door for me to climb in. He would wait for me to pass each of those initial boundaries of touch and intimacy, then follow up with his own soft kisses combined with genuine smiles that would make your heart melt. I felt giddy much of the time.

If I had paid any attention, I might have recognized some of the warning signs of being with him. A significant sign was how well he was able to pinpoint where I was all of the time. Whereas most people just got a feeling for where and when their loved ones were at any given time, Keith could find me anywhere. I would be sitting in an outdoor mall food court, and he would walk right up to me and say "hi," then sit down, kiss me, and start sharing lunch with me. I was thrilled he was there because I was always thrilled about his company. The fact that I had not told him where I would be and that I was actually outside my normal pattern for the day should have worried me. It should have made me wonder if he had surveillance on me, to have found me without even a pause. Instead, I simply ignored that flicker of good sense and jumped into his arms. I convinced myself he had simply been shopping and seen me unexpectedly, right? I could have convinced myself of anything in order to see his smile again.

Another intensely important issue was simply that I knew almost nothing about him. He would erect the subtlest of walls between me and any of his personal life. When we hung out, it was at my place. If we went out, it would either be to places that I selected, or we would take drives away from the local area. He learned my habits, patterns, and had me figured out. I simply knew that he bought me gifts and treated me well. Just like with everything else, that felt like it was more than enough. It felt like love to me.

There were times I found it frustrating, but I never pushed him that hard. Typical conversations with him wouldn't go very far. Once, I asked, "So, do you live with any roommates?" I asked.

"Yes." His answers were always short.

"Do you have one roommate?"

"No, I have two roommates."

"Will I get to meet them someday?"

"Probably not. In the military, they don't like us to mingle with civilians while we're in training. My superiors would prefer that I stay on base and focus on our mission as much as we can." The excuse was ready on his lips, as if it was rehearsed and planned for the moment I finally asked.

Of course, I wasn't noticing that. He was struggling to be with me, casting off the rules just to be by my side. To me, it wasn't a warning sign. It was romantic. "So, will being with me be a problem?" I asked it breathlessly, wanting him to say how he was willing to fight past any odds to be with me. It played right into my fantasies.

He knew it. He had the right answer ready, and he fed it to me. "Yes, but I don't care. I want to be with you." With a rush of passion, he grabbed my belt loops and pulled me closer to him.

He was a master of deflection. That was only one example. Another time, we were sitting in a park, kissing on a bench. There was a wicked thrill of doing something nearly indecent, even though it was little more than snuggling. Despite all the trials I had been through, my choices and thoughts on intimacy were still quite traditional. I remember sitting on his lap facing him, and suddenly thought to ask, "Will I get to see your place?" I asked.

"Why? It's just a bed and a dresser. Nothing big," he answered.

"You're always at my place and I want to see yours."

"I'm sorry babe, but we're not allowed to bring anyone on base."

That seemed strange to me, but then again, I didn't know everything. I thought to question him, "My uncle was in the military. My mom and I would go on the base all the time."

"Yes, some bases are open to military families and friends. The type of base I'm on is a training facility, so there's no commissary or PX for you." He was so smooth and had an answer for everything. He could see I was clearly disappointed, and so lifted my chin to look into my eyes, "Besides, I love being with you at your place. You make me feel at home," he smiled.

I loved the idea that he considered my home to be his. He put all his focus and attention on me, and so it never seemed to matter that he never reciprocated. The great lovers in movies always focused on the women, asking them questions, and never went on about themselves. He was fulfilling a role I thought he was supposed to play. I had no idea where he had spent his childhood, who his family was, or anything else. He was so interested in me, my family, my background, my culture and my life. With all his effort to invest in me, my hobbies, my interests, and my love of music came the feeling that he cared. It was almost perfect. We didn't fight or even disagree as far as I can remember. He wasn't much of a talker. I was the loud mouth and he was the quiet one. I literally believed opposites attract. If I wrote a poem, he would listen. If I felt the burst of energy to sing, he would let me yodel. He was my prince and I was his princess.

One day, he surprised me. He invited me to travel out of state with him, supposedly to meet his family in Florida. I was not strong in the area of geography, so I didn't really understand how far away from home I would be going. I didn't make sufficient preparations, and he never encouraged me to do so. Indeed, he made it feel like a short trip, like a day trip where we would be back in no time. I remember going on the car ride and feeling giddy to finally be seeing behind the curtain of his life.

I was brimming with joy to be meeting his family, and the fact that he was going to surprise them with my arrival was an added element of fun to the whole event. I remember him breaking open what I thought was a briefcase, but it was actually a cellular phone. I had only seen them in the movies. Such technology was still new, and this was the version that required a full case just to carry the battery, transmission gear, and broadcasting unit. He held up a finger to request my silence to make sure I couldn't be heard on the phone. I recall it being so much fun to be keeping his parents in the dark, and I giggled silently to know I was in the car and he was giving nothing away. He answered in his typical way, with one word answers like "Yes" and "Soon." I just figured he was playing the whole situation up. It wasn't that I didn't think anything was strange. I was thinking that he was actively clever and the whole situation a fine, wonderful play-act.

We drove into the driveway of what looked like an abandoned house. Some of the windows were boarded up with white wood while the blue pastel siding was faded and dingy with creeping moss. My mind flashed first with the first thought, "*I hope his parents don't live here.*" The place looked scary, but I wanted to trust my boyfriend. I remember feeling guilty about that thought, thinking I would sound awfully elitist to look down on them for living in such a rough place.

Instead, trying to break the tension of him maybe letting me know of his poor background, I tried hard to make my voice cheerful as I asked, "So, do your parents live here?"

"No. I have a friend that I help out once in a while. That's why we're here." His tone was different. I didn't notice this until later, or simply brushed it aside as a petty concern.

"Okay, well, I'll wait here while you go and visit your friend. I'd like to be getting to your parents' place before dark, wouldn't you? Can we be there in time?" I settled in with both of my hands in my lap, patient and willing to give him a little time.

He got out, shut the door to the driver's side, then he walked over to my side and opened the passenger door. Everything happened so fast I didn't know what to think. He leaned in, his face filling my vision. One of his hands came up and settled on my neck, clasping tight enough to choke me a little. His cold voice came at me like a stranger's would.

"You'll get inside with me *now*. You'll do as I say, and wish you could have done it faster, understand?"

He was angry and I didn't know why. My first thought wasn't "escape." My first thought was "fear of losing him." Was meeting his friend that important to him? Ragged fragments of thought flitted through my mind, "*Did I do something wrong? Was I being too snobby about his friend's home? Oh, my God, I was, wasn't I? I can't let him stay mad at me.*"

I followed him through the door with little need for him to drag me. He made sure I went in first, giving me a little shove through the entry as I stepped over the edge. There was a ratty, faded-green, patchy couch along one wall. Some of the couch cushions were on the floor so I could see the supporting coils under the thin supporting material. The room was dank and had just enough light to see clearly because of the strength of the sun streaming in around the edges of the boarded windows, but there was no light to turn on. The room smelled like mold or old moisture alongside a stale scent of the unmoving air. The only other furniture that had been in the room at one time was now broken apart and tossed into a corner. There was another room further in, but the doorway into that other room was covered in a dark-colored bed sheet. I also remember another exit into what looked like a kitchen.

I was still trying to absorb the deplorable conditions when Keith grabbed hold of my wrists. He pushed my back up against the now closed door and snagged my wrists with handcuffs. He locked me to the doorknob and let me fall to the floor. I was beginning to realize that whatever he was to me was evaporating and that I had been trapped. I began to cry, but any hope of that helping was far gone.

I remember watching him pace back and forth as if waiting for something. I was all but ignored, despite any of my pleas or questions. When he needed to go back to the car to get the other items he had brought along, he would push the door open to get past me, making me scoot out of the way as if I didn't exist. He brought the phone-briefcase in from the car among his other things. He pulled the receiver out, activated the mechanism and dialed a number.

Someone must have answered, for he soon began to talk. "Yeah, it's me." Silence, but I could hear the muffled sound of talk on the other end. Then, "Yeah, okay. Got it. Bye." He hung up the phone and put the briefcase near the covered entrance to the next room. He began to move with brutal efficiency. He ransacked everything about who I was. He went through my purse. He went through my pockets. My luggage. Everything. I watched in horror as he destroyed my social security card, naturalized papers, driver's license, and anything that could authenticate my identity. Every sensitive document that proved I was who I was, was shredded right in front of my eyes. In reality, I was unaware of how important those documents were at the moment. Oddly, I watched with strangely-twisted anger as he burned my Blockbuster movie card and erased the free rental I had built up with the points on it.

After all the documents were destroyed, he settled in front of me and pointed at the ashes and tiny pieces that were left. "See these? This is what let you walk around here like an American. Without these, anybody who you talk to will just ignore you or even get you deported. You're nothing to anyone anymore. You're here until I have to take you somewhere else, and that's all you need to know. Get it?"

I had no idea what to say. I had no way to adjust to everything that was happening. Instantly, I was cut adrift in a world I had not even imagined, much less had any ability to understand. How had my boyfriend turned into this cold, calculating monster in but a few minutes? I still couldn't connect the fact that he had always been that way, that I had been played, conned, and fooled. I couldn't admit that, not yet.

The confusion was just the beginning. The real torture soon began. I don't recall the exact length of time I was there, and in truth, I don't care to. Minutes faded into days, then became weeks. I didn't know why he was holding me, and I didn't know what his purpose was other than it was some sort of task. The phone calls would come now and again. He would get instructions and there seemed to be a plan. To me, the plan hardly mattered. I was raped continuously beaten, sodomized, and tortured in ways I never expected.

Through it all, I was treated like an animal or an errant pet in an unclean home. I wasn't always handcuffed to the doorknob, I was left to wander at times through the unlocked rooms. Keith, or whatever his real name might have been, had no fear of me. I remember walking through the kitchen and seeing that there were no countertops or sinks. There were just pipes sticking out of the wall. When I walked to the bathroom, there was no tub or sink. There was a toilet, but it didn't work and had no water. There was no toilet paper or towels to wipe myself after nature called, or showers to cleanse myself from the filth of my captor's foul attentions.

When Keith was home, he would unlatch me and warn me that if I tried to leave, I would be beaten. Of course, I didn't listen. Now, I am sure he was waiting for me to try as part of some training regimen. When I did, he knew me well enough to read my intent, stop me, and make sure I regretted it. After several attempts, I stopped trying. He would bring food and sometimes had to spoon-feed me literally to ensure I ate.

Now that he was sure I wouldn't try to escape, he would spend time in the other room, watching TV and ignoring me. I would receive canned beans and other simple fare for my meals while he ate fast food and generally did as he wished. His food would smell so good, after days living on far too little, that I would vomit from the need for a simple taste. I wasn't allowed to enter in his other room. When he would come out, I could see past the bedsheets that he was living his own simple existence. He had an unshelled mattress on a bed, as well as the TV that I could hear. At that moment, I had no wish to see any deeper into that room. I had no desire to be close to him. Often, he'd come sleep on the couch with me. His arm would curl around my neck, so that if I moved he would choke me to make me lay still. I would wish for him to just go back to his own bed and leave me alone.

So many days had passed that by now, my nose was dead to the odor clinging to my body. I had no idea how powerfully I reeked, and scratching at the filth on me was part of life. On this day, he dragged me to the front door and made me stand still.

He looked at me rather seriously, and said, "We have to leave." Leave? The concept of being outside was beyond my understanding at that point. He had beaten it into me that getting out of that house was to be feared, and I nearly soiled myself at the idea of trying to step out the door. I hadn't been outside since I was locked up. It sounded like an alien land we would be visiting. "Listen close to me. If you try anything, I will catch up to you and you will face consequences, do you understand?" I nodded my head. He took off the handcuffs and opened the door to take me out. I ran as fast as I could.

I remember as a young child, seeing horror movies and thinking *"Don't turn around. Just run. Run fast and the monster can't get you."* That's exactly what I did.

I didn't care where I was going. I just had to get away. I don't remember how I got to this shopping mall, but I charged through the glass doors and burst into a clean, elegant world that felt completely wrong. People were walking everywhere. They stopped to stare at me like a wild zoo creature that was loose in their midst. I must have seemed hideous. I hadn't showered or bathed in weeks, had soiled myself a few times, and had food stained on me everywhere. Disgust and horror were rising on all of their faces, and they all started to back away from me as if I was insane.

I tried to reach out for a few of them. They backed away, pulling their children away from me. I screamed and sobbed at them, "He's coming and he's going to kill me!" People continued to back away.

"You don't understand, he's going to kill me!" I continued to scream. I might as well have been yelling in a different language. My emotions were a torrent of confusion and frustration and fear. I couldn't make them hear me.

Then, Keith was there. He came up and grabbed me by the hair from behind. He dragged me down to the floor. I grabbed his hand and tried to pull off his fingers, but I couldn't. I had this vision of a security guard mollifying the crowd, telling them Keith was simply there to return this out-of-control person back to the lock-up where she belonged. As Keith dragged me out, I remember seeing the security guard saluting him as if he was taking out the trash.

When we were outside, he shoved me up to a car and in through the passenger door. I collapsed onto the fabric of the seat and began to cry uncontrollably. My chance to escape was gone. He got into the driver's side, and I knew I was going to be punished. Instead, he didn't yell. He didn't smash at me with his fist. He leaned down until his face was right close to my head, and spoke with cruel, deliberate sincerity. "Did you see anyone trying to rescue you?" His tone was so calm it was unbelievably eerie.

I shook my head, answering him instinctively. Not answering him meant pain.

"I have told you, you are nothing to anyone. Don't try that again." He pulled back and put the car into "drive." My shock was made worse when I realized he was taking me back to the house. Where had we been going before? I couldn't go back in there!

I did. He made me. The moment he shoved me across the threshold, I was revisited by his belt, fist, and anything he had within reach. I pleaded and begged through sobs that I would not run away again. The abuse reminded me of my mother disciplining me. I cowered on my knees, rubbing my palms together and asking for forgiveness, the way I was taught in the Korean tradition. It lasted forever.

I don't remember how long my stay was exactly, but I remember he told me we had to move. At this point, I no longer fought. I felt so numb that I didn't care if I lived, died, or if I even starved. When I was raped, I no longer screamed. I no longer flinched or fought back. I just laid there and drifted off into a distant part of my mind.

The city was making renovations to the small neighborhood and the dilapidated house we had squatted in was being remodeled or torn down. At the time, I didn't care. I just followed the orders as they were given to me.

We moved to a quadruplex apartment. We lived upstairs. The hallway had hardwood floors with French doors for the main doors of the entrance. Had I been in a better state of mind, it might have felt like walking into heaven. The complex was much more sanitary compared to the one we had left.

He tugged me in through the apartment unit door and I saw where we would live. The unit had an open concept, white walls and bright hardwood floors throughout. It was a one-bedroom apartment, although the bedroom was separated from the living room with French double doors. The bathroom was an older design, outfitted in black and white tiles. The tub was a claw-foot design, and there was even a pastel-blue, pedestal sink. The kitchen resembled one large ceramic tub in its color scheme with an antique retro faucet. The counter was ceramic with rigid lines. All the cabinets in the kitchen were white-painted metal with black handles. The tile in the kitchen floor was also retro with an off-white color. The windows had white trim. It was almost overpowering, but it was clean.

Not everything changed. When we moved into the apartment, Keith first covered the windows with blinds followed by a thick curtain so that the shadow from outside looked right. Then, he boarded up the windows over the fabric. He reversed the door knobs in every room so the lock was on the outside, letting him section me off into any room he wanted while he could come in whenever he wanted, including the restroom. I had no privacy, but at this point, my mental state was completely numb to it. We ate poorly, but it was far better than before. At least I got basic food like eggs, bread, milk, cereal, canned goods, sugar, butter, Ramen noodles and a bunch of instant made food. I didn't have much in a way of a real homecooked meal. If I ate any meat, poultry, or fish, they were either canned or hotdogs. At least I was no longer living completely out of cans.

I don't remember how long it was, but there were moments he would leave me home alone. I didn't pay attention to the pattern of Keith's frequent disappearing acts. When Keith planned to be gone more than 24 hours, he would handcuff me to the doorknob in the living room. If it was less than 24 hours, I was free to roam around the apartment, but that didn't make me any freer. There was nothing to do but wait for his return.

I felt absolutely subhuman. I tried to think if anyone would ever look for me. Would my family fight to find me? If James knew I was taken, would he look for me? Where is my voice? Why can't I lift up my hands? Why can't I fight back and try to get to them? But, then I would remember that I had tried, and only blank stares of horror had looked back at me. I was lower than the lowest creature. Not even worth listening to. A strange sort of self-loathing came over me, and I didn't even think about running away. Where would I run to? My family could never take me back after this. I wasn't worthy of them anymore. This was no fairytale where your mom and dad accept you back after being so tainted. This was a result of my choices, and I was responsible for all of this. If I had listened to my strict upbringing and not been a horrid daughter, I wouldn't be here. It was a vicious cycle, but I had nothing else.

One of the neighbors in the complex had witnessed the abuse through our walls in the unit. She had called the police to rescue me. In their attempt to save me, I felt relieved, but also very frightened. Still unsure that at any moment it was too good to be true. I remember the officer speaking with me, but I couldn't hear him, I was in a state of shock and just numb. By the time I was escorted to a local domestic violence shelter, the intake staff handed me an application.

Rolling her eyes, truly annoyed that this seemed to be a case she would actually have to handle, she asked, "Got any ID? Have to photocopy it."

I swallowed and shook my head. "He destroyed them all. I have nothing!"

There was actually a flash of relief in her eyes. She settled into her chair more completely, "Can't help you, dear. You could be an illegal looking for a place to crash. We don't need that kind of trouble."

My mouth dropped open. I was speaking clear, unaccented English to her. I was ragged, half-dead from fatigue and grossly tormented in every way. I was the poster child for how a battered woman would look, and she was ignoring me because I wasn't white and might be an immigrant without papers?

What else could I do? I staggered away, my mind going completely blank. What was I going to do? The officer who dropped me off left his card with the intake staff, there was no way for me to retrieve it. My effort at the shelter had proven that. They would think of me as an undocumented trespasser into a country that had been my own since I was an infant. I had no proof of anything. I had no money and no idea where I was. I knew I was not in Florida like Keith had said, but I had no idea that I was still trapped in northern Oklahoma.

Eventually, I ended up at a gas station. Enough time had passed that the raw panic had died down. Keith was here, nearby, but I was in this same small town somewhere. He hadn't found me yet, and maybe I could stay hidden. I had seen signs that said I was in Oklahoma. I felt miserable that I couldn't remember anyone to call, then I didn't know how to explain my situation.

"Are you okay?"

It was a woman's voice. A kind voice. It reached out to me when I was completely and utterly lost. I turned to see her leaning out of an older Monte Carlo. The exterior was dark, with a plush, red velvet interior that screamed "rich." Her dark hair and high, refined features reminded me of a well-aged Elizabeth Taylor from her best years, now living well through her late fifties. Her make-up was thick, and a heady perfume surrounded her. She was a piece of society, and she was reaching out to someone cast out of that society.

I tried to say something, to apologize, but nothing came out.

She stepped out and shushed me softly, her arms coming around to hug me despite how disgusting I must have appeared. It was the embrace of a mother to a daughter, and I had no idea how she could have stepped past the boundaries of familiarity so quickly. It was like she had found me. Like she had known the description of one she was looking for, and having seen me was quick to embrace me before I could slip back into the smoke of the city.

It turned a key in me, and I fell into her arms with a sob. She led me back into her car. It was a shelter of a whole different sort. All the rejection from before melted away, and I had found a place to let it all go. All of it came spilling out. She was a stranger, but my life story itself flowed out of me in jagged stories and gasps. None of it made all that much sense, I'm sure. Not right away. The woman would have plenty of time to piece it all together later. We would know each other long enough.

Her name was Kat (as in Kitty Kat). There was no hesitation in her. I needed that. She consoled me and took me in. She took me to a motel and got me a room. I was beyond grateful. I felt saved.

Somehow, she steered me away from any thoughts of calling anyone. She painted everyone I knew as having betrayed me, being unreliable, or not worth talking to. "You can only count on yourself. That is not a mistake you want to make, my dear. You have to get yourself home. You have to make your own way."

Home? A place that no longer carried comfort, escape or permanent recreation. Even if I had returned home, would my roommate be there? How long have I been away? Where have my belongings gone? All these thoughts rambled in the back of my mind while I was watching Kat giving me directions in a muffled tone. I watched Kat lay her purse on the table that was set in the corner of the motel room. She sat in one of the plush chairs and crossed her legs.

"Now, what are your plans?" She asked.

"I don't know, I don't have any money, I don't have any identification . . ." I murmured.

"Money won't be an issue, you just have to find work." She comforted with a confident smile.

"How? I…" Sure, I guess I could get any job, but I was so lost that it all seemed impossible.

She smiled, "Do you know what an escort is?"

Most people might not believe it, but I had no idea. My life was a traditional one despite all the terrible things that had happened to me. It certainly was not part of my upbringing for my parents to sit me down and instruct me in the manners of the underworld. My television was filled with classic romances and PBS. No, I didn't know what an escort was. I told her so.

Kat actually looked pleased to hear it. "Well, it just means you have to go out on dates with men."

My mouth fell open again, not believing she could be serious after what I had been through.

She must have recognized my look of horror, for she jumped to reassure me, "Oh no, my dear. You don't have to take them to bed. They want companionship. That is all. We never sell our bodies, not ever. Understand?"

I nodded, still numb from the momentary fear. She didn't convince me right away, but she kept at it. She was a Madam of an elite escort service, which I was not aware of at that moment and she wanted me to work for her.

Working for her meant she could look out for me. I wouldn't have to go through this alone. Once everything began, where I started to service my clients with fancy dates and public appearance as the eye candy exotic girl, money was coming in ways I didn't fathom. There was a 60/40 split for the first three months then it switched to 40/60. I was also expected to purchase cocktail dresses, make up, feminine products, and etc. I reminisced about the time when I was a dancer and make up, lingerie, and perfume was bought from Walmart or some Family Dollar, but the items Kat had me spend were from Department stores which left me with almost nothing. It was a revolving door of making money to spend money, but that didn't stop me from stashing some cash away for immigration fees that I eventually planned to retrieve.

The old adage about "sounding too good to be true" is old wisdom for a reason. This was no exception. I was out on a date with an older, business-class gentleman. He was in a suit that likely cost more than a month's rent at my old apartment. Thus far, everything had gone pretty much as every date with any other man had gone while I was working that job. We had enjoyed a nice meal and were in his car on the way to a show. He received a phone call, and after that said he had to swing by his place on the way. I was on his time and thought nothing of agreeing.

We arrived, and he gave me a more lascivious smile over the center console. He leaned in and tried to kiss me. I pushed him back, objecting immediately, "Hey! I don't do that. You know that."

He put on what he likely thought was a charming pout, "Hey, baby, don't be like that. I paid for this. Go along with it, and you won't regret it."

I was naive in some ways, but I had been mistreated far too recently to actually given in, even if he had been half as charming as he thought he was. "You didn't pay *me* for that. Other girls might do it, but I don't. If you want that, you have to go looking for someone else. Kathryn's girls don't do that sort of thing!" I felt so certain invoking her name, believing her to be as upstanding as I felt in that moment.

He gave a theatrical sigh and nodded. "Fine. I thought you liked me."

"I do, but not like that. We are having a good time. Let's keep it to that, alright?"

"Fine. Hey, you said you liked kittens and cats, right? Well, my cat just littered. I have to go log into my computer and do five or ten minutes of work. You could sit out here, or you can come play with them. Call it an apology?"

Looking back upon that night, I was thoughtless and naive to the extreme. To allow myself to be so easily mollified was ridiculous, but I felt like I was under Kat's protection. He wouldn't dare hurt me with her behind me. It wasn't something I reasoned out. It was something that I felt instinctively. I just happened to be entirely wrong.

I went into the house with him, and the first thing I knew he was grabbing me and throwing me to the ground. He forced himself upon me and had his sick fun. When he was finished, he threw crumpled bills on my body to pay for that fun. I was still laying on the cold, marble floor. The material was sticking to the skin of my back. He walked over to the door and ordered me to leave. I got out the door, somehow.

A cab was waiting for me. The driver simply waited there patiently for me to get in. I climbed in the backseat of the cab and the client spoke to the driver. I said nothing. The rape had put me in a state of shock. I was being discarded, and at the moment I was willing to let it happen just to get away.

Once clear of the house, I managed to ask the driver to drop me off at the police station. When I got out, the cab left. I didn't have to pay him. Apparently, it had been covered. It was hardly enough compensation for what had been done to me. I walked in and an officer approached me.

"May I help you?" he asked in a polite tone.

"I've just been raped." I cried.

He actually responded. No disbelief, and even some concern. He led me to a seat and handed me some papers to fill out and told me to wait until he could get a detective to meet with me. After I filled out the form, I held on to the clipboard and waited in the lobby. The room was old. I saw wood panel throughout the lobby with wooden hollow doors. The same officer who instructed me to wait in the lobby came out of one of the rooms down the hall came towards me.

"If you'll follow me, I'll take you to meet the detective." He gestured his hand, directing me to go first. When I walked into the office, I saw a man who looked in his late 30's or early 40's with a dark mustache and brown hair with a bald spot on the top. The officer took the clipboard from me and handed it to the detective. I sat in one of the two seats that were sitting across his desk.

The detective looked through the papers and took out a yellow legal pad and his pen. He started out with general questions like my name, date of birth, and other simple details.

"How do you know your assailant?" he asked.

"My who?"

"Assailant. Your attacker. The guy you said that raped you."

"Oh... I met him through an escort service." I responded.

Then his demeanor began to change. He half-dropped, half-threw the legal pad on his desk along with his pen.

"Ma'am, if you don't leave right now I can arrest you for prostitution."

"Wait a minute! I was raped!" I began to get irritated.

"No, you're a whore. Whores don't get raped. Now get out of here," he ordered.

Furious but without options, I stormed out of the station crying. I went to the nearest payphone and called Kat. After talking to her on the phone, she came and got me took me back to the motel.

She seemed most alarmed that I had gone to the police and relieved when she realized I had been turned away. She explained it all away, "The police are all corrupt in this city. They're paid off to ignore things like that. Listen to me, I don't know what else we can do, but give me a day. I will try and find an honest detective and tell them the truth. Leave it to me, alright?"

I trusted her again and watched her leave with regret. I wanted to *do* something. I was hurt, but I actually didn't feel totally powerless this time. I wanted to take action, but there was nothing to do but wait.

I made it to the dawn somehow. I was climbing the walls and couldn't wait any longer. I couldn't do anything about my rape, but I could do something to take the next step to regaining who I was as a person. Kat was now busy trying to help with my attack, so she didn't have time to assist me in getting my documents back. I decided I could do that on my own. So, I gathered a few things and went down to the Immigration and Naturalization Services or INS offices.

I was shown into a caseworker's office, and told her what I knew, "My papers were destroyed by an abusive boyfriend of mine. I need to get the documents back. Could you please help?"

She was young to be an agent there, and her prim, polite attitude felt condescending from the very start. She looked down her nose at me, and replied with an exasperated sigh, "OK, what you are going to have to do is head back to your home country and obtain your birth certificate there. Once you have that, I'd be *happy* to help you exchange that for your American documents."

I had no idea then, but that was not correct. She could have helped, and those very documents could have been requested and hunted down for me. She looked at me like an irritating bug she wanted to squash, and like I was less than worthy to be there in *her* country. For one in her INS profession, I could hardly believe she was speaking to me like that. I tried again, "Can't you look me up on your computer? I mean, I know my social security number. Won't you see my picture and see that I'm a resident here?"

She took a long breath as if counting to ten to avoid losing *her* temper, and huffed theatrically. When she spoke, sarcasm dripped from every word, "Do you *understand* English? I told you what you have to do."

I lost my mind. I admit that. I totally and completely lost my cool, and that cost me so very much. Her thoughtless resentment and hatred for who I was just cut right to the core of me, and I screamed right in her face. I climbed at the table, trying to get at her and just ripped and crumpled any papers that were within my reach just to anger her.

Security was called, and I was dragged kicking and screaming out of the building. No one thought to ask what the trouble was, and to be fair I gave them little enough reason to see me in a good light. I had just been thwarted by a stupid, racist woman and I had no more weapons to fight her with. I wanted to rage at them all, and so my ability to talk reasonably was taking a vacation.

I went back to the hotel and prowled it like a trapped cat. When Kat returned, I half-screamed at her about what had happened, not angry at her but needing to vent.

Again, Kat looked increasingly worried. This was the second time I had gone to the authorities instead of trusting in her. She tried to act insulted, but in reality, she was simply aware that I was pushing at the edges of her control. I wasn't being a good little girl any longer, so she knew her game was up. She said, "Listen to me. It's clear I need to push harder for those documents. I'm not sure what else I can do, but I'll go and push harder to get them. Just give me a couple more days, alright my dear? I'm so sorry I let you down."

To hear her apologize made me want to cry, and calmed me down in the moment. I told her that there was nothing to forgive and that I'd try and be patient, but begged her to hurry.

The next day, Kat came to me and said I needed to go see someone. She said it was all part of the plan to get things moving along. Bowing to her expertise, I thought nothing of getting into her car. We took off and drove until the Monte Carlo pulled into a parking lot that was all but empty. A dark van idled in the middle of it.

We got out and approached the vehicle. Kat gave a bang on the door, and the back-door opened. I had a fleeting image of two large, powerful men. Kat gave a curt, simple nod my way. It was clear what she was saying with that gesture. "*Yes, this is the one.*" She summoned me to step out of her vehicle and motioned me to walk towards her with the gesture of her finger. When I approached both men, they ordered me to stick out my wrists. At the moment from the corner of my eye, I watched the cash transaction go through, they handed her large rolled up cash and she accepted it without any concern for me. When she returned to her vehicle, somewhere in the pit of my stomach, I knew I wasn't going to leave with her.

A potato sack bag was thrown over my head, and my vision was obscured. One of the men spoke with a heavy European accent that I couldn't identify at the time, "Be quiet. If you yell, you won't yell for long. You can have a nice trip or you can be in a lot of pain. Either way, you're going where we tell you. If you want to arrive alive, shut up and be still."

The van jolted into motion and pulled out of the parking lot with a soft squeal of the tires.

Kat was suddenly out of my life. The Madame of that escort service had just sold me for a finder's fee. I had finally started showing independence, and she knew I was getting too hard to control and wasn't accepting the life she wanted me to accept on my own.

So, I was taken. My experience in being a true, trafficked human-slave was about to begin.

CHAPTER 5

TRAFFICKING

Before I begin, what must be understood is that nearly none of what happened in this period of my life comes out of my memory in one, continuous, unflawed stream. I am not sure my mind could take it if it did. Maybe that is why it comes out in fits and starts with flashbacks bursting into existence within my life whenever a memory trigger happens along.

I understand that some of what I am about to say will sound and feel jagged and uneven. The events and the torment I endured were exactly that. Jagged and uneven. I have tried to piece together this work into a coherent explanation, but I know there are gaps and inaccuracies. I had no clock or continuous view of the sun. There was a constant stream of physical torture that seemed unending. This period lasted months, but it felt like years… decades even.

The Ride to Vegas

What began in that parking lot didn't end for a couple of days. I didn't know it at the time, but I was finally leaving Oklahoma and Texas behind. Keith had lied to me about Florida, but this time I was truly heading out of state.

The van bumped and swung out of the parking lot and made for the open road. This was the critical moment for them. We were still in an urban area, and I was so freshly under their control that I might be unpredictable. But Kathryn had just betrayed me, and I was still stunned. They used every trick in the book they had to keep me off-balance and compliant.

I wore a potato sack over more had more often than I did not. I soon hated the smell of that burlap bag. The few times it was removed, it was for splashes of water. I don't recall eating the whole time. After all, they weren't particularly concerned with keeping my strength up. It was a big van without side windows and the view up front was obstructed. I have no idea how many days went by on the trip. There were always a couple of men keeping tabs on me. They spoke fast and in a foreign language that I am pretty sure was European, but otherwise paid me little attention. I was cargo and they were tasked to deliver me.

They did. As we arrived, I had no idea how much worse it could get.

I was still so naive. But how could I have really understood?

The First 24 Hours

The door to the van rolled open with a crunch of its wheels, and I immediately heard sniffling sounds outside. My heart started to palpitate with fear and anxiety and began to get the best of me. I was quaking and barely able to walk. I was now blindfolded in addition to that damned potato sack still pulled over my head. I was tugged out of the van, and deliberately moved and made to stand on a specific spot as if on cue for some movie.

The roughness of the sack scratched across my skin, and then it was gone. The blindfold was taken away as well, and the gift of sight was returned to me. I flickered my eyes around, wanting to see and know where I was, but I also knew if I moved too quickly or jerked around, I'd be beaten or screamed at or something worse.

From what I could see, I was in front of a line of various different girls. They were all cramped together, standing up against the wall in a submission position. Their hands were deliberately at their sides, heads bowed down as though they were expecting us.

We were in a storage unit of some sort. It was drab, concrete, and without any detail other than assuredly being a warehouse or other storage unit for holding bulk cargo. That was us. My heart sank even further. The two men who escorted me to the unit shoved me in and said this was my new home.

I just couldn't fathom the reality I was facing. I wanted to believe in my heart and soul that I was only dreaming and this was but a nightmare. Somewhere in the pit of my stomach, I knew this was anything so simple as a nightmare. Reality was being peeled back, and the ugliest part of it was dragging me in so that I could see it first-hand so that I could become a part of it.

They pushed me forward into the storage unit within the warehouse and rolled the garage-like door shut behind me. They left me there. After the doors rolled shut, the lamps hanging from the ceiling by a cord continued to glow. I remembered my father would use these types of lamps in the garage at night so he could see what he was doing. They stayed on for a half hour, and then they would go out on their own until the door was triggered again to save electricity. Only the thin line of light under the garage-style door allowed in a meager string of light. You could see the silhouette of someone's feet walking by.

The girls relaxed just a little the instant the men left. Most of these girls were from foreign countries, separated from their families and their homes. I had just become one of them. I was not aware of our purpose there, nor did I have any clue what was going to happen from that moment forward, but the passive way these girls were standing around didn't keep me from deciding there had to be a way out.

I turned and pounded my palm against the cement walls and screamed out for help, hoping someone on the other side could hear me. I screamed until I was hoarse, but of course, no one came. The other girls didn't try to stop me. They had all been there before me and knew what would happen. Eventually, I tired myself out and sat down on the floor in misery.

It was difficult to determine the time of day since there was no light from the outside. I didn't really pay attention to how much time passed. I was still in mental shock from being ripped from my other reality just when it had seemed to me that I was headed for a way out. Kat's betrayal felt all the worse given how she had played me. I sat on the floor staring at the other girls, watching them. One girl was laying on a mat talking to herself. Two other girls were playing with each other's hair. Yet another girl was standing against the wall and simply staring at the floor. A few of them fell asleep on the mats while some curled up in ashy, forest-green blankets in the corner.

The moment I heard the clanking sound from the other side of the rolling door, the other girls immediately shuffled in the darkness to stand in that same line with their hands to the side. I remained on the floor, confused by their behavior. There was no one demanding that they stand like this, and what chance was there to run away if you just stood meekly away from the door like that?

Suddenly, the doors flew open. Light streaked in and blinded me for a fateful moment. I couldn't see in order to act, even if I had had the courage. One of the guys grabbed my arm and pulled me up off the floor. My head tilted crazily to the side and my cheek exploded in horrid pain as he backhanded me on across my face. He pointed at the others and said "When you see the others stand, you follow. Whenever this door opens, you stand like they do!"

73

I spit in his face. I tried to bolt past him, but he snagged hold of my hair and dragged me back into the storage unit. With another vicious blow, he slapped me again. Now seeing I was dazed, he pushed me into line with the others, and said again, "Stand there!"

I stood there with the other girls looking down. Tears fell from my eyes. My nose ran and tears fell over the raw skin where he had hit me on the cheeks. My chest heaved heavily with every breath, made painful by the exertion, fear, and anger all mixed together.

Now that I was taken care of, the men went about their business. They moved down the line behind us, tapping those on the shoulder they wanted to select. Those picked would be shuffled out of the door and taken somewhere else. I had no idea where. Shock can do all sorts of terrible things to you; I still hadn't figured out what was being done to us or why. I wasn't picked because I was new and remained new for some time. It began to twist in my brain; I wasn't sure if what was happening out there was good or bad, but I wanted out. I knew I couldn't do anything in that storage unit in the dark, and I wanted out. In that twisted way, I found myself wanting to be picked, and angry whenever another round went by without me. Girls were brought in and taken out six or eight times a day, but I never went.

We were fed about three times a day with sack lunches; inside each sack would be a plain hamburger or a white bread sandwich with turkey baloney, a bag of chips and a cookie or fruit. It was about the same thing all day long. I wasn't very hungry; I had lost my appetite since my arrival here. Some of the girls were in far rougher shape than I was, and some even looked completely starved. I would share my food with the youngest girls in the room. Then, I would just sit in the corner, my knees up to my chest and my arms resting on my knees. I watched them all eat and wondered who they all were. There were two buckets in the corner of one side of the room. One with a towel over it which was used as our bathroom, the other filled with water and a silver bowl like the rice bowls I would have used in my youth.

I was drifting on the edge of sleep when I heard the knocking and clanking of the door being unlocked. I immediately stood up and waited for the door to roll open. The door scrolled out of the way, revealing a powerfully built man. He stood about a foot taller then me with a very wide shouldered frame. His thick eyebrows almost covered his eyes. His hair was combed back in a slick style that was considered cool at the time, but with strands of gray filtered through it. He had a trimmed beard with the mustache coming down off his mouth to touch the beard on either side, all of it a deliberate style meant to look in touch with current styles. He wore a 3-piece suit, nicely pressed and cufflinks that portrayed an expensive taste. His fingers were thick and his hands looked so big they could crush a can with no problem.

He strolled around in front of us, looking us up and down as if examining us to see what we were fit for. Then his eyes fixated on me. He leaned over to the other guy standing nearby and whispered something in his ear. My shoulders were tapped. A few others were selected as well, but I hardly even heard that happen. When they were done, I felt myself being prodded out of the unit and ordered to march in a single, straight line. I had my wish to be picked. Now that it was here, I was terrified.

We were brought out to the front lobby of the building. I saw other girls and boys standing in different spots, taken out of different units around the facility. They were keeping us in order so they knew where to return us when we came back. If we came back.

My stomach started to turn. There was no freedom here. I was being carted around like cattle. Frankly, the cows had a better chance of escaping. I saw a warehouse truck pull up and the door swung open. The men laid down a wooden board for us to walk on to get into the back of the truck. As we all got in, we could see blankets and gym mats which resembled the ones from the floor of our units. Different location, Same minimal comforts. We didn't have to wait long before the truck pulled out as I suddenly felt the vehicle bump to life on the rough road and the heat of the outdoor sun hit the sides of the truck and managed to find its way through holes rusted into the sides. It was daylight.

I was mixed up with a completely different selection of girls now, some of them recognized from the cell but most from some other unit. It resembled a candy store for predators, different ethnicities and gender for the specific request. Just the thought of it made me nauseous. The vibration of the truck tossed us about, and we could do little but hang on. Some of them were looking around in fear like I was, which marked them as being new. Others just clung on in listless, hopeless agony for what was to come.

They were the ones who scared me the most. They looked like they had been part of this strange procedure for years, and had no hope of seeing it end. I started to wonder about others who knew me. Would they know I was gone? Were my family concerned about me? What about my friends from school? Did anyone notice I was missing and did they miss me? When we got to our destination, I was more dazed from my spiraling thoughts than I was from anything else.

The door swung open, and we were given the same board, but this time to walk down and away from the truck. We were in front of some abandoned motel in the middle of nowhere. All you could see was the desert in every direction. There was no other house or store in sight. As each one of us got out, we were made to follow one the recruiters. There was no real chance at flight. Even if you wanted to risk running across an empty desert in the middle of the day, there were 6 or 8 of the men. Each of them held military-grade rifles and could have shot us a dozen times before we reached anything like shelter or cover. We climbed up the stairs and were assigned to a certain room.

As I was pushed into mine, the recruiter said, "20 minutes." Then, he slammed the door behind him.

Twenty minutes? Until what? I looked around. There was a bathroom with an open, partially clean sink. Next to it, there was a basket filled with makeup and personal products: condoms, lube and other sexual novelties. Laying across the foot of the bed was a lingerie dress. It was nicely folded, waiting for me to put it on. I just sat at the edge of the bed and started crying. It was hitting me now, even though on some level I must have suspected. This was when I could no longer deny it. I knew I was going to be raped. As I held the garment in my hands, I clenched my fists and just cried.

The door swung open without warning. The big man was there again. He stalked over and stood above me. He commanded me to disguise myself as a Japanese girl, and to act as young as I could act. He said I was to speak no English. He was clear on that. If I were to utter any words of English, he delivered a promise of consequences. My time with Keith had taught me well what sort of consequences he intended. Then, he turned to go. Just as he was about to leave the motel room, he looked back once more to warn me against escape attempts. He said something like, "I have powerful friends, and they run this area of the world. Understand? Whoever you talk to, I will hear about it. You will just be sent back to me. Then, there will be those consequences I spoke about. Only, worse." He left.

As soon as the door closed, I tried the doorknob. It was locked, and I was shut in. I hadn't heard him actually turn a lock. He had just walked in. I realized the knob on the door was tricked so that I could not leave. This brought déjà vu from the times I was imprisoned with Keith, I felt an eerie chill come over me of that reminder. I wasn't even given the privacy to be myself. Whatever sick game he wanted me to play, I had to start playing it then and there, or I was going to be hurt.

Twenty minutes… Time was running out. I hadn't even changed or applied the makeup on my face. I knew punishment might result if I was not ready, but I couldn't bring myself to move. I just sat there feeling extremely numb. I didn't know what I was going to do. I was operating purely on instinct.

The doorknob turned, and I spun towards the bed. My hands closed on the alarm clock, tugged it out of the wall, and lashed out at whoever was coming to have his way with me. I bashed him right on the head and he fell to the ground in a lump.

What I missed was the recruiter who was with him. He hadn't been walking in alone. The powerful man grabbed me by hair and slammed his head viciously into my own. I blacked out from the force of the impact.

It was a merciful unconsciousness.

Training

I woke up in a dark, cold room. I wasn't alone. There were others around me. I stirred, issuing a soft moan.

Immediately, my arms and legs were pinned to the table. I screamed, but the effort earned me nothing. There was too much strength in those limbs. Even my panicked motions did nothing at all. Multiple hands were on me, everywhere.

I was raped again and again by unknown predators. I lost count about how often and in what ways they abused me. I cried and begged them to stop, but it did nothing. I was sore everywhere, and a strange moisture blended with the burn of my forced loins. I was bleeding, but I didn't know how badly or from where.

It stopped. They reached some point. Whether they had made their point, done as they had been told, or were just sickly satisfied, they stopped. Footsteps walked away from me. The door to the room swung open, letting in the staggeringly bright light from the hallway. Six men walked out and shut the door behind them.

They hadn't tied me down. It had only been their hands which held me. Now, I began to scream and throw tantrums of rage. I slammed my body against the wall, scratched the wall, and screamed hysterically without response from the outside world. I was tormented and broken and the fits of raw anger drained me. Despite all the pain, I finally fell asleep, unable to keep open hour after hour in the dark.

I awakened sometime later to be forced onto the table and raped again. And again. The process repeated itself, and I have no idea how long it went on. I had no idea how long between each session, nor when they would let me sleep for hours or only minutes. Sometimes, a stream of men would come in. Other times, they were already there. I had no idea about their patterns or identities. I only saw their backs as they exited the room.

I was in a state of extreme exhaustion. For hour after hour, I lay on the cold floor and just stared into the dark room, visualizing that I was somewhere else, maybe in heaven. I prayed at that moment that my life would end so the misery of this so-called life would be over.

I heard footsteps. I ordered myself to get up, but I was too shattered to do what I commanded. I could only crane my neck in the direction of the door. Light washed over me, and I saw the silhouette of a tall man with two others behind him. The door stayed open this time, but I could barely make out any details of their faces. My eyes burned with irritation from long being in the dark and hours of crying. He leaned down, his breath close and hot on my face. "Are you willing to do what we tell you this time? Do you believe me about consequences this time?"

I was desperate to get out of that room. I agreed to all of his commands and warnings, nodding my head fast and sure.

He grunted, "Good." He gave a silent wave of command, and the two guys lifted me up. I could barely stand. They escorted me to another unit. All of the walls and the doors all looked the same so it was difficult to track back where I originally came from, but I remembered many of the turns we made on the way out. I knew this was a different spot.

Maybe they wanted to further unbalance me and not return me to where I was even mildly comfortable. Maybe they just didn't care, and I was filling a hole in their count. They didn't change anything. The door rolled open, and there stood a line of girls being submissive. Different girls, Same obedience. They stood there just like I would stand there, waiting as if being selected was their sole purpose in life and always would be.

CHAPTER 6

MIA

In the end, there was something different about this unit.

A lot of it was the same. We all slept on the dated mattresses with old stains that smelled like a combination of stale urine, vomit, body odor and dry-stained feces. We had the same dank blankets to wrap under and around ourselves. There were no windows to look out, and time once more fell to being a matter of little concern. We were given white hospital scrubs to wear, changed only when we finally got filthy enough that it was necessary to prevent rampant disease among us. The occasional hose-down and change of clothes were almost worse than being filthy. At least when you were dirty, you couldn't smell the other filth around you. When you were halfway clean, the reminder of the humanity you lost was enough to make you cry.

I learned this group was all those who had been particularly disobedient. We had been stripped away from our original units. At first, it might seem strange to group us all together, but there was a reason for that. They had a special control mechanism for us, you see. They had threatened us once, and it had not worked. So, even while they proved those threats and made it clear those threats meant something, they took those threats to the next level with our group.

Locked in with the rest of us were a smattering of young girls. Most were around the ages of eight to ten, and varied in heritage from Spanish to Russian, to others I couldn't identify. I comprehended very little Spanish from high school, but nothing else. Many of the girls only spoke their own first tongue, meaning we only conversed with them in simple gestures and facial expressions.

Each of us was given a little girl. Once assigned, the girl was ours. I don't even really think they knew why they were there. We were told if we messed around or disobeyed, it wouldn't be us that suffered. At least, not *only* us. I am sure those sick bastards would take any chance to punish us. But, they made it very clear that the girls would suffer as well. Our crimes would be theirs to endure. The very idea of that haunted my dreams.

At least they gave us a little light so we could care for the girls. We would sit around and play with each other's hair, play cards, or make paper dolls. The men provided the girls with crayons, paper, but no sharp objects like scissors or pencils. The scene would almost be considered domestic if it were not for the horrid conditions and fear of being dragged out to be made into a sex-slave. I would drift off to sleep while watching the children play and share food with the older girls. I tucked up with my own little charge on the mattress for warmth. I would dream of pleasant things, like eating Mom's home cooked meals, smelling the aroma of soy beans being boiled with oysters, shrimp, and tofu spiced just the right way. I could almost hear her soft voice calling to me in the voice she used when she wasn't upset with me.

I would moan in my sleep, "Oma..."

My charge would nudge me awake. She thought I was having a bad dream. She smiled up at me with her lovely smile. She was so small. I assumed she was the youngest, for she was indeed the smallest among the group of children locked in with us. She loved playing with my hair. She had her own beautiful, long, black hair down to the middle of her back. She smiled at me and whispered some soft words of what sounded like comfort. She only spoke in her native tongue and knew I didn't understand her. It didn't matter. She would hug me and I would understand. I called her "Mia," even though I wasn't really sure what her name was. She never offered any other name and would answer to the name I called her.

There were nights when Mia was afraid. I would let her sleep with me on my mattress. To calm her, I would sing "Dreaming of You" by Selena or "Somewhere Out There." I would repeat the song until I knew she was asleep. She reminded me of my baby sister, Melissa. She was so young and the thought of what those men would eventually use her for angered me even more. They were being used to control us now, but they were as much trafficked slaves as the rest of the girls. There was no way those men would let them free without using them in any way they wanted to make money. I would pray (not knowing if my voice would be loud enough for God to even hear) that would not happen to Mia. There were times I hated God. I hated him for what I was witnessed every day. I couldn't fathom how this was happening and why God couldn't blind these men and set these girls free. Even as I hated, I begged God to do exactly that.

The two mattresses closest to mine were inhabited by Russian and German girls; both could speak some English with strong, foreign accents. Heidi was 16 and she was the Russian girl. At least, that was her best guess. She was taken when she was much younger than Mia. She had no idea about her birthday, age, or any holidays that might have passed. She was tall, slender, and with skin that was soft and the color of ivory. Her cheeks were lightly pink, and when she smiled her dimples were achingly beautiful. I recall she kept her red hair short and straight. She chatted with me most often, and we talked about our dreams of what we would do once we were free, or what we hoped to be in our next life if we died. We tried to keep it cheerful and we would fantasize about a fairytale rescue and how we would all live together and protect one another. We never mentioned anything about what we all knew awaited the young girls.

Now, she smiled over at me, gesturing at Mia. "That's the first time she's slept so peacefully."

The German girl was less complimentary, saying sharply, "It's too dangerous for you to be close to her like that." I never got her name since she and I weren't very close. Given what she said, maybe she avoided giving her name out to keep us all at a distance. I understood why she did it, but I couldn't think that way. Especially, not about Mia.

I replied back as calmly as I could, not wanting to wake Mia, "She's too young. I won't let them hurt her."

"Then they will kill you!" She scolded with straightforward simplicity.

"I don't care," I got angry. Tears began to form in my eyes as I pet Mia's hair in her sleep. "I can't do *nothing*. I... I have to do *something*. Anything."

Heidi heard my conviction. She reached over and touched my shoulder, "Please, don't fight!" she begged.

I looked down watching Mia sleep. As I continued to caress her face and stroking her hair, I whispered, "I won't let them hurt you, I promise."

The German girl hissed with exasperation. "That is a stupid promise. You can't keep that promise! You should be trying to help us all! You could get us out!"

That took me completely by surprise. I blinked in disbelief. "What?" I thought she was transferring blame onto me.

She actually had something of an idea in her head, no matter how insane it sounded. "You're an American! You speak their language!"

"So? Did you think that helped when I got tossed in here? Do you think I didn't scream at them to let me go? Saying it in English or German doesn't matter. I'm the same as you!"

The German girl pressed on, "You are here for a reason, don't you see?"

Heidi was not fully on her side but also didn't speak up to stop her. Obviously, the two had talked about this before they came to me.

The German girl went on, "They make you work in two places. That's not the same as us! We only go to one place, where they know we are foreigners. No chit-chat or anything. Same thing with you when they make you be a Japanese girl. But you get taken to the other place where they know you are American with the other girls who are from here."

"Are the American girls like me? Asian?"

"No, they change. They have Black girls, girls from Mexico, they are like you."

"I don't understand? How are they like me?"

"They are American just like you, not foreign like me. They speak two languages."

"So?" I was listening but still didn't get her point.

"So? You know American men that like oriental girls like you. Sink your claws into one of them. You can get him to buy you! Make him fall in love with you and you become his bride. Then you buy us out and then you free us."

That sounded completely impossible. "That can't happen!"

"Of course, it can! You don't know. It might work!"

Heidi interjected with what sounded like an old argument from having discussed this before, "It'll take too long. We'll be dead before she got back to us."

I had a different thought, "What if he doesn't marry me and he just keeps me as his toy? Then what? I wouldn't have money or any freedom to come rescue you, and I wouldn't be able to protect Mia."

"Then you keep at him until he loves you and buys you things. Us."

"Even if I make him love me, he's not going to let me buy the same girls I was trapped with!"

"It doesn't matter if it's the same girls or not. I want out of here, but you just start freeing girls, understand?"

A muffled sound came from outside, and we rushed to quiet ourselves and return to our mats, laying down to pretend to be asleep. I left Mia on my mat and I slept on hers to ensure they didn't wonder why we were huddled together. They hated it when we did that. The door swung open and two men walked in. The lights flared on.

They walked through our ranks, tapping or kicking those they wanted to get up. I kept pretending to be asleep, counting the girls being taken but not trying to say anything about it. My heart was pounding and I had prayed they didn't wake Mia. It was always difficult to explain where the girls went, and I hoped Mia would sleep through this selection.

After the girls walked out, one of the men stayed and stood there watching us for a good half hour. The door swung open again and I smelled food. Apparently, it was mid-morning, not night-time at all. "Time to get up!" the man shouted. "The food is here." A box of bagged lunches was tossed on the ground and then they left. We all gathered around the box and took our bags and returned to our spot. I woke Mia up and gave her a bag.

We were just settling down to eat when the door rolled open again. This time, the man who entered looked like he was on a specific mission. Mia scooted closer to me, and I held her close. The man projected his evil intent, and we had no wish to capture his notice. The illusion didn't last long. It was clear almost immediately that he was walking our way. He came closer and reached out to grab Mia by the arm.

The moment had come. I just reacted. I cried out, "No!" I tried to pull his hand off her arm.

My struggles frightened Mia further, so she started to yank and pull and try to escape on her own. The man tried to drag her closer, yelling at her, "Get up!" He raised his hand to strike her.

I stepped in between them, trying to break the hold. The man used his backhand and slapped me. "Get off of me you, bitch!"

I remember feeling the pain, but I remained standing. All I could think of was Mia. "Take me! Please take me!" I cried.

The commotion brought in two more men. They walked up and separated me from Mia. She looked back at me, still trying to break free and all I could see were tears from her eyes.

"No!" I cried. I felt like I was chained to a wall as I watched my world crumble around me, and I couldn't do anything. I never felt so helpless in my life.

I heard Mia's voice crying out "Mama." Then, my world came crashing back to the immediate present as a punch landed on my face. My mouth was bleeding and I didn't care. The pain didn't compare to the fear I had for Mia. I sat there and cried and I just couldn't stop. The men retreated, hauling the door shut again, leaving me there.

"I hate you, Lord!" I screamed. My clothes were drenched with my tears and sweat. "Why? Why these girls? Why Mia!" I remained on the floor right beside the door crying. I lost all track of time. I just sobbed and railed in my mind over and over, going back and forth between damning the Lord and begging Him for salvation for Mia.

I must have fallen asleep eventually, my mind overcome with the stress of the moment. One of the men woke me up with a nudged of his boot. "Get up," he summoned me.

I looked up. He punched me without warning. I fell back to the ground, shaking my head as dazzles danced around my vision. I saw that the lights were on, and the girls were lined up against the wall, looking down at the ground. Two men each took one of my arms and dragged me out of the room.

"Where is Mia?" I asked, my fear and focus dimmed by sleep and time, but my concern still on my young charge.

"That isn't her name," the man replied, offering nothing else.

"Why hasn't she come back?"

"You ask too many questions." The men brought me to another barren room. At the center was a few terrifying implements. There was a free-standing tub without plumbing attachments. Next to it was a table with several items on it. A leather belt. Wrist straps. A whip.

The Master Recruiter I had seen several times before was in the room. He paced back and forth, clearly agitated. "You like to give me problems, young lady. I thought we had an understanding."

I recognized this for what it was, and my fear spiked high. I tried to wrench free, but the men holding me clenched down and held me in place. They picked me up and threw me in the tub. There was no water, but the porcelain was already cold from being in the dark, chilly room.

The Master Recruiter gestured at the other two, "Restrain her!"

"*No!*" I cried. I kicked at them and bit them and screamed. Trying to fight my way out, I ended up just bruising myself against their massive strength which overpowered me. They managed to get my wrists and ankles both tied to the legs of the tub. They were ordered to rip my clothes off, and soon I was shivering nude against the cold-tub interior. There was a large lamp swinging right above me on the ceiling. I couldn't see anything but the circle of light around that tub, and the men who walked in and out of the circle.

The man came into view at the foot of the tub and began to talk to me. "I tried to be nice. I gave you a second chance. Instead, you create problems. You scare the others when we want to keep everything calm. We thought the girl would keep you in line, but instead, you just act like a mother cat protecting her kitten. Well, my people don't like getting clawed. So, here is your punishment." He stepped aside. His tone wasn't cold. It was calm in an eerie, practical way.

The two other men stepped forward and upended a large tub of ice onto my body.

I immediately let go a scream, trying to curl up on myself but unable to move from the restraints. I laid there and cried. I could feel my body freezing as the sharp corners of the ice scattered over me. Sharp tingling pain lanced into my nerves, and I could feel the cubes sticking to my skin. Some of the cubes that were broken were poking me and there was nothing I could do.

I started to sob apologies like, "I'm sorry!" They didn't listen. They just continued to pour the ice on my naked body and only stopped when it got to my chin. I just prayed to die. I prayed that day for God to take my soul. They left me there for what felt like hours, shutting the door behind them to leave me to freeze. I wasn't sure they would come back.

I nearly died. I don't know how many times they had done that to know how long to leave me and still be able to save me. I thought they were going to let me die for sure. When they came back, I wasn't sure if I should be relieved or curse them for not letting it end right then and there.

They dragged me out. I can't really remember if they tried to warm me up or just let me lay there until I recovered on my own. I have to admit, I didn't believe I could make it. I was constantly shivering. I felt extremely nauseous and everything in me was in extreme unfamiliar pain that I just couldn't describe. It had to be God, it just had to be. There was no way I could've survived being in the ice and I know it had to have been more than an hour. Somehow, I found my way back to consciousness. I had blacked out from the pain several times. Now, I was trying to focus as the Master lingered near me.

He finally flickered his fingers in front of me and caught my eyes with his own. "Listen to me. I like baseball. This is America, right? Three strikes. Then, you are out. You've already got two. If you piss me off again, I will make sure you go to hell screaming, because you will die very, very slowly. Do you understand me? No more tricks. No more chances. You listen, and you play my game. Now, think very carefully... and tell me... do you understand?"

I nodded.

The Master looked into my eyes a long moment. Then, he looked at the others. "I think I actually believe this one." He motioned for me to be dragged away.

They hauled me out and dressed me in another pair of scrubs. I was dragged around for a while. I didn't have the strength to care too much. Finally, I realized I was standing against a wall, and there were other girls around me. I tried to focus because the Master was speaking to us.

"Some of you have been disobeying. I have told you this is not acceptable. Every once in a while, we have to make our point a little more clearly. I hate doing that. It's a waste. You will watch this. If you utter a word about this moment to anyone, you will be discarded as well. Don't talk about it. Just watch, and think. Don't think I will even hesitate if you push me on this."

He summoned forward two of his men, who dragged forward another girl. She was in a daze as well and looked like she had just been through a similar hell as I had been. For some reason, I thought the Master was looking right at me. "I didn't believe this one."

He raised a pistol and shot her in the head.

I should have screamed. I should have lost my mind. I didn't. They had nearly killed me several times. I was sure they had killed others, and this would not be the last killing I would see. She was too slow to play their game, and she had lost. So, I did nothing but blink, and keep watching as he had demanded. I had no wish to pay any further price.

He turned back to us and nodded in satisfaction at the resounding silence. "Good. Now, let's talk about the next selection and next assignments. Who was told they were next?"

Two girls stepped forward immediately, coming forward to present themselves.

I hated that smirk he had on his face as they came forward. He grinned, and said, "I love when you come when I call." We were his possessions and his pets. We all looked down at the ground and submissively waited for what he would do to us next.

Doing as Ordered

The voice of a stranger breathing into my face lingered over me. "God, you feel so good, so warm and juicy."

I just tried to survive until his hour came to an end.

He continued his outlandish charade, pretending in his fantasies that I was speaking back to him and giving him what he wanted. "You like American cock? You like, huh?" He continued through heavy breaths as he struggled to finish. Thankfully, this was my turn in the motels where

I was playing the foreign, Japanese girl, and it was part of my role not to speak any English.

I closed my eyes, pretending that I was somewhere else. I wanted to cry so much, but I scolded myself instantly, silently, "Don't cry!" That wasn't part of the act. That would get me punished.

I tried to see the clock. It kept flashing "12 o'clock." There was no time in here. I couldn't really see the outside. I just wanted to know the time! It had been so long. I stared at the ceiling and just imagined I was somewhere else.

As soon as the man was finished, he jumped up and went straight into the bathroom. I laid there feeling helpless and numb. He came back and began to put his clothes on. He was hardly anyone's image of a dashing figure. He was stocky and had a slight beer gut. His face was clean shaven, spotted, and his dark brown hair had a dusting of silver in it. Naked, he was unimpressive. As he dressed, it was clear he had money. He put on a well-pressed suit, expensive shoes, and a black sports jacket. With his clothes on, he was the image of a semi-powerful businessman. He must have been to afford such service. He leaned over and kissed me on the forehead. Then, with long, exaggerated tones as if he was trying to translate the words from English for me simply by speaking slowly, he said, "Thank . . . you . . . for . . . letting . . . me . . . see . . . you." It was doubly insulting. Had I not understood him, I certainly wouldn't have because he spoke slowly. He obviously didn't care to know any better. He didn't care what language I spoke as long as he could buy me as his plaything.

I got up and raked fingers through my hair. I didn't have long. Usually, they gave me no more than a few minutes. At best, twenty minutes, but usually only at designated longer breaks so I could take a quick shower. Those only came after particularly long or disgusting calls. Otherwise, there wasn't time. A girl could average a hundred or more calls in a day when summoned to work at the motels. The last call had been an hour-long marathon compared to some of the quick in-and-outs I was forced to do.

Not knowing, I didn't move. I wasn't causing trouble. If they came in and said I had time for a shower, I would take one. I was past resistance in that moment. I had no idea what I could do to resist. Part of me tried to bicker about that, to tell me that I had been given an idea by my two friends back in the cell with Mia, but I couldn't see how to pull that sort of thing off. It felt hopeless, and it felt like a game I would be punished for playing.

I vaguely wondered from time to time if anyone was looking for me in those days. Had my friends or family filed a Missing Person report? I remember shows like "Unsolved Mysteries" and imagined being listed as one of those missing girls. I called to mind all the bad things I had done, the things I had stolen, those I had lied to or manipulated, and all the grief I had given my family. I used all of those things as reasons for them not to care, and to do nothing to find me. Then, I hoped that they wouldn't listen to that. Would it be worth it for them to file a report?

I could only hope they had, for in that moment I had no recourse. I could only try and survive. If they weren't looking, then my whereabouts would never be discovered, especially if I turned up dead.

Sad thoughts wandered through my mind, and perhaps some few words might be written to offer poetically what could not be expressed any other way.

Silenced

There, she stands,
In the corner,
Peering through the window;
Freedom is only a dream.
She's nonexistent,
The disassociation from a
Haunted past:
Always escaping the voices of terror...
She longs to speak,
But words escape her...
Wanting to cry out,
Her tears have become silent...
There she stands, a victim,
No one perceives.
Reality, an enemy,
Predators strip her innocence.
Though called by many names,
The decision is not hers.
To the left, to the right,
One is in question:
Auction, or the chopping block?
A chameleon of colors,
submitting to their command;
In that hour, evening, or day.
A paralyzed puppet until the dance,
they seal her lips;
Catatonic words...
Hearts torn asunder;
Feelings are just a memory...
Her body is owned by the predators.
Set her soul free,
Less you empower such slavery.

CHAPTER 7

LOYALTY

When you live your life around filth, it becomes impossible not to become drenched in that same filth. This is something I have learned, and something I have had to come to terms with. Perhaps, this is how all those who traffic in human slaves or anything else get their start. They are taught the business and slowly placed under pressure and expectation in the same way a lump of coal becomes a diamond over the slow, weight of time. Those who are predisposed to that sort of terrible lifestyle then come to glory in it, enjoying their superiority with relish. That's what I became. At least, for a while.

You see, I was slowly going insane. How could I not? I had no power or choice or ability to determine my own path. I couldn't shut off that part of me, the part that needed a way out. Some people suffer for longer, while others fade away. I honestly don't know how anyone could survive being mere property to someone else. Yet, I was trapped. I had been violently shown the punishment for rebelling against this system, and yet neither could that inner core of me simply lay down and submit to an endless existence as the puppet of my then masters. Yet, where was the other path? There is an old axiom: "If you can't beat them, join them."

It was a terrible thought, but the idea had already been planted in my mind by the two other girls in my holding cell. I had tools, ways to interact with these men that the other girls didn't have. I had education, language skills, and the will to use them. I had resisted them right to the point of being bluntly told I would be murdered unless I shut up. I had strength inside me that was not yet tapped. Now, there remained only the morality of what I had to do. I had to sacrifice that, and I couldn't do that and remain who I was.

So, I didn't remain who I was.

I am not sure if this falls into the category of Split Personality Disorder, or Dissociative Syndrome, or any other real psychological term. I don't know if this was a choice to permit myself to follow the path of insanity, or if it just came to me slowly over time. I recall a flip switching in a way, and that will be part of my story you will see, but that moment was perhaps when I finally could not take any more and decided to act. That is when "Jules" came into being.

"Jules" was everything that I was not, and she was the one who would be able to survive this world and eventually escape it. She is a tragic figure, for she also had to perish as soon as I found my way free because I had to go back to being me. She would help me to survive, but she was a terrible person, lost in a world awash with sex, drugs, and every other type of hedonistic business known to the American underworld. She was my own personal savior even as she was my personal insanity. I owe her everything, and yet spend every day hating what she did, and ensuring she never resurfaces again. She saved me, and I survived her as much as I survived any of the other traffickers around me.

Marco

Life had become the very worst sort of monotony. Each day, I either lingered in my cell or was called to do what needed to be done. I didn't resist any longer. If I was called, I stood up like a good girl and placed my hands to my side, got led onto a truck, and taken where they wanted me to go. As I became more compliant and filled two of their needs as both English speaking and visibly foreign, there were more days I was selected than not. I didn't question it or try to keep track.

Something was breaking inside of me. Other girls had broken. There were always ways to commit suicide. You could simply stop obeying. Those girls died. You could try and escape. Those girls died, too. We were commodities, so they tried to keep us alive as long as they could, but if you weren't worth the trouble they would simply shoot you and bury you or dispose of you. You became forgotten forever. There was no need to try and do anything as dramatic as hanging yourself—but I didn't. Somewhere inside, there was a part of me that demanded to be heard. That part of me demanded the right to say this was not to be the sum of my life. Yes, there were times I wanted to die, but those would fade along with the presence of those bastards who would use me as they wished. When it was just me, the part that wanted to live somehow always won.

At times, the inner part of me that wanted to live would get a boost. I recall one such time being when I saw Mia again for the first time after she had been taken away. They took me to a hotel room one day, and when the room opened, Mia was there. Little Mia. She flew into my arms and hugged me, babbling away in her native tongue that I still didn't understand.

Seeing her nearly overwhelmed me, but I fought that back. No! If I acted foolishly, like before, I would be dead. Survive. I needed to survive. At the same time, I *couldn't* survive if I witnessed Mia being used. Oh, it was foolish. I had to know she had been abused a dozen times since we had last parted. I wasn't saving her from anything, and it was a stupidly dangerous thing to do, but I couldn't watch her being raped and hated the idea of being raped in front of her.

Acting on that, I took a stupid chance. It confirmed the old core of me, the part that could love, was still inside me somewhere. I took Mia into the closet and hid her there. I tucked her up into the shelf so that none could find her, and tried to forget how wonderful it felt to feel her pulsing heart against me as she hugged me.

The johns who had been given an audience with me started to arrive, and I performed even more enthusiastically than I ever had. I wasn't exactly willing, but I wasn't exactly lying still, either. I did all I could to keep them interested even as it sickened me. I protected Mia. This might be the first stage for what would later come; this is where I had the understanding that I could take some power for myself if I changed how I acted. If the johns stopped to question why there were not two of us present, they would find Mia. I knew that, and I couldn't let it happen. So, that day I gave as much as any two might give to those men, and not one complaint was had.

When they came to take us away, Mia was once more with me, waiting as well. She was cramped but unhurt for that day. It was a silly victory, looking back, for what would the next day hold for her? That didn't matter. On *that* day, she was safe, and I had made a difference. It was a victory and cemented, even more, the way that I fell into that new role. It was not an illusion. I could change things for the better if I stuck to this path. How much more could I save if I got out of here? How many more children confined in unknown warehouses in scattered cities could I help free if I could just get the hell out? But, these were just small ideas then, and I still was not sure how I could possibly do it all.

There were the times I nearly gave it all up. Mia was also central to that as well. It was a while later. This time, I couldn't stop anything. There was no private way to hide Mia that time. I can only remember being brought into one of the units from the storage facility. I was bewildered at the reasoning for my presence. I had complied to all the commands, I had not received any punishment. When one of the handlers sat me in a metal folding chair and strapped my wrist towards the back of the chair, immediately came Mia. She smiled and waved at me, but I couldn't smile back. Something in me felt aghast. I knew that being there simultaneously in the same room was not a welcome of any sorts. They wheeled in an unshelled mattress and bound her wrists, at that moment I knew what she was going to receive and the haunted nightmare that would never escape from my conscious. After hours of screaming, crying, begging, and cursing, I continued to watch her until she stopped screaming herself. She was gone. I was gone. My fury had surfaced in ways I never imagined. I didn't have the opportunity to grieve, say my last "goodbye" or even knew if Mia ever received a proper burial. I fell into an apathetic desolation. The plot of vengeance consumed me.

Days or maybe weeks later, I was lined up with the other girls as usual, and I remember feeling emotionally exhausted beyond any other day from that routine. I could hear the trafficker's command start to fade. I didn't have to hear them. I had memorized the rest of the orders. In that moment, I was all worn out of hope, faith, and prayer. I despised God and felt the empty chasm of nothing else being out there. I would have embraced Atheism as a way of thought if I knew what it was called. Then, something unusual happened.

I was standing there, wavering back and forth on my feet, and thinking inside, "If there is a God, I hate you. Do you know that? If I die (which I hope I do), I don't want to be in heaven or hell with you. Better yet, just leave my soul alone, just leave me alone." I was crying softly, thankfully not noticed by the traffickers.

I wasn't called. I didn't really care. I just leaned against the wall and slid down to the floor, holding my knees up and crying into my arms. It was hot outside, but I felt so cold inside. I could still hear the traffickers barking orders to those who they were taking with them that day, and I had my hand down, staring at my legs to keep away from their attention. I was folded over, with my legs to my chest, and wished everyone would leave me alone for just a while so I could simply fade away.

Something of an unknown force nudged me. I looked up. In the midst of the treacherous atmosphere of those warehouse units, I saw a blue butterfly flying towards me. I felt entranced along with an overwhelming peace inside of me. It's something I couldn't explain or describe. I reached out my hand in the air and the blue butterfly landed on my finger. I slowly moved my hand toward my body and used the other finger to gently caress the wings. At the same time, I heard a soft whisper in the air along with a cool breeze that brushed against my skin. "Everything will be alright." said the whisper.

I don't know if it was God because, at that time, I didn't believe. It was simply a moment of wonder. But, I heard the voice and it gave me a calming feeling at that moment. When the breeze came in the butterfly flew away. Mia was still gone, but I was not. She couldn't be helped, but that didn't mean I couldn't survive.

I needed a way out. That striving for life was tearing me in two because there seemed to be no pathway out of this other than death. I was breaking in two from the hope and hopelessness that was at war in my heart.

On day, as I heard my name being called, "Jules" emerged. I didn't yet know her name, (for her name would be given to her by the one she would call Master), but it was her. Yes, "Jules" would become my new name.

When the buyers would ask for our names or how we were being introduced, we had various pseudo names. Most of mine were a mixture of Asian names that weren't accurate like Hong Su Shimoshi, which is part Korean and part Japanese. What ignorance the traffickers displayed. The name they called out to summon me was "Sukki." I knew right away that this would define what my mission would be this time around. When they called that out, I would be used in the "foreigner" sense, pretending to not speak English and be the *Oriental* fantasy for those who wanted it. A racist fetish for those who longed for me to play up all the ridiculous Asian stereotypes. This strained me even further, as it was a role I despised. I wasn't even able to use my voice, instead reduced to an object to be used merely for sex. It simply added that much more pressure on me.

The other names were assigned the same way to the other girls based on skin color, and we were loaded up on our truck that would take us out to the remote desert motel in Nevada's landscape. As was normal upon our arrival, we were ushered into our separate rooms and given the half-hour needed to make ourselves ready for our first visitor. Usually, this was a shameful last bit of torment as I donned the evening gown and make-up they left me, crafting myself into a strange mockery of beauty.

This time, I looked into the mirror and saw something different. Always before, I turned the sad girl in front of me into a broken puppet to be played with. Puppets did not act on their own, and they always had a master. Puppets couldn't ever be free. As long as I was one of them, as long as I thought *like* one of them, I could never be free. I recalled the German girl's suggestions, saying that I should find a suitor and play him to my tune and get him to buy what I wanted. It was a terrible, unformed, impossible idea. But, the one part of it that suddenly struck as *possible* was that it wasn't *passive*. I wasn't just letting things happen to me. They could kill me for suddenly doing something new, but the new persona that was breaking free wouldn't accept that. A tigress was taking over, demanding that the gentle swan give way and let the predator rise up and tear open the cage.

With a frantic haste, I began to paint my face as if I was the "China Doll" these men were requesting. Usually, I just put a little base on, eyeshadow, and some lipstick with my hair down. This time, I felt the need to do something more. I heard that other side of me suggesting, "*Why not go a little further? Play with the colors and put your hair up in that geisha style American men always lust after? Play as if you are on stage! They don't know you are an American as well. They are stupid fucks that deserve to get played!*" I giggled at my own thoughts, thinking them so delightfully sinful. Don't fear these men! Sure, they had power because they paid for it. They were the ones who were too worthless to know anything about me and had to pay for sex, and they were the ones who should be manipulated. I actually saw myself grin. I was the wolf, not the sheep.

My first conquest arrived, and he had no idea what he was in for. He came in like dozens of others have entered, expecting to see a sad girl with eyes lowered. He would have to demand precisely what he wanted and fill in the holes in his fantasy with his own imagination. He was like all the rest tended to be; about 6 feet tall, middle-aged and in business attire. Well-off, bored with his current job and life, and using his wealth to buy a sick fantasy. He was like so many others.

I was not. Not any longer. When he came in, I was calm. Sitting on the bed, legs folded and dressed like the perfect expression of what he wanted to see. I smiled at him, innocent yet ready as if I wanted to be there.

Right away, he was taken aback. He smiled back at me, "Wow you are the first girl I've seen smile since I arrived."

"Come. Sit. I give you what you want." My tone was slow, using poor grammar and broken English with an oriental accent as strong as I could manage. I wanted to push him, but also knew I was not supposed to be American or know anything. I walked a fine line, but I was willing to risk it to get the upper hand. I softly patted the bed next to me with a further grin.

When he started to lean in closer to me, I grabbed his face and kissed him. Hard. I heard him moan in surprise and pleasure, and this brought on a different rush. My own self tried to scream out, "*Oh my God! What are you doing?*" The new me squashed that immediately. I began to strip away my dress, exposing my naked body. Rather than stop, I sought to drive his lust even higher. "So, mister… you like Japan girls?" I played on every stereotype I could think of to make him lose his mind.

He lost it completely. It worked perfectly. He lunged at me and pawed at me and dove into his fantasy in a way he had never been able to do before with mute, inexpressive girls. I felt dirty to give him the exact thing he had always wanted. "*What am I doing?*" I would scream at myself in the depths of my mind. Instantly, I rejected that thought. This was not about him! It didn't matter if he should or should not want to be doing what he was doing. This was about carving myself a path out of this waking nightmare of a life! There was only one way to do that, and the new side of me stabbed a single thought back at me, "You make sure you are the best fuck he has ever had, and you do the same for any one of them that comes in here. You make them bow down to your games instead of having to play *their* games. That's how you play them. Once you make them weak in your hands, then they will notice you. Once you are noticed, things will change. You will have *status*! Status is power."

The john that was with me finished, and I didn't let him go. Instead, I started to get aggressive with him again. I started to bite him and scratch him, playing right on the edge of sexual play and real violence. He had to hold on for the ride. This made him more intrigued and he became aggressive as well. A huge part of me wanted to scream and cry, so I used sex to vent out my anger. I allowed him to beat me and slap me so that I could scream. I could feel my head getting hot and I just wanted to tear him to shreds. I inspired him to all sorts of wicked acts, and through it all, I heard that new voice telling me to "*Let him fuck you however he wants. He's the one that's stupid. He has no idea who you are. You're in control. You've got him, baby.*"

I just ranted and rode him and was everything he wanted and more. I spoke filth, said things that matched every stereotype there was, and did everything I could to bury him under a flurry of sex and imagery and need that would make him totally become my own sex servant, in a way.

I hated him no less. By the end, it was me who was choosing the positions and him that was saying he had had enough.

He didn't expect any of it, and in the end, I thought he looked completely flustered as he lay on the floor after finishing him for the last time. I immediately jumped up and walked into the bathroom. I stood over the sink and stared at myself in the mirror. What had I done? I squashed that thought again. Maybe he would report me to the traffickers. I didn't care. I had made him dance to my tune. Sure, I hated the music. Sure, I didn't want to be there on that dance floor, to use the same metaphor. But even if I hated it, at least I was the one who had been leading!

A knock on the door summoned me. I called back in my broken English, "I come out." I splashed some cold water on my face and dabbed it dry with the cheap towels hanging on the rack. I expected that the traffickers might already have been summoned, and this might be where I was dragged away to be quietly killed. It didn't matter. I still felt like a success. A dirty success who had just traded a part of her soul for a chance at life.

The gentleman was still standing there in the room, and he was alone. He was half-dressed now and getting towards being a little tidier as he talked. "Man, you were fucking awesome!"

I was shocked. I tried to look meek, but it was difficult. I had won! "Me?"

"I want to see you again, tonight." He kissed me on the forehead and walked over to the last of his clothes lying on the chair. I could see the bruise on his shoulder from where I had kicked him at one point, and another from where he had fallen on the floor. He looked a little awkward as he got his shirt on, but his good cheer never faded.

Half-stunned but also half-thrilled, I waited until he left and then darted back into the bathroom. I didn't stare at myself. I got ready for the next one. I washed up, recreated my make-up, and got ready for the next client.

When the next one walked in, I repeated the routine. Then again. Days turned into weeks, and as far as I knew those weeks turned into months. It didn't matter. I had no proof my plan was working, but the new side of me was fanatical. She *believed*. What was more, I suddenly felt like I had some measure of control. I had little and was still ferried around like a slave, but one by one I made my johns succumb. My regulars wanted me and demanded me more often.

Finally, what needed to happen happened. We were standing in line waiting to be selected for the day when one of the recruiters walked up to me specifically. He smiled, touched my arm, and drew my eyes up to his face. It was a gentle touch, and I was shocked he was being nice. Usually, this particular head trafficker was one of the coldest among them, never smiling unless we were in pain or about to punished. This didn't feel like either was the case, unless my antics had finally caught up to me. His dark brown eyes pierced into my own as if trying to see what games I was trying to play. I let him look, saying nothing, letting him judge me. Finally, he caressed my face, took a last long look, and then took a step back to talk to the rest of the group. "All of you get your assignments and get going. Except for this one." He stared straight at me.

This broke the tense moment, and the other traffickers all began to move. The other girls were summoned either back into their units or onto one of the waiting trucks. I was left in the middle of the room like a London soldier waiting for the change of the guard. All alone, and feeling very exposed, I just stood there. I was only a few feet away from where the other girls I had seen shot had fallen, bleeding out the last moments of their life. Was this it, then?

The others finally finished their work. The lone trafficker was pacing around, impatient for it all to be over. We were finally alone. He waved at me to follow him, and so I did.

I wasn't in restraints, but it had been a long time since they had figured I needed any. I had been compliant for so long, they must have thought of me as one of those that was sufficiently broken. They were both right and dead wrong, but the path to freedom was not through direct violence. I knew that, so there was no threat from me. They must have recognized that.

I followed him through a dark hall that was like a tunnel. I was led outside for the first time in a long time. It was also the first time in a long while that I felt nature's air burning my skin. The coolness felt refreshing while it stung at the same time. He took off his coat and wrapped it around me. There was an SUV that was parked sideways and a gentleman waiting outside. When he and I appeared, the gentleman immediately opened the door. Throughout the car ride, this particular trafficker distracted me from looking out the window by talking to me about something regarding business, loyalty, and trust.

We went to a building which resembled the alley in the back, away from other buildings. We entered through the back door which led down a hall to an elevator. He looked me over as if he was considering how I was being presented. I stood there, staring away from him. I knew we were going up but didn't see what button he pushed.

The doors scrolled open, and I blinked against the lights. I looked down the length of the hallway beyond and was surprised to see it was fairly well-fashioned. It looked like the inside of a fancy hotel. I followed him without question. He walked down the hall and slid a card into the card slot of the door, turning it from red to green so we could enter. It was a nice room, well-maintained and freshly cleaned. There was a fireplace against the wall, black leather couches surrounding a glass coffee table, and another room to your left.

I stood there by the door not moving, waiting for him to give me commands. He seemed to be in no rush. He took his coat off of me and waved his hand as if he was showing me some type of exhibit. "Do you like it?" Deciding it was best to just agree, I looked straight at him and nodded. That actually drew a laugh out of him, as he realized the game I was playing. After all, it was a game they had demanded that I play. The game of instant obedience. He should have expected that response. Realizing his error, he laughed and said, "You don't have to pretend with me. I know you are American and I know you have a brain inside that head of yours. You don't have to be afraid. You see, I want you to be my personal concubine." He plopped himself on the edge of the couch and waved me over to him.

When I came closer, he took my hands and touched them. "You have very soft skin, I like that very much." He had an accent of Italian or Latin descent. I wasn't sure what his ethnic background was at the time, but I didn't care either. To me, he was worse than the scum who were his customers. He was also precisely what I needed to get out. So, I let him touch me and said nothing.

He gave me a tour around the hotel room; it was very extravagant and large. There were curtains on the windows, but when I pulled the drapes there weren't any windows. He stood there behind me, watching my every move as I explored a little at his encouragement.

As I finished, he said, "We don't rent out this room to anyone; this is my personal room for you. You won't have to go back and stay in the cells. You can stay here with me. There will be guards that will be there for your protection. If you need anything, you tell them and they will come and get me."

It sounded frightening. It also sounded like the first step down the road I had been planning for. I cringed at the idea of what he wanted me for. The unnamed tigress side of me purred in satisfaction. She was making progress. "What are your plans for me?" I asked.

He laid it out for me precisely, "I will be your personal master and you will be my concubine. You will now serve me and those who I wish. I have my personal client list that you will serve as well, but I would think this is a far better way than working out of the basement, is it not?"

I nodded, of two minds about the whole thing. Partly the idea of being with him on such a personal basis was terrifying. On the other hand, this was certainly progress. This place would let me feel clean again. I would feel like a human and far less like an animal. I was not yet my own person. I was still being abused. I was still a slave. Yet, it was different.

He lured me into the bathroom and showed me the towel and the evening gown I was commanded to wear. "Take a shower and relax. This is your new home. If there's anything you need, don't hesitate to ask one of my men." He pointed to the door. "Knock, and ask. If they refuse without calling me, tell me when I come back. They have to answer to me. If you irritate them, I'll hear about that, too. Don't be a fool and screw around with them. I like you, and don't want to lose you."

I had value. I was still a slave, but that statement proved I was making progress. Before, he would have killed me without even blinking. Now, he was offering me protection from his own men. I wanted to crow in victory and cringe in fear. I was walking a tightrope, and the heights were climbing. If I fell off, I would fall so very far, but I could see the top of the pit I was getting closer to being in reach. One part of me laughed, thinking this was just a different type of slavery. I mocked the whole idea, thinking this was no further to anything other than being abused in a different way. The tigress derailed that train of thought, "*We are closer. Those johns were all mine. Someday, HE will be all mine.*"

For the moment, I was all his. There was no getting around that. He walked out, and I followed his command by turning on the tub's water faucet. Admiring the bath walls and the marbled tub, I admitted to myself that I had never seen anything so extravagant as this. I sank to the edge of the tub, trying to see this trafficker's face in some new light. I tried to imagine seeing it near me more often and trying to please him. To serve him as a master.

His name was Marco. At least, that was what he was called in the few times I overheard him talking to the others. Until then, it wouldn't have mattered. Now, it mattered more than anything else. What else did I know of him? What was he to me?

*   *   *

Marco's face hovered in front of me, screaming, "You belong to me! Do you understand?"

Two men were holding me up, propping me there so my legs wouldn't crumble. I babbled back at him, drenched in fear that I would be hurt further, "I'm sorry! Chalmo tes say you, tashi an goo day yo!" I murmured the Korean apology my mother made me memorize until it was a mantra I uttered while she whipped me.

Now, it was Marco who whipped me again. "I feed you! I clothe you and this is the respect you pay me! You stupid cunt! You do not defy me!" He continued to rant on, screaming in my face.

My legs became limp and I could barely stand. My hair was damp from the sweat and tears and it covered my face.

"Drop her!" he commanded, "Leave us!" The two men stepped back. I laid on the cold floor, crying as he stood over me. I felt the tip of his boot kick me in the stomach. Then he leaned down and grabbed me by my hair to pick me up.

"Do you know why you are here? Cause your family doesn't even want you. Am I right?" he screamed. "Say it!"

"Yes," I sobbed, "My family doesn't want me. That's why I'm here!"

"You are a bad girl, you have no friends no allies, and you are alone. Everybody hates you! Repeat!" He screamed in my ear.

"I . . . I'm sorry!" I cried. Then he slapped me and I fell on the floor once again. A pleasant knock sounded at the door. That wasn't right. What?

*   *   *

The flashback broke as the door swung open. There was a primly dressed hotel maid standing there, her expression inquisitive and polite. "Do you need towels?" Her accent was heavy and European, but I could understand her. Was this another way out? Had she pleased someone as well, and become a maid instead of being trapped below? Was this what she could hope to be?

I shook that thought off and thanked her. Taking the towels, I waited for her to go. I tried to center myself again. Whatever Marco had been to me, now I was his. He was my future and the path to something else. That was all there was to it. If I failed with him, none of the others would try with me. He might even kill me. I had no options. I had set myself on this path, and I had to follow it.

Jules

My life became a series of inches. I had to claw forward each day, one at a time. Marco was not exactly a fool, even if I had convinced him of something that I was really not. He didn't immediately embrace me completely to his heart or anything so romantic. He bought me expensive clothes that hung on my closet racks, and compared to the daily abuse of being in the basement, modeling clothes for him and dressing for the approval of his friends was hardly the worst thing I had endured. But he was always careful.

I wasn't instantly free me from all of my other duties. Marco still had his own quotas to meet and clients to impress, and to many of them I was still "Sukki." Marco was as trapped as I was in those moments, and still gave me up to them when they called. Over time, I had the impression he was trying to wean them off of me so that he could have me all to himself. I was trying to help him accomplish that too, but it took time. It was so strange, trying to slowly eke a little loyalty out of him even as I gave myself to him, even when that was the last thing I wanted to do. I was being pulled in a dozen different directions. Jules got stronger each day, for she was the one with the strength to handle all of this.

When they took me to my appointments, things went a little differently. First off, they were appointments now, not simply being caged in a motel room waiting to be attacked. I was sent out with purpose. I was led down to the basement but loaded into a car instead of a truck. I would see the other girls, ones that I stood with before. The only difference was, they were still in the scrubs I had once worn, now they see me in a glamorized cocktail gown. They often looked at me as if I was betraying them, but I tried to shrug it off. What else could I do? Would I remember, some day in the future, not to betray them? Would I come back for them? I tried to tell myself that I would do all that I could. At that moment, those thoughts were still preciously few. My focus had to be on staying alive, on playing the game. Jules knew that and knew she had to be strong. I had to be strong.

When I returned to the hotel after each appointment, I was that much more Marco's concubine and servant. I had to get into his good graces so that I didn't have to endure the others anymore. More resolved than ever, I was his. His appreciation began to show. Marco started to shower me with luxurious gifts, designer handbags, and unlimited quantities of cocaine on elaborate golden platters. It was sinfully ridiculous. I slowly began to confide in him about parts of my life. Most of it wasn't true, but it didn't matter. I made him feel like he was special. It wasn't an overnight task. It took me weeks and maybe even months to convince him to open himself a little further and trust me a little more.

With each of those weeks, I would gain more and more exclusivity with him. Instead of going to the motel to be with other clients, he would take me there and pretend to be my client. He would fluctuate wildly from cruel to kind but began to confide in me as well. I started to understand him, and that was the most dangerous part of all. I loathed the idea of loving him, but I started to know him as well as a lover should and in a way only a lover normally does. I learned how much he needed someone emotionally, and I became the outlet for his suppressed emotions of loneliness.

Marco was very much attached to a woman who was not only his legal partner by marriage but who was also the mother of his children. He never hid the fact of his marriage, but it was estranged, according to him. He kept his family far from the life he and I were living. It was far too dangerous and it was a risk he knew very well not to entertain. Many times I watched him (from a distance). I observed his demeanor with curiosity, and often wondered how he became the monster he was?

It was the opening I was waiting for, I began to play on that. One evening we were laying in this huge king size bed with the lavender see-through canopy above the bed. My body was wrapped in the silk sheets. I felt his hand softly caressing my arm as my back was facing him. Every time he touched me, I was caught between disgust and the longing to have anyone touch me in that kindest of ways. It was falsely tender with him and always led to intercourse. He was, at his core, a cruel and callous creature who could understand no other expression of love than sex. Knowing what he needed, I pretended to be asleep and ignore him touching me.

Like he said so often before, he once again whispered, "You are unbelievably soft. I love your skin."

I still said nothing, making him come to me, knowing this was a moment I could draw him even deeper into my game.

I felt him scoot closer to me. He began to kiss my shoulder down to my arms and to my hands, then sensually kissing my fingertips. I pretended that I just woke up from his kisses and I slowly turned and pulled my hand away from his so that I could stretch the rest of my body. I turned and lay on my back and just looked into his brown eyes. He watched it all with fascination.

"I'm going to give you a name," he whispered. "I want to call you Jewels, 'cause you are a "jewel" to my heart."

Sappy poetry from him felt twice as wrong. That was a line I remembered delivered from old movies I had once loved. "Will it be spelt J-e-w-e-l?" I asked.

"You can spell it however you want, but you will be my jewels, understood?"

I laid there and nodded my head and thought about the new name. He was trying so hard to be tender, yet couldn't even see how forcing a new name on me couldn't have been further from what a true man would have done for me. As if to drive home that point, he turned me over onto my back and forced himself inside of me. I went along with him and even my body language gave him the message that I wanted him. I was so practiced at being his.

Instinctively, that part of me that was the tigress knew it was time. She had a name now. Jules. Spelled the way I wanted. She was alive now and had a plan. "Marco?" I asked. "Do you think I'm pretty?"

He lifted his head and caressed my face and stared at me as if he was looking at a work of art and he smiled at me. "You are unique. There's something about you that inspires me, which is why I want you all to myself. Other men see it too, and it makes me crazy when you are with them. I hate that."

I couldn't ask outright to be spared from that sort of thing. Not so blatantly. Instead, I knew what had to happen. I had to fall into him, and confess my loyalty to him. I had to be his. "Can I tell you something crazy?" I asked. I went carefully, choosing every word knowing that if he didn't believe me, I might be killed. I said the words so sincerely that the part of me that was Jules maybe even believed it a little. "Ever since you brought me here, I feel like Cinderella rescued from below. I can't thank you enough. When we spend time together I don't feel like your concubine anymore. I'm falling in love with you." My tears began to fall as the inner-most part of me roiled and snarled, yelling out, "*What the hell are you doing? I could never love this fucking beast!*" Jules only remained calm, and bared this private and completely false face to Marco, confessing a love that was somehow both fake, and yet completely and necessarily real.

He caressed my face and held on to me. He kissed me and I kissed him back as if he was the love of my life. When he slowly pulled back I was worried that he figured my game out. Instead, he flashed me a smile that was as genuine as any could be on a monster as such as he. "I'm falling for you, too." He smiled, "I'm trying to resist, but there's something about you that makes me feel young again. You are so innocent and soft."

It tortured me inside to have to get closer to him. I could sense the darkness in him, and his talk of innocence reminded me of pedophiles and their twisted urges spawned from whatever dark core was inside of them. This was what I wanted, and I encouraged him by emphasizing the qualities of myself that he liked. Showering after our sex sessions was a cleansing ritual that I needed, though I never let him see how I scrubbed at myself.

Over time, he spoke to me of other things. At first, it was only in vague terms, but I tried to encourage him to get more specific. Marco was one of the lead traffickers for that business that was being run, answering up to an unknown set of superiors. He was inside the inner circle and had his own aspirations to grow and become more powerful in the underworld. He would use me as a sort of sounding board for what he was thinking. This only grew more common as I showed curiosity about the business. I used him to learn their underground schemes. I tried to pry little details out of him, like who else was involved and who in the government was aware of this slave trade happening. I tried to find out how things were kept secret, and what pockets were lined with silver in order to keep the whole thing in the dark. The more involved I became, I knew this would be far more difficult than I had first thought. If I ever chose to escape this underground world, I would then be a threat to these people. In the meantime, I had to do what I felt was right at the moment. The height was getting dizzying, but I was walking that same tight-rope. There was simply no going back. I had to either keep my balance as I got higher and higher or fall to devastation.

One day, the time felt right. He was particularly annoyed at some decision his superiors had made, and it had been days since I had caused him the least bit of suspicion. Trying to sound casual and yet intrigued, I asked, "Why don't we make our own money? Instead of just getting a percentage, why don't we open up our own entertainment industry and make an empire out of that?"

He had been sitting in bed just reading a newspaper. He gave a low chuckle, and asked, "Sounds good, but how do you plan on doing that? What type of entertainment business are you wanting to open?"

I scuttled closer to him, trying to play the enthusiastic, cute woman he wanted by his side, charming him as well as I could, "This kind of business, sort of. More reputable, higher end clients. We could be like "Bonnie & Clyde!" I could be the Madame and recruit the young girls while you run the contacts and keep the hired men in line. We can split the money 50/50, even. It can be our own escort service."

He laid down the paper, chewing a lip and looked intrigued. Immediately, his own twisted nature began to put a mark on the idea. That couldn't be helped. "We can do an international industry with young pre-teens as well," he offered.

Even the Jules side of me wasn't sure if she could handle that. "Why do we need to have kids? What's wrong with girls fresh out of high school? It's legal and you don't have to worry about being tried in court for soliciting prostitution to minors."

Now, he laughed again, as if that was the least of his concerns. "My dear Jules, you are so vibrant, and yet so naive. If you are worried about the legal aspect, you haven't understood everything I've tried to tell you. I have connections that will protect me."

"But do you trust them? How do you know they are going to be there for you? I just don't want to lose you and I really want to be there for you."

He sounded utterly confident. "I have worked with these people for many years and they have never betrayed me. So, I know. Besides, most of them have partaken at least once or twice in visiting a girl here and there. Mutual destruction, get it? If they don't protect me, I won't protect them." He smiled at me, then said more seriously, "As far as this Madame idea goes, if you want to do this, then you have so much to learn."

"You are going to teach me?" I asked.

"If we are going to do this together, then we can't make any mistakes, do you understand?"

"Yes, I understand. I really want to do this!"

"Why are you interested in doing this now?"

This was it. I had to sell this. Jules knew it and demanded to be given free reign. I gave it to her, not wanting any part of this. I felt it more and more; I was becoming each day more this creature and less and less myself. It was scary as hell, wondering if I would ever be myself again. The excitement that came out of my lips with Jules in control was almost so real it hurt to hear the words spoken with my own voice, "Oh my God! Are you serious? Hell, the money, the power...I see how people treat you when we go to the casinos and the shopping malls. The security guards and the limousine drivers all give way to you. It's like they bow down to you. I want to know what it feels like! Besides, how much sexier do you think I'd be to you if I had that sort of respect and on the surface, I look like the perfect lady, but behind closed doors, I can be your Asian concubine. I don't want to see these other customers anymore. I feel like I'm cheating on you." This was it. I had said the words. This was the play to belong to only one person.

He gave me a knowing smile, but he actually spoke a word or two of caution that seemed out of character for him. "You are beginning to understand the power it gives, but you must also remember not to let it seduce you. Money can be very powerful, but you must control it. Do not allow money to control you."

I thought this was odd coming from him since I believed he allowed it to control him and helped turn him into the animal he was. His tone was so firm, but it felt cold and calculating that I wasn't sure he was excited at all by the prospect. He didn't hurt me or say that he didn't believe me, but I didn't want to push the issue. I didn't bring it up again, knowing I had planted the seed and that I had to let it take root.

After a few months, that is what happened. He took me on a ride and introduced me to a commercial tax agent for training. Marco bought me business attire for me to wear when we went out in public. Suddenly, I found I was no longer doing calls or servicing my body to other johns. When he took me to the tax agent, he treated me in a whole different way, even introducing me by saying, "This is my fiancé, Jules Costatos." I could see both men sizing me up, judged me as the typical young gold digger they assumed me to be, but I didn't care.

At first, I was taken back by the name. I sat there quietly listening to the conversation that was traded back and forth between the two gentlemen. I had up until then only the vaguest hope that this was regarding the escort service I requested months ago. Finally, I heard the question I longed to hear: a confirmation that they were indeed talking about exactly that and that I was going to be a major part of it. Throughout the conversation, the other agent and I caught sudden glances at one another.

"Jules, what do you want to call this start-up of ours?" Marco asked me.

Secretly thrilled, I was somewhat surprised he was offering me that sort of choice. I think this was like a gift for him, treating it like a romantic gesture. I asked with real surprise, though I added an element of excited delight as would a proper girlfriend or fiancé, "Oh, I get to name it?"

The details they passed back and forth went quickly. I understood numbers and could handle details, but it was clear this was not their first time speaking. They skipped over whole elements, and I became quickly lost. This was not a good trend. I needed to become invested in the business, and continue to take on a larger and larger role so that I could earn a little freedom. To do that, I needed Marco to trust me with more than just naming the business and using me as a mascot. I had to truly be involved. I passed the time enjoying how handsome the young agent was. After so long servicing middle-aged and wealthy businessmen and politicians, his face was enjoyable and refreshing.

Once our meeting was over, I walked with Marco back to the limousine. He filed away the information into a briefcase, and I could see his organizational method was about as orderly as his personal life. I saw another way in. I offered, "Why don't I be your secretary?"

"Do you know how to organize?" he asked.

I nodded back, "I use to volunteer at a college when I was 17. I know how to make Xerox copies. I can type over 75 wpm, file, take notes, and answer phones."

"You can do that?" he asked.

I tried to laugh, making light of the stab of pain that rippled through me as I joked about my abduction, hating myself every moment, "Well, it wasn't like the big boss asked for my resume when I got stuck into this situation in the first place, right?"

He chuckled back, my humor helping him to trust me even more deeply. The less resentment I showed, the further in I pulled him. "You have a fine sense of humor, Jules. Don't change that. I like it."

I began to take on the project of keeping Marco's finances organized, and that only deepened my hold on his life and his expectation that I was going to become an integral and permanent part of his. Now, do not be deceived, I was not alone in this task. He still directed additional eyes on me, for security reasons. Once more, there was a strange set of feelings that surrounded that time. I was doing work, and there is satisfaction in seeing the files come into order and the numbers add up. As well, there was a satisfaction in seeing my plan coming together. Insidiously, my feelings for Marco grew more complicated. I despised giving him my body, but this joint endeavor gave us other things to discuss and deepened our relationship.

I don't want to give the impression I was actually in love with him, or even flirting with the concept. Not in any traditional sense, that is. There is a term that I learned called the Stockholm Syndrome, and perhaps this was the beginning of that very phenomenon. As I said, this was an insidious process that came by playing the game of loving him even as he combined our efforts to make this new process work. I never forgot he was an animal, but all of my hopes for the future rested on his success at that moment, and it becomes so very hard to separate one thing from the other: to wish both for his downfall in the end, and yet also to strive for his success in the present. The idea even more complicated knowledge that, given how woven I was into his finances when I left, I would leave a hole a mile wide from which he might not recover given the less than forgiving personalities who worked in his business. They were not likely to forgive errors. The interconnected feelings of potential fear for his safety and warm thoughts of revenge were wound so closely in on themselves that it was impossible to untangle.

After a few weeks of ongoing visits with the agent, Marco couldn't attend these meetings anymore; he had other tasks he was obligated to do. So, I began to go alone, chauffeured by the limo driver. My meetings with this agent became more and more personal. I developed a friendship with him. "Jules" saw an opportunity there which the less-practical, less-daring side of me would never have seen, much less taken advantage of. He liked me and started to look at me in a rather fond light. So, I began to share my body in exchange for information. He might never have shared some of it, afraid that Marco would not want him giving away all of their secret dealings, but our softer relationship soon had him confessing everything to keep my interest intact.

Eventually, it had to end. I admit I didn't want it to. He was pleasant, and even if he was involved in helping keep illegal businesses flowing, he was not the same type of vicious criminal I was surrounded by day and night. He became my fantasy man when Marco was in bed with me and helped make those times more bearable. Our time alone was an intense affair, but when I caught a few signs of him starting to get into the relationship more deeply, I knew it had to end. He bought me a gift here or a gift there. I was able to pass it off as gifts Marco had given me but that he had forgotten. He gave me so many. I saw it was only a matter of time where he would try to give me something larger, and I would have to turn it down. Marco would notice it, and I wasn't ready to run, yet. I couldn't risk him losing his life, and I also couldn't risk him being uncovered or losing his job. I needed him for the contact he was. So, I eased him down as much as I could and stopped seeing him. I had learned all I could anyway. It was tough to lose that physical contact, but in the end, he wasn't my goal. He wasn't freedom.

From that point, our meetings always tended to be with other attorneys or consultants in the room. It was as if we had an unspoken agreement that to be alone again would not be a good thing. Feelings still existed on both sides, and the "Jules" side of me recognized the power that granted me. In a way, I guess I was terrible to him. We both accepted the danger of what we were doing, and when I flirted with him he still smiled and couldn't resist his own flirtatious replies. I knew that if I asked him for something, he might risk a lot for me. That was a tool and power. I cringed at the idea of what that meant to me and felt bad. "Jules" saw just how far that could be pushed, and she was the one in charge. I let myself become more and more her because she was my strength that would see me through those moments.

So, the tax agent wasn't the only gentleman I traded my body for information. It became a regular trade for me. It was the one bit of power that was completely mine. Marco controlled my money and made all the final decisions in our business deals, so I couldn't trade favors that way. So, my body was what I had that he could only control if he discovered what I was doing. So, I used private meetings and secret liaisons to push my knowledge outwards, and earn what might be future favors from those who would have good reason to remember me very, very fondly.

Once the business meetings were over, I would always return to the hotel. I had some autonomy at this time, but only in my ability to move. Marco gave me the keys, a pager, and a large cell phone to call him. I didn't have any papers or drivers' license. He told me that if I ever got in trouble, just take the ticket and he would settle it with his own contacts. I had security surrounding me at all times, wherever I needed to go. Often, they wouldn't ride with me, just following me at a distance. I always had to remember to have a good reason to be at each venue where I got together with my various male contacts so that none of it would look suspicious to Marco. I even got my own female consultant to help me make a business plan.

I was waiting to meet with that consultant one day when the concierge came to tell me she was a little late. He smiled and went to close the door. My memory cued on a sort of feeling of familiarity. He was the same size and shape as my father, and it reminded me of him.

*　　　*　　　*

"Why are you leaving me?" I asked him. At that moment, I felt like a small little girl afraid of losing her daddy.

"Daddy?" I was awake in the middle of the night and saw the headlights fading away from the window. I plopped on the floor near the doorway and cried. My mother woke up and ran to me.

"Song Ja! What's the matter?" My mother picked me up.

"Daddy's gone!" I cried.

"No, he went to work." My mother tried to comfort me.

"I wanna' go with daddy!" I kicked and screamed. My mother finally put me down. I ran to the front door and planted my hands on the glass window pane at the center of it. My tears were falling endlessly on my face. I wanted to go with my Dad. I didn't want to stay home with Mom.

"Jules...?"

Song Ja was my name. Why didn't she know that? Mommy knew...

*　　　*　　　*

"Jules? Ms. Costatos?" The lady called my false names. I looked around and I was in the doorway to the hotel conference room where I was going to meet her. I tried to shake off the flashback. They were coming more often, and I had the good sense to wonder what was causing them and if they would ever end. I feared I knew the answer to both.

Still not certain about me, the woman went on, "My name is Emily Strauss. I'm the consultant your fiancé called to schedule. He informed me that you have no experience in starting up a business, so I am here to help you."

I tried to plaster on a welcoming smile and allowed her into the room. I pointed at the couch.

"Would you like something to drink?" I asked.

"Coffee is fine." She said. Then she pulled out some papers, notepad and a pen. We got to work.

That kicked things off, and within two months I couldn't even recognize where I had been before. It felt like so suddenly, I had 32 young ladies working for me. Marco was the "supervisor" and I was the leading Madame of the local escort industry.

Madame

My duties were both simple and yet challenged the very core of who I was. Before, I was a victim. True, I still was. Every night in Marco's bed, I remained a victim. But now, I was also one of the ones making the system run.

I was taught how to train the girls, and they trained others. I watched out for the good cops and gave reports on which ones were amiable and bribable and which ones would not play the game. I would talk to the customers and learn how to draw out what they really wanted in order to keep them happy, and gave them the rules to keep them in line.

In short, I learned how to make the selling of a girl's body marketable. The flow of cash was incredible. The service retainer alone was $1,000, then anything after the initial meet, it was up to the young lady's command or the client's request; it ranged from expensive wining and dining to weekend getaways, kinky live sex shows, full service (meaning anything goes), to simple, innocent companionship. The prices ranged for the girls anywhere from $1,000 up to $50,000. Each girl had their own price and it wouldn't matter if you requested the same service from two different women, they were allowed to quote different prices. I only urged the ladies not to accept anything below $1,000 per hour of any service. If, and when, the customer wanted more, the price rose steeply. Full service packages ranged from $1,500 to $10,000 per hour depending on what they wanted and could fuel any need from intercourse to oral or anal sex. Show dates were priced at $1200; a live lesbian scene in which clients were forbidden to partake in any sexual schemes. A threesome with two girls was labelled a Liquorish Lush and went for $2,500 per hour, per girl. I sold the dream, not just the price.

Most of our requests were via phone, so we came up with pseudo names in case our phones were tapped. We never asked for cash, always using names like "Candy" for cocaine, "Collect" for cash, or "Plastic" for credit cards. We even moved into the realm of Dominatrix calls which could range from $2,000 to $10,000 per hour due to the risk of health and bodily harm. The girls' compensation only involved the direct service they were to provide, meaning the retainer was 100% ours, not the girls'. After the retainer, then it became a 40/60 split. I kept 40% and they took home 60%, and of course, tips were 100% theirs. All transactions went through a zip money bag. We had a counter who was literally hired to count the cash and record it. Once the cash was in the zip bags, one of the men who worked alongside Marco would collect the zip bags.

That is to say, Marco got paid. I never actually saw any of the money. He still kept me on a tight leash. Security still followed me around, and despite all my lavish lifestyle, I rarely had more than a few dollars of actual money in my purse. Marco gave me an authorized secured credit card, which became my life, and I knew Marco paid attention to those beyond almost any other element of the business finances. There were alerts on specific purchases, it wasn't about the amount I spent, it was the item. I was given freedom to buy an $8,000 Gucci purse, but heaven forbid if I decided to buy a plane ticket, rental car, or anything that remotely resembled *"escape."* I never had any freedom and was always watched.

We were a new and rising element on the underworld scene in that area. Marco had connections everywhere. One of his old friends from the traffickers worked a day job as a United States Marshall and Marco paid off an FBI agent directly to keep us informed of any pending busts or raids. The trafficking world victimized various cops, law enforcement, and other governmental agencies that included a vulnerable price that they did not want to come to light. This would range from back child support that was over $20,000 to millions, gambling issues, or financial repercussions. Even a few of the vice agents informed us of information. They would tip us off regarding those who were in witness protection that could possibly hinder our business. They would also funnel information to us about where we might find potential markets of girls to tap into. The very people that were supposed to be protecting society were filtering off the vulnerable elements of that society into our arms so we could take advantage of it. I was continuously startled, amazed, and terrified even as I used those advantages to push Marco's interests.

I ran my business like few others ever did, and I think that is why I was successful at it. I never understood the pimp mentality to have the girls all reside under one roof. Marco tried to explain it once, saying that in an escort business, especially an elite one, you had to mentally train the women to depend on you so they remained loyal. Rather than do that geographically by housing them together, I would do it through getting them hooked on unlimited amounts of cocaine, heroin, opium and meth, along with large compensation that no pimps could beat. I had over 30 girls working under me, but I trained 10 of them to watch over the others and treat them like products. These girls had a freedom that even I didn't have. They could spend their own money, live in their choice of residence, and see who they wanted to see. If there was a leak of information of what the business was about or if the girls tried to steal clientele, they were terminated from the business. I got the impression Marco made it clear to them that they would lose far more than that, but I tried to ignore those deeper threats.

Most of these young ladies were college students in their freshman year, or high school graduates barely turning 18. The quota for them to meet with each client varied between 12 to 20 per day. I hired drivers to provide transportation and security for them while they were on the clock.

I was continually engaged now, and never bored. My daily routine would consist of getting up around 2 p.m. and not going to bed until around 5 a.m. when I wasn't manning the phones. Most of the time, I didn't get to sleep at all for days. My girls were not the only ones who were hooked on those drugs. "Jules" was not a stable personality, and I was trapped in a serious self-destructive spiral. I was constantly pumping meth and cocaine in my body to keep me awake. I met with my protégés on a daily basis for status checks, and they would hang out in the skyscraper office I rented to keep me company and allow me to influence their actions. They would help me answer the phones and recruit more girls. Money poured into Marco's pockets like a waterfall. Jewelry stores knew my car and welcomed me whenever I drove up. Casino managers and supervisors ushered me into the VIP lounges without pause. It felt like I was one of the elite. If I could only ignore the fact that I was constantly under watch.

Marco was always there, bringing his own harshness to each moment. When a man betrayed them, like trying to make off with one of the girls to resell her to another market, he would make sure the malefactor was punished. He would bring me along to witness the man being tortured so that I would be aware of the penalty of anyone "betraying" him. At that moment, I didn't flinch, cry, or move my body when I saw them being beat almost to death. It was almost satisfying seeing these men get tortured. In my mind, I tried to justify what they were going through compared to what they had planned for the girls they were trying to profit off of by selling them to new slavery and away from my protection. I stood there, watching the torture, and almost enjoyed it.

*   *   *

"Ma!" Mia cried out. She laid on her stomach on the old mattress. Her wrists were bound to the bed rails. I saw the men line up and her panties torn off her.

"Stop! No!" I screamed. She was crying out and my heart was filled with rage. I wanted to jump out of the chair, but I was bound by chains wrapped around my wrists. My arms were pulled behind the chair as the two recruiters held me down. My mind was spinning and my heart felt as if I had been stabbed multiple times. My head was hurting so much from crying.

I kept looking into her eyes as she screamed, begging me to do something. I couldn't but I wanted to kill them. I wanted to save her and I couldn't! I hated them, every one of those fucking assholes! "Stop it! Stop it!" I screamed. I cried even more.

*   *   *

Fortunately, that time, I had not cried out for real. I came back to reality as the man passed out on the concrete floor of the basement in one of the casinos. I shook violently, nearly getting sick. The damned flashbacks were starting to strike at the worst moments. It was getting worse. The drugs, the alcohol and the life I was leading was taking an unknown, terribly emotional toll on me. I wasn't sure how long I could continue with this façade.

At that point, it had been somewhere between six and nine months since I had taken over as Madame of "Jules Escort Services" in Las Vegas, NV. The business was expanding, and I hated where it was being taken. Marco was now fully ensconced with expanding along the lines of international child slavery which he had mentioned to me. This was at a whole new level of illegality, and yet he wanted me to be a part of it. I tried to stay clear of it, but he needed my help in some ways. As well, this was something like an ongoing initiation through mutual incrimination. He had explained it once to me: his contacts helped him and he helped them, and everyone would go down together if anyone spoke. So, he got me in so deep that I was one of the guilty should any of it ever come to light.

One of the worst moments was when he decided to show me one example of how they got children from other places, and how their parents were not actively concerned for their welfare. Marco took me in his vehicle with him and we drove south towards Arizona. When we approached the border gates, there were lines of them along with cars waiting to enter Mexico. I remember seeing Marco staring at a crumpled folded paper with numbers. I tried not to notice, but the numbers didn't make sense to me. Then he looked up and drove down to the booth that was towards the far right. When he pulled up, he spoke in Spanish. This was the first time I had ever heard him speak in a foreign language. Without suspicion, the patrol officer let us in. I don't remember showing any form of identification. After the long drive, we drove up to a house where he changed into a suit that was all black. His attire looked familiar, and then I understood when he announced himself as a "Catholic priest." I was summoned to follow him, and he dressed me up as a lay nun, long skirted with a top that covered my neck. My appearance had to look welcoming and innocent, and I made it work.

The house he had chosen was a small wooden house. It resembled a patch work of quilt built into a home, with discolored wood and metal sheets that created four walls and a roof. There was a young girl about five years old and she was playing outside by herself. I got out of the vehicle once Marco got out. He knocked on the door and a lady approached it. The moment she saw his "Roman collar," she immediately opened the door without hesitation. She and Marco spoke back and forth in Spanish. I had no comprehension of the conversation, but I watched his demeanor and it was unlike anything I had ever seen. He pointed at the young girl that was playing outside and the mother kept nodding her head as she smiled. I heard him mention "America" a few times in the conversation.

Something inside me just felt lost and helpless. I wish I knew Spanish so that I could find some way of hinting to her that the man she was communicating wasn't real. She had tears of gratitude in her eyes and she continued to thank him with "Gracias." He put his arms around her and prayed for her right then and there as if he cared for her. Once the conversation was done, she walked out with us and called her daughter to come over. She introduced us, and I knew what was being decided.

We got back in the vehicle, and Marco spoke with real satisfaction, "Someone will pick her up tomorrow or sometime this week."

"What is going to happen to her? What did you tell the mother?" I asked.

"That's a step too far, right now, Jules. Leave that for me to know. This is just the first step. I'll show you more later. But you need to keep building your ways of drawing in new business. Every person's style of entrapment is different. All you have to know is that this child is worth over $5,000 per hour. She's going to make a lot of money for us." Then he peeled out of the driveway and off we went.

When he mentioned "us," I was nearly sick right there in the car. I had no idea what to do, and yet I could hardly deny that I was helping make this possible. I was in so deep that I could not think of escaping. Not yet. I wanted to be free, and this had felt like the path in the start, but I was so lost in this lifestyle. "Jules" ruled over my life. The more I didn't want to give up the power, the more I *became* "Jules" each day. The escape route I had always envisioned for myself grew fuzzier and fuzzier.

My girls were my life, and I lived for the work and play that surrounded them. They called me "The Queen of all Bitches," and I was satisfied with that reputation. I was firm with the girls and kept it strictly professional. They were the product and I was the distributor.

My perspective changed as well when it came to men. Marco continued to own me, and as a way to lash out, I started to want to see some of those men beg for more. They came to me for my girls, but that wasn't enough power over them. I started to drift even further into the world I created. There were times when I went on calls with some of my girls. When men requested show dates including girl-on-girl action, I would join in. I did anything from lesbian porn, strip dancing, dominatrix and bondage/domination/sadism/masochism (BDSM) displays with the girls. With the men, I went even further. When I would get calls from customers requesting to be beaten, kicked, or punished for being a "bad" boy, I took those calls personally as a way to vent. Some of their requests were extremely volatile, and I was not really that violent at heart. Neither was I really a lesbian at heart, even though I tried to throw myself into that lifestyle as a way to break away from the constant heartache my male relationships had caused me. So, to allow myself to do all of this, I was constantly drowned in cocaine so that I couldn't feel the physical pain or the emotional or mental guilt. I wanted to be the woman every woman envied and the woman every man wanted as a fantasy doll. I was turned on by the idea that I was a "million-dollar bitch" and not a "two-dollar whore."

The more involved I was, the more lost I became. Some of the lessons I learned were ones I wished I could forget. I've learned about the dirty politicians who benefited from this type of operation and gained a certain percentage that came into the industry. I learned how deeply the justice system was bought and perverted by those who could use cash to stay free of jail. Worst of all, I learned that the young girls that grew pregnant were culled, separated out, used for the fetish by those who liked pregnant women, then sent up to a different cell until the baby was born. Then, the infants were ripped out of the arms of their mothers to be sold online fraudulently. That thought haunted my nightmares and set the stage for how I would finally manage to get free of it all.

There were moments where the "old" me would come out. I would wake up in a bathtub drenched in alcohol, surfacing from a night of having drowned myself in meth, acid, and cocaine. Naked, pale, and feeling like I was wrapped in dead flesh that was no longer my own. I would walk over to the mirror and try to see anything that resembled me in the image that stared back. I had fallen into my own sort of enslavement, beholden to myself more than any other. Had I sabotaged the very thing I had hoped to find: a normal life?

Into this chaos came JC.

Jules seemed impervious to the idea of love, and I have no idea if my relationship with JC could be classified as something to straightforward as that. For Jules, she was about control, and "the old me" had little control in those days. However, the time with JC was as soft a moment as I ever felt while lost in that world.

I can't remember why I was out in the rougher area of town that day since the ultra-urban lifestyle was not my stomping grounds. I was fascinated with African American culture and admired heroes like Dr. Martin Luther King Jr., Rosa Parks, and Harriet Tubman, but I was not part of that culture in any way. I knew how protective some neighborhoods could be, and I knew when to get out when I wasn't welcome. This time around, I didn't react quickly enough. I was confronted by a tall, black man with a muscular build who clearly thought I was trespassing where I shouldn't be. He was pulling out a gun when a friend of his stepped in, calmed him down, and maybe even saved my life. That was how I was introduced to JC.

He played his game as perfectly as I played mine. He waved at me, saying with an easy tone, "Hey girl, where ya been? I was wonderin' what happened to you!"

The other guy stared at JC, disbelieving.

JC just looked at him right back, saying, "What? She's with me, T." He motioned to me to play along. I was so clueless. I was so slow on the uptake that JC must have known his friend was getting suspicious. So, he came over and jumped in my car so casually that he had to be welcome, saying, "Let's go! I promised you a night on the town, didn't I?"

Now, this is a critical point, "Why did I ever trust JC? Why did "Jules" trust him?" My track record was clearly poor when it came to finding healthy people, but at this point, I had little choice. If his friend "T" figured we were lying, he would probably kill me. If JC was worse than he seemed, he might hurt me. At that moment, maybe he just seemed like the lesser of two evils.

I followed his lead and drove off. He took me to a nearby train track that led me to an exit to a highway. Instead of doing anything to me, he was instead focused completely on my car. It was a 1996 Mercedes SI500 black Roadster, and his mouth was dropped open. I knew it was a sweet car that had the envy of many and didn't tell him what sort of torment paid for it. I recall he said something like, "Damn girl, you got it made! You must be married to a rich man, huh?" I couldn't bear to tell him the truth.

I will never forget his heavy-slang accent or his light-colored eyes. His braids were unique and his medium-dark, complexed skin was wonderfully different from the pale, listless-gray skin of the elderly businessmen I serviced. I didn't feel afraid or defensive with him. He was alert and intelligent, but simple in his emotions. There was no hatred in him or duplicity. He was just who he was, and unapologetic for any of it. I was in awe. I wanted that freedom. That might be what burned inside me in those moments. He was the living icon of the freedom that I hadn't tasted in what felt like years. He noticed my blatant, frank stare, and quickly looked away as if embarrassed.

"I bet your man is white, huh?" He smiled.

"Yeah," I answered. Another quiet pause fell between us.

"Yeah, well, I wanted to get you outta the hood before anything nasty happened. You want to come down there again, you find me or use my name, but be careful. Take the 215 from here and I'm sure you can find your way back, 'cuz it circles to wherever you're goin.'"

The way he gave directions, it sounded like he was waving me onwards. I had a sudden spike of dismay. I didn't want our time together to end so soon! I leaned my chin on the edge of the door's window and felt tears suddenly well up in my eyes. The emotion came on fast and far heavier than it should have, but the idea of him leaving then struck me deeply.

JC blinked in surprise and his voice held with real concern, and only made my tears come faster as he asked, "Hey, girl, what's wrong? I know I didn't touch you?"

I wiped at my tears and then tried to smile through them. I must have looked so foolish, but the vulnerable depths that lurked inside me had been touched by his sincerity. It was so strange. I saw white businessmen who were supposed to be so "normal" and "respectable," and all I saw were the faces of my abusers. Here, I saw JC, whose laid-back mannerisms and ghetto background made him shunned by so many people, and yet it was he who was trying to treat me right. I managed to say,

"Please don't leave me."

His eyebrows rose in surprise, "You want me to stick around?"

I didn't want to stop our time together so soon. "Want to go for a ride?" I asked.

His surprise only grew. "Yeah. Are you sure?"

I laughed, trying to banish the last of my tears. "Of course, otherwise, I wouldn't have asked."

Later that evening, we climbed a fire escape to the top of an old abandoned business building and found a quiet place to recline with each other. He sat holding his knees to his chest in a relaxed position and we stared into the valley as we watched the sun go down.

It was a moment of peace in a flurry of months where I had known very little. I shared with him that when I was little, I used to listen to the song, "Up on the Roof" by the Drifters, and it always made me feel safe.

"Man, you are into some old stuff."

"I'm sorry," I looked down and felt disappointed.

He gave a kid chuckle, "No, no that's not a bad thing, I think it's cool."

In that moment, I was carried away by his smile. I so admired the way he spoke, his accent and his constant smile. He also took notice of my stare. I believe I made him blush, but he continued to ramble on. It was a sense of peace I wanted.

From that point on, I felt like I was in another world. I didn't want this moment to end. I wanted to escape reality and he was my distraction. Of course, that is when my pager went off. It was a call for me to come home. It showed just my call number "22." Double Deuce.

"That's probably your man, checkin' on you?" JC guessed.

I wanted to throw that pager off the roof at that moment. It was more of a slave monitor or dog collar than anything you could stick around my neck. My heart sank in disappointment and pain. I knew any involvement with me would be dangerous, but when I looked at JC at that moment, I knew I couldn't say "goodbye" forever.

After that evening, I would sneak off whenever I could to see him. I would lie to my master, pretend I was with girls on a call, and head off to see JC. It was stupid because, of course, I was being followed. I figured the security guards wouldn't know the difference. I was routine to watch because I never did anything or tried to run. Besides, things went slow at first. JC and I just hung out. We respected each other enough not to cross any personal boundaries. It was a strangely wonderful, slow pace. Even when I initiated the first move, like holding his hand, it made my heart flutter in a way Marco's closest, most intimate touch couldn't manage.

I was so entranced by him. JC thought it was odd and intriguing at the same time about the way I looked at his life compared to the luxury car and clothes I was prancing around. There were moments he felt embarrassed that he hardly had much.

I also remember his one bedroom apartment well. Someone was always at his place. I wasn't sure if they were roommates, but he kept the bedroom. There would be two to four guys in the living room playing video games at all hours of the day. They would talk loud or even yell at each other over the game, but the yelling wasn't threatening. It was fun, brothers at rough play with each other. There was no coffee table, but there was an old couch, a big TV, game console, and a few remotes lying around. In the kitchen, he hardly had food but there were always a few 40's in the fridge, alongside an old fried chicken box and an opened box of baking soda.

His bedroom was just as simple. There was a full-size mattress on a box spring, some sheets, and a blanket for extra warmth. I would see ashtrays for the marijuana and some Newport cigarettes I'd smoke with him. He had a cardboard box set next to his bed, placed upside down with a little radio on it. Cassette tapes were scattered around on the floor. I was fascinated with cooking hot-dogs in the microwave and the simple life he was living. He didn't understand it, but I believe he was more fascinated with me. It was like watching a kid in a candy store as I soaked in this strange, real, "normal" life away from the high-class charade I had to live every day. It was almost to the point where I had been brainwashed of my pre-existing life before slavery that I forgot existed. Of course, I knew how to cook hotdogs, but it was so long that it felt simple and pleasant.

I felt addicted to JC and started to risk more and more to see him. We got closer and closer, and it wasn't long before we were in bed together. This wasn't my first time having sexual intimacy with a black man, especially during my time with Kelli, but those men were only looking for sex. Nothing about it was every intimate or sincere. JC was gentle with me. His smooth skin rubbed against mine. His lips kissed me all over. This was nothing in comparison to the white elite monsters who would savage me with their pasty-white, ashy skin and rub violently against mine. Making love to JC was a new tenderness I had never felt and I drew more into him. I didn't want this night to end. I was unaware, but it also wasn't long before I was pregnant with his child. It also wasn't long before Marco found out about the affair.

I was so crazy for him that I nearly stopped being careful enough. Eventually, the security guards around me picked up on cues they couldn't ignore and began to question the simple lies I invented. They saw through it all and brought Marco into the loop. After that, what followed was all my fault.

I hadn't been truly beaten by Marco in months. He was rough with me in bed sometimes but that was hardly the same thing. I could feel his desperate anger in the way he thrashed me that time. It was more than just my disobedience he was punishing. I had taken long measures to convince him that he was my true love. Any other man I was with was only for money in the course of my work, to help the business succeed. He could see that JC was different. So, he hit me with the anger of one being betrayed, and who had no other way to deal with that anger other than to strike at me physically. What topped it all was the mere fact that JC was black, and that angered Marco even further. He cursed at me using racial profanities of how dare I share my body with a black man and described JC as "a low disgusted animal." His racism didn't surprise me, but in my mind, JC was not the animal, Marco was.

"You are not to see him again or I will make him disappear without a trace! Do not think for a second that I will hesitate to destroy him!" His command and threat felt like a scythe of doom on my heart.

I screamed back through the pain, "Please don't, it's my fault! I kept chasing after him. Punish me, it's my fault!" I pleaded and cried. I could not imagine JC being hurt, even though he could take care of himself. The problem was that the more I spoke, the more I hinted that JC wasn't just a fling, but that I truly cared for him in a way Marco had never been able to bring out in me. That only made him strike me harder. He struck so violently that I lost the child I hadn't even known I was carrying. If I cried from his blows, I cried even harder that night when I saw the bleeding.

I cut ties with JC then and there, truly in fear of his life. I stopped answering his pages. I never called him back, and I hoped for his sake he would stop trying. There wasn't a moment I didn't think about him. My pager came with a voicemail and listening to JC's messages tore me apart. He was completely oblivious as to why I stopped communicating with him. He begged and pleaded to for an answer from me, but I couldn't risk it.

Despite the tragedy of losing him, it was also the first wedge in helping pry me loose from the life I was trapped inside. Some of the magic that "Jules" saw in the control and power she wielded as a Madame ceased to matter, and the "old me" found a little more room to surface. When I was sitting in my lavish hotel room with marbled floors reflecting back at me, I would see the cracks in the facade of that life around me. I would see the windows without windows so I couldn't get free. I would see the security guards everywhere when before I just ignored them. I began to cry, missing JC so much that my heart was torn. It was the type of pain that I hadn't felt in years, a pain of love that had been buried since James broke my heart. Business went on as usual, but I couldn't fake it like I had before.

One morning, I woke up feeling nauseated and extremely sore and fatigued. I had this overwhelming feeling that I might be pregnant. What had terrified me before about girls in the business who got pregnant suddenly hit home in a whole different way. Already, my drug and alcohol use had fallen off considerably with my utter disenchantment with that life. This became the splash of cold water that shocked me fully out of the illusion of safety "Jules" thought she had in that life. I couldn't allow my baby to go through that. It was the final key that turned inside me, and I knew I had to get out. I immediately made my plan to escape.

The problem was, even if I wanted to go, could I? After knowing what I knew about the underground operation, it wouldn't be easy to get out. They certainly would never let me leave. Marco tracked my every movement, especially after JC. Where could I go? How do you go back to a life knowing there is something else that will continuously linger in the back of your mind? What about the children and would anyone even believe me if I shared what I knew? It all felt like a landslide waiting to crush me, but the same thing kept coming up again and again. I had to find a way. My child was coming, and that would not wait. What could I do? How far was I willing to go?

I was riding around in my Mercedes and came across a teenaged, single mother who was begging for work in order to take care of her child. My reputation was well known on the streets, and when she saw me she got my attention.

"I'm 16, but I can definitely do the job." She pleaded.

The idea of dragging her into my life now sickened me more than it ever had, especially seeing the child she was carrying with her. She was so desperate. I wondered what I would do, and here was this girl willing to sell herself into what I had done unwillingly just to protect that child. "Are you in school now?"

"No, I dropped out and got my GED. Do I need that to be an escort?"

Her naivety reminded me of myself earlier. I let her into my car, and faced her in the front seat with serious eyes, "I do not tolerate bullshitters, do you understand me?"

"Yes, ma'am."

"Where is the father of your child?" I asked sternly.

"He left me." She stared down in embarrassment.

"What is it that you want to do? Really, what do you want to *do* with your life?"

"I want to go into nursing."

"So what is holding you back?"

"I don't have any money."

I handed her a box of Kleenex, then started up the car. With her in tow, we went into one of the finest casinos in Las Vegas, one where I was owed plenty of favors. We walked up to the front desk.

"Ms. Costatos, how can I be of service to you?" the gentleman grinned.

"You see this young lady here? I want you to give her the best service. If she needs anything I do not want to hear any complaint is that clear? I want a room comped for her for as long as she needs to stay here. Can you swing that for me without anyone asking too many questions?"

"Yes Ma'am." He nodded.

After he gave me the key to her room, I walked her up to the elevator and escorted her to her room. It was beautiful, with a glorious view of the strip. She laid the baby on the bed and she was so stunned. For the first time in years, something in me felt very serene at the sight of her.

I held onto her shoulders and said, "You can stay here as long as need be. This is all the cash I have on me, and I'll get the front desk to set you up with a job somewhere in the hotel. Probably as a maid. I will go and pay for your tuition for nursing, and then check back to see if you enrolled. If you stop going, I will have them throw you out. This is your chance, so...don't mess it up. It's a chance I never got." I may have been harsh, but I wanted to sound serious. I used the "Hard Bitch" weapon that my girls saw from me all the time. She might fear me, but at least she would respect my word and do what I suggested. That was the best that I could do for her.

I saw here standing there in astonishment, her tears kept flowing, but she was speechless. I was not a hugger, so I just left. I never saw her again. The chaos of my life would soon grow worse, and I never had time to check back. I recall pulling over at the side of the road and just cried for a while. I had saved her and her baby or at least given them a chance. Now, I still had no way to save my own. I wished someone could've saved me from my situation, but I had no guardian angel like that. They would never let me go. I was either going to die as one of them or die betraying them.

As each day passed, Marco became suspicious of my behavior. Quotas weren't the same anymore. I wasn't working the girls the way I was taught. He started to demand that I stay in my room until he could further deal with me on a more personal level. During that time, I was locked up in the suite with very limited access to go anywhere. Security was outside the door at all times. The only visitor I saw other than the recruiters or the security guards was a maintenance guy named Roger who came to check on the vents. When he pulled my dresser away from the wall, I saw for the first time that there was a huge vent in the wall, easily large enough for me to slip inside.

It was so foolish. Real escapes and real people didn't involve things like vents! That was for the movies! I loved those movies, but they were so unreal. Right then, it felt like a master plan, and I knew it just felt *right*. To go down there, and emerge out from the dark and into a new life. It was just so romantically perfect.

I did everything I could to create my escape as carefully as I could. First, I took out the cash I had managed to secretly stash away in my tampon box. It wasn't a lot, but it was enough to live on for a little while and help me get somewhere else. The maintenance guy was some blue-collar chump, the same age as those I had charmed a thousand times except without the money. I noticed he kept looking at me and smiling at me, and it was not hard to work my way into his good graces. This took some time, more than a few weeks actually. A few minutes with him, and he was chatting away about the vent tunnels and where they went and how to get out. He was a little shy and took longer than I wanted, but in the end, he even drew me a map. I promised I would never tell anyone or cost him his job. If everything went well, they would never figure out how I did it.

In the late Fall of 1996, I made my escape. I was so scared. Every time I heard noises or if it sounded like someone was saying my name "Jules," I would stop and just crouch real still. My heart continuously pounded in my chest with fear.

I remember whispering in my mind, "Please Lord, I am seriously begging you to protect me now. Wrap your wings around me and make me invisible just this once, please?" I prayed in silence, hoping Someone up there would answer my prayer. I was so afraid that at the end of the tunnel the men would be waiting for me. I didn't know Roger and he didn't know me. For all I knew, he could've blown the whistle and gave me away.

No one was waiting. I could see the fountain outside the hotel, and the parking lot full of cars. I took a final moment and whispered one last prayer, "OK, Lord. I need just one last thing. As I walk out, please don't let them stop me, please?" My prayer came out through clenched teeth, and then I walked across the pavement. I was in a night evening gown with stiletto heels and a duffle bag. Of course, I didn't look like someone that was traveling so I tried not to be so conspicuous, which wasn't an easy task to do.

As I came up to the entrance, I pretended to be one of the street hookers and waved down a man to get him to stop his car. He did, and I had him drive me to an alley nearby. Once we got to a secluded spot, I pulled out my shoe and bashed him over the head. I hit him so many times that I lost count of it all. All I could see was red, and all I wanted to do was escape. Once his head was unconscious over the wheel, I pushed him out and stole the vehicle. My heart was pounding so fast I thought my heart would explode. When I got out of town it was nearly dawn. I abandoned the vehicle at an empty church parking lot and went on my way from there.

I walked away from that life and didn't bother to look back. I had a new purpose and it was inside me.

CHAPTER 8

MY ANGEL

There was no hiding if we were what the traffickers considered defective. We wanted to hide. After all, there was no hope of medical care, nor hope of being treated with kindness, or retirement. We had seen them dispose of girls for simple disobedience. Sure, the traffickers would spring for the cost of curing you of the clap or some other non-lethal disease, but what could they do with AIDS? It was a death sentence, and they just carried it out that much quicker. As for pregnancies, well, I knew from watching what was done to girls with child. We wanted to hide it all, but not even that was an option for us.

They had us stand in line for a health examiner to test us for that sort of thing. AIDS, other STD's, and pregnancies. We stood there not saying a word, watching each girl go through the door in turn, then come back out a half hour later with even less dignity and suffering from a different sort of violation. They would file to the other side of the room and fill another line waiting to be sent back to their unit.

It was my turn. I opened the door and saw the examining table with stirrups. There was a short, heavy set gentleman with a bald spot and black-framed eyeglasses that made his eyes look larger than the rest of his facial features. He held up a syringe and grabbed me by the arm. I had been through this before, so I was not surprised by the callous procedure and lack of any bedside manner. These men were being paid to do this under the table, and I wouldn't have given any hope that their medical degrees counted for much in any real hospital. I remember the burning pain in my upper right arm and feeling very nauseated and weak in a matter of minutes as blood was drained from me for testing. I remember lying on the bed and looking straight up, seeing the light bulb that was cupped with a silver-rusted light shade. The more I continued to stare into the light, the more the light became very dim, and I began to gasp, wondering if they were draining too much from me that time, drawing my life's blood away...

*   *   *

I awoke gasping for air. Damn! The flashbacks were still with me. I was free. I was out of Las Vegas having walked until my feet bled, and yet I still wasn't free of it. Disoriented, I peered around, trying to remember where I was and why I was there.

I found myself in the backseat of a car that was parked in a middle of nowhere. It was an old, golden Pontiac Grand Prix from the late 70's or early 80's. Not a nice car, and without any modern protection devices. I couldn't remember whose car it was or why I had decided to crash in its backseat, but now the car offered an opportunity. I leaned over between the front seats to see if there was a key in the ignition. No. I opened the glove compartment and found nothing but the instruction book and some store receipts. Nothing.

I was covered in sweat as the heat beamed through the windows. The bright sun was going to turn the car into an oven, soon. I had to either get out and start moving or cross over the line again into illegality. I wasn't so far from Las Vegas yet that I was past all fear of being found, so survival was still primary in my mind. Without too much of a moral dilemma, having no wish to trust in any stranger to give me a ride, I took a final sweep to ensure no one was in eyesight. I slid forward to the driver's side and stuck my head under the wheel. My father was a mechanic at home, and one of the few things I had learned from him of real value was how to hot-wire my car if I ever lost my keys. He saw it as a tool for a bad day, not as a carjacking skill. Fortunately, it worked well in both situations. I worked the wire ends together, and soon heard the engine start. I put the car in gear and began driving.

It took me an hour to get clear of the back roads I was on. Once on the main highway, I headed for the sunset. Throughout the drive, I kept trying to remember how I went from a black sedan to this car? It was haunting me. I wasn't good with geography and had little idea of where I wanted to go. Away. That was all. So, I headed for the sun and tried to chase it towards its bed.

What followed in my life was a series of chasing moments. All of it was a blur, and none of it grabbed at me or stuck with me beyond a couple of days. The car I was driving died, and wouldn't start again. So, I began to walk. Then, I hitchhiked. A few times, I jumped on the back of a pick-up truck without the driver noticing when they stopped for gas and made a little distance that way.

I only had limited funds from what I had ferreted away from the hotel, and I knew it would only last so long. I bounced from house to house, living with men I barely knew in order to make ends meet. As much as I had broken free of Marco, my addictions continued to roar their ugly heads. I would use drugs and partied, and lived my days as if there were no tomorrow. I was drunk on being away from my captivity and somehow, strangely, bizarrely alive.

That could only last so long. My pregnancy moved along, and I knew I was going to start to show soon. I had recently ended a short-term relationship with a boy named "Liam." I manipulated him into thinking he was the father so that when the first bump showed around my belly he was forced to deal with it. I really didn't care if he would step up and support me. What I needed was a signature. I was already thinking I would give the baby up for adoption. In my mind, anything else was unthinkable. I was a mess. This was Marco's baby, and how could I deal with that and be free? What was more, I was living on shoestrings with a serious drug addiction clogging my life. I had no future and could not see how I could help this baby to survive. So, I needed Liam for a signature, to agree to the baby being placed for adoption. There was no way I was going to Marco to ask for his agreement!

Liam agreed to give up the child easily enough. He was nice but nowhere near ready to take on a family. We were not going to last, and he was happy to sign away responsibility. Now, I needed to find a place that could care for both me and my unborn child. I ran through the advertisement and found a place called the "Maternity Home for Women."

They had a 1-800 number, and I made the call. A caseworker took my information and instructed me to head for the "Church of Christ" facility in Las Vegas. They would pay my way to Texas where I would be kept until the child was born. I had some trepidation about even passing through Las Vegas, but I convinced myself I wouldn't be walking through the same circles where I used to frequent.

I found the location and started to feel a little more at ease. With each step, that feeling grew more powerful. I had lived so long in a place where anyone around you would sell you out for a dollar. Now, helpful smiles greeted me at every turn. The church in Las Vegas purchased my bus ticket to Texas and then brought me to the station. I had never ridden on a bus before and felt uncomfortable with all the terms and procedures. Instead of mocking me, the front desk clerk was very nice and encouraged me to board towards the front so that the driver could inform me of the whereabouts, break times, and boarding times. The driver did exactly that and even tried to chat with me along the way. Kind faces met me everywhere, and it made the whole trip seem a little surreal.

On arrival, I was greeted by one of the social workers of the adoption agency. She took me to the maternity home and showed me to my room. She introduced me to other pregnant moms that were there and encouraged me to ask questions as they came to me. I did, and she informed me about the procedures that would follow. I was even given an ongoing advocate that would walk me through the process. I know especially now in hindsight that it was not completely for my benefit. It made sense that they would have that sort of help to ensure no legal issues arose that would confuse or stop the process. At that moment, it felt like they were ushering me through with the gentlest of hands, and I remember feeling entirely grateful in a way I had never been before.

I remained in Texas for the remainder of my pregnancy. The further along I was, my attachment to the child grew. A part of me was scared and sad with the thought that I would carry this child to full term and not be able to take her home with me. I was eased through withdrawal from my addictions, and life began to feel a little more wholesome. True, I still had no job and no prospects, with a terrible background waiting to swallow me up. My flashbacks still came and dragged me back into the darkness. I would wake up screaming at night or even in the broad daylight, but that was no longer my whole life. My mind was clearer by the day, and with that came the wonder about my future, and the sneaking suspicion that I might be able to care for the baby. Maybe, even, that I would want to do it.

But in the end, I stuck to my plan. Part of that was because I could pick the parents. Candidates were given to me, and I selected who I wanted to get my child. I met them, and we started to become friends. That helped immensely. I never told them the full truth. No one at the maternity center knew about my past in Vegas, nor did anyone ask. I made up a past that involved domestic violence so that they would know how important it was for me to see the child sent somewhere safe. So, I chose a couple—Greg and Trisha. A fine couple with kind smiles. They were the ones. I felt it right from the start.

Very little caused me concern in that time. I was well taken care of and knew where I would live safely for nearly a year of my life. It had been a while since I had had that sort of stability. I was even allowed to stay at the maternity home for about six weeks after the delivery. I grew to have friends in the area and enjoyed passing the days. My greatest worry came from health concerns for the baby. One blood test unveiled a chance that the child was at a high risk for Down syndrome, so I was sent for an amniocentesis to diagnose the issue. The test returned as negative, but also with the news that I would be having a girl. I cried at that news, knowing how much it would be wonderful to be able to have a baby girl all my own.

I decided to name her then and there. I couldn't guarantee her safety and I knew I couldn't keep her alive with me, but I was going to give her to her new parents with a beautiful name. I opened the book filled with potential names and began my search. After careful consideration of the name I wanted, a name that would ring with true meaning for me. I called her Angela, "Angel" for short. My Angel. I remember wanting her to know that I wasn't letting her go because I didn't want her or because I wanted to continue in youthful fun and not be tied down. I was desperate for her to know that I was placing her because I loved her so much that I had to put aside my personal feelings, a sacrifice that only a mother could do for her child.

I alerted the adoptive parents of the test results and together we went through the adoption process. Even though I was aware that my relationship with the parents would be short lived, they gave me hope. Seeing their home and seeing how my child would live gave me a happiness for which I could never truly thank them enough. I was always welcome in their home, and Trisha and I had serious conversations about what we both wanted for our daughter. I wanted a mother that would fight for my daughter as if it was hers and she agreed. I recall feeling a shadow of regret that I had never been placed. It was not quite jealousy, but a vague wish that I had never been under the harsh fist of my mother, but instead had known the kind smile of a new mother like Trisha, who was grateful to receive her because she truly wanted another child. She would never abuse My Angel because to her, the child would be a gift and not a burden.

It was the summer of 1997 when I was scheduled to be induced for labor due to toxemia. I had high blood pressure and the doctor couldn't afford to let me deliver on the due date. I became so eager for this moment to happen, but at the same time, I was afraid of the emotional and physical pain that would follow. Trisha was there the entire time, and we shared the joy and fears of the moment. I went through nearly 10 hours of labor and then found out I had to have a caesarian delivery. Frustrated, fatigued, and in pain, I only remember passing out eventually as they put me under anesthesia.

My daughter was born at 7:53 p.m. She was so beautiful when they brought her to me. I didn't want to let her go. I wanted to spend some time with her since these few moments were my last. I laid her in my hands and cupped her tiny body and let her face me. She made small moans and yawned at me. I felt her soft skin and kissed her on her tiny forehead.

Tears fell from my eyes, and I said softly to her, "My dear Angel." The words were hard to speak, but I had to speak them around the lump in my throat. I had to say what was in my heart to make it real. "I'm going to miss you so much. I know you just came into this world, but there's so much I want you to know. I wish I could sit here right now and tell you everything about me, but we both know that could take forever."

I began to admire her beauty. I saw parts of her that came from me shining out in her face, and that was the best thing of all. Then I moved her to my left arm and her head was close to my left bosom. I allowed her to grasp onto my finger in her tiny hands. My heart felt thick in my chest, and I wanted this moment to last forever, so much did I cherish it. "You are my Angel. I gave you that name for a reason and I don't ever want you to forget that. Because of you, I am now free and so are you." I began to caress her face with my finger and wiped the tears from my eyes. She peeped up at me with one eye open, then closed them and slid off into sleep.

I smiled a happy smile and gave a soft laugh. She was charming and cute. "You go ahead and sleep. I'll just keep talking, okay? I know none of this is ever going to make sense to you right now, but I hope someday you will come find me so that I can explain everything."

I took a long breath, sorted out my thoughts, and then let my heart spill forth with all I wanted to say, "I don't ever want you to think I gave you up because I didn't want you. I only wanted to keep you safe. This is the only way I know how. If I'm wrong then I'm sorry, but this is all I can come up with. I made sure you would have good parents; they had to be better than mine. You will have your own room, two parents that love you very much, and even a big sister which I never had."

I smiled then, thinking of a gift I wanted her to have, "Do you know what Mommy's favorite song is? It's "Somewhere Out There." If you ever hear it, I want you to know that it's me singing it to you, okay? Mommy won't be here in Texas for long. I must be on my way once I get better. That doesn't matter. No matter where I go or where I end up, I'll always think of you in my heart. I pray that you never have to go through what I went through. I pray that you'll get to wear pretty dresses and have bright pink ribbons in your hair. I pray that you will achieve all your dreams and that you'll be happy with the family I placed you with. I want you to be happy and have a childhood. I want your parents to spoil you like crazy because you deserve it. Greg and Trisha are their names, but you'll call them Mom and Dad. They're going to see you for the first time tomorrow, and I know they will love you immediately."

I took a long breath, knowing the next part was hard. "For the rest of the week, Mommy has to heal, but then I am going to go my own way. You'll stay with them. I want you to remember something, ok? If you ever want to find me, just look out your window at night and look for the brightest star. There I will always be, right above you wherever you are. Promise me you'll do that, okay? I promise I'll do that for you. Every time when I see a star in the sky, I will know that you will be waiting for me, and I'll be there for you with both arms wide open."

I softly pressed my lips to her forehead and held her in my arms closely. It was our last time alone. That evening, I held her and cried, "I love you, Angel." I whispered to her as I held her in my arms in the lonely hospital room, on and on, until I could speak no more.

ANGEL

From the moment,
I knew it was true.
My tears over flowed
With happiness for you.
I couldn't wait to share the news,
That this very day,
I would soon have you.
As time went on,
I fought my best,
To have you near,
But the only option left,
Was to give you away.
It broke my heart,
A difficult decision.
But I could not bear,
For you to carry my tears.
For so long,
I kept a promise deep in my heart,
That I'd find some way,
To break the cycle.
I couldn't have you
In the situation I was in.
So, I asked God
If he could take you in.
Nine months later,
And here you are.
Right in front of me.
In Mommy's arms.
I had to hold my tears back,
Knowing the decision
Was already made.
But loving you,

Would never end.
Someday I hope,
As you read this in your hand,
That Mommy always loved you,
And prayed that you'd
Never forget.
My precious, Angel.
So innocent and sweet.
Never knowing
Where life may lead you,
Never to stop wondering,
What you are doing right now.
Someday, I pray
That you will find
The courage to seek me out.
How I would love to see the very eyes,
That looked into mine
That night in July.

CHAPTER 9

FUGITIVE

After a week in the hospital, I returned to the maternity home. The week had not been enough, and I was still in emotional disarray. The pictures of me around the room with friends, pregnant and happy, didn't help much. I sat on my bed and cried for hours. I tore the pictures apart one by one. A huge part of me wanted my baby back.

"Why?" I cried out to God, silently and even aloud once or twice. "Why me?" I sank onto the floor with the remnants of the pictures in my clenched fists and all around me on the ground. I pounded at my chest, trying to keep the hurt in my heart going and even make it worse. A twisted part of me didn't want the pain to stop, because if it stopped then she would really be gone. It had taken all my strength just to wait until I was clear of the hospital to lose my reserve. I couldn't let Trisha see my pain or she would have reconsidered. She was a true friend, and I had given her the gift of going away thinking she had done me a great favor without any pain. Now, I released all my frustration. I threw a violent rage in my room, tossing everything off my dresser and tearing everything in sight.

One of the house managers came in and she held me so tight. She was used to seeing such displays and knew how to try and help. "It's ok," she tried to calm me.

"I want my baby! I want her back!"

"I know. I know and you can scream all you want. Let it out." She began to rock me back and forth. It took time, but my cries calmed. She continued to hold me in her arms and caressed my face as if I was the small child. It felt very comforting and soothing.

Some measure of reason returned to me, and I realized other girls were running over to my room to see what the matter was. When it had started, I hadn't cared, but now felt a little embarrassed. I wiped at my face, trying to regain my composure a little. I stayed huddled in the housemother's arms, not yet ready to move away.

"Do you want to talk about it?" the house-mother asked.

"No. I just don't know what to do. I know I did the right thing, but it hurts so much to lose her."

"You are grieving and it's normal. You're going to feel like this for quite some time, and you are not alone. Everyone feels this way after giving a child up for adoption. It is not natural to lose a child, and that means you are normal like any other mother." She was trying to reassure me and help me feel like I was not a lost soul for what I had done. I owe her a lot for that. She was more than kind, and her voice was exactly what I needed. "You are right, though. You did the right thing. You thought about it and did it, and because of that you made another couple very happy, and your baby will have a wonderful life." It was no judgment against me. She made no comment like "which you couldn't provide," even though she knew most mothers there couldn't. She played the caring diplomat well, which I needed. She might have been trained, but at that moment I thought she was being completely genuine.

The housemother's name was Louise, and she continued to prove her genuine nature over and over again. At one point, I confided in her that my identification had all been destroyed. Not being able to prove who I was continued to be a thorn in my side and a pang to my heart. I had started off with pride in being an American and felt like having that called into question again and again especially when trying to get help deflated me. Hearing that part of my story, Louise decided to take me down to the Department of Motor Vehicles (DMV) and help me regain at least one piece of it.

We walked up to the counter at the DMV and I explained the situation. He asked if I knew my Social Security Number (SSN), and I provided it. He typed it in, and then grew a little more circumspect. His deference and customer service went away, and I was starting to get afraid I would be tossed out again because I couldn't prove who I was, even though I had known my SSN off by heart and my picture had to be right there on his screen! Had I changed so much? Maybe he couldn't recognize me. He kept stalling.

Then, I found out why. I was trying to casually talk to Louise and not take the delay too seriously when several officers came up and took me under arrest! They handcuffed me and started to take me off to be detained. Louise objected, demanding to know the reason. When they replied that it was for "hot checks" and prostitution, my heart sank. These were not racist or trumped-up charges. They were real, and I was in real trouble. I had written bad checks on an old bank account I once had. When I wrote those checks, I was surprised cashiers even accepted them. In my moment of desperation, what I had done in my past could have been noted as avoiding prostitution at some point.

Whatever the details, I knew there was truth in the charges, and I thought immediately on how it would damage how Louise saw me. I thought for sure this friend and all of those friends at the Maternity House would vanish and never want to hear from me again. They had my baby, didn't they? I was a reminder of that, a lingering person they would kick out of the house soon, anyway. I was sure this would be an easier way to see me gone that much earlier.

Louise didn't leave. I was shocked and crushingly relieved all at once. She fought to stay near me and not let me get dragged off to be alone. She was allowed to chat with me before I was taken to a holding cell. She comforted me and reminded me of God. It's funny because usually I didn't care to hear about the Gospel, scriptures, or about God, but this time I felt I was in His mercy. Louise was very gentle and I saw the sad look in her eyes. If she dug further in, she might find out. I had no idea what to say, so I went mute as they dragged me off to be booked, fingerprinted, and photographed. I left her there to do as she wanted, and left it to fate. Fate had never been on my side and I was sure that she would abandon me.

I honestly don't remember how long I was in the holding cell. It was probably three hours or less, but it felt longer.

A bailiff called my name sternly, "Song Ja Bak?"

I got up with a start from my seat. "Yes?" I was shocked to hear my name so soon. There were two other women in the cell and one was enormously huge. She had looked at me and said I was yummy. Added to the rest of the fear and uncertainty, my stomach was turning circles. I was thrilled to get the hell out of there, even if it was to get tossed in a courtroom and sentenced to deeper in the prison system.

Instead, the bailiff said, "You're free to go."

He started to rummage for his keys to open the cell, and I blinked in surprise. I thought for sure I was dreaming. "I can go? Are you sure?" I hadn't made my one free phone call, my parents had no idea I have been arrested even if they would have cared, and I had never shared to Louise and the House regarding my past. How could I be released?

The bailiff made a crack about there not being much doubt between me and the others in the room and then walked me out to the foyer. When I came out into the open, I saw Louise still waiting for me. She was an older woman in her late 60's, and waiting in that uncomfortable atmosphere with only plastic seats must have been hard on her. She met my eyes with concern, making sure that I was alright and paying no mind to her own discomfort.

Still, in shock, I blurted out, "Did you bail me out?"

She smiled back reassuringly, "I tried, but your bail was too high. I called the Director of the maternity home and she bailed you out."

Now I thought I was beginning to understand. My heart sank. Of course, I had been a slave for too long, and then a Madame who used all sorts of pressure to keep my girls in line. Sure, normally I used drugs or fear, but money worked as well. Now, I owed her. Even worse, I owed her in the legal system, so everyone *knew* I owed her, and she could prove it. I didn't make the assumption because of the director being particularly mean or strict. She had always seemed like a nice sort. But, given my past experience and tendency to judge people incorrectly at first meeting, I was sure I had made the same error all over again.

I tried to put on a brave face. Louise was still looking at me as one of her own kids in that caring way of hers. She asked me, "Are you okay? Did they feed you at all?"

I was taken aback by her genuine concern for me and hadn't seen that if ever. I got a little teary-eyed, not used to anyone caring for me at all. Whatever tomorrow would bring, I could just be happy now that someone cared for me. "I'm alright, I guess."

Louise smiled, seeing that I was trying to look strong when I wasn't at all. She got a sly look, and said, "Tell you what, you need to take your mind off all this. How about we go do something bad?"

Just being liberated from jail, her choice of words momentarily confused me. Then, I recalled what background she was from. The maternity home was a Christian establishment, and they had some fairly strict rules. "R" rated movies were pretty much forbidden, and our diet had been somewhat controlled.

So, it made sense when Louise lowered her voice with joyful conspiracy and said, "Let's go get some sugar ice cream and watch a Mel Gibson movie, alright?"

I nearly laughed out loud at the ridiculous definition of "bad," and yet the wonderful innocence of it also felt refreshing and light. Oh, if only that was what "bad" meant to me as well! I loved Louise even more at that moment. I recalled that Mel Gibson was her celebrity idol, and she rarely got a chance to see him as many of his movies tended to be rated higher. In a way, this was her way of joining me on the "wrong side of the law," and sympathizing with me even as she comforted me. She felt like a real mom, and I nearly wept at my love for her.

We enjoyed our night, and I even got a little sleep. The next day, I was to meet the director. I managed to hold off my fear until it was almost time to meet, and then I started to shake a little. This had been a wonderful home, and I was sure it was about to be tainted by being strong-armed into some sort of payback of the bond money. I was afraid that whatever punishment I was about to receive would cost me more than I could survive. I was consumed by my own personal version of Post-Traumatic Stress Disorder (PTSD) that I reacted as poorly as a little girl. I ran in sobbing, "I'm so sorry! It's all my fault and I don't know how to explain what had happened!"

Instead, the director consoled me in her embrace. The director went on, "It is NOT your fault!"

My thoughts went wheeling through my mind erratically, *"It's not? Does she have any idea what I just went through? Does she know about me being a madame? Or exploiting other girls? Or about the fraud, the theft and everything else?"*

Aloud, I could only ask nervously, "It's not?"

A calm sternness now entered the director's voice, as if commanding me to see her way of thinking at this, "No! Everyone who comes to us has a past. But, you are a different person now. You've sacrificed a lot, and done a great good. Whatever happened in the past is in the past. It is Satan and his kind that want to hold your blunders and mistakes over your head." She was not cruel as she spoke, but merely direct and devout.

This was *not* the type of Christianity I understood or was acquainted with. In my mother's version of Catholicism, it was all about repentance and being severely persecuted for your mistakes. Who are these people? What type of Christians are they? Is this even real? This was so foreign to me, but I instantly wanted to embrace it. I loved it. I hate to think my practical mind wanted this, too, but the "survivor" in me (that was Jules) jumped all over the idea, *"Take it! They'll help get you clear of the court system!"*

They did exactly that. The court proceedings were terrible, and I was told I would have to pay a large amount of money in restitution. I didn't object and plead guilty, not wanting the rest of the details of my life to come into the light. Instead, I just accepted that debt was about to become my burden. During the arraignment, I was instructed to have a court appointed attorney since I had no income to afford one. Louise was there every step of the way.

Now, I had to figure out what to do. At first, I could only think of small things. I took up a babysitting job that hardly constitutes employment. It was just an additional cash flow to help me obtain toiletries, personal items, and such. That job wouldn't put a dent in my debt.

I received a phone call from my caseworker that the church had gathered the funds needed to set me free of the burden altogether. I wanted to fall on my knees in thanks. I didn't even have to report back to court, and I was free to go.

I went in to see the director, and asked how I could thank her; I wanted to let her know I was going to pay her back.

Once again, she shocked me. "In true friendship, bargaining is not a factor. With Christ, how could it be so? You don't have to pay us back, and nor would we want you to. I want you to utilize this experience and when the time is right, share it with the world." She smiled, "You have a powerful story that could change the world."

At that moment, I thought it completely unfair to her. There was no way I could ever be viewed as an advocate or any sort. I knew my own weakness and I wasn't ready for a positive change. I still wanted to party and was not giving up narcotics as well. I admit this gives me cause to smile even today, especially as I write this book.

The kindness of the home didn't stop there. Returning to the maternity home, the director was aware of my stay and knew it would soon be over. Her concern of my well-being took refuge in her heart. The maternity home itself was forbidden to house or favor one client over the other, so the director asked her church to assist me. That is when I met Nash, the minister, and a recovering addict. We would meet once a week just to have a conversation in his office. Through his support, I was given an apartment and the congregation paid my rent for the first three months. With that solid foundation of support, it didn't take long before I landed a job at a call center through the help of the church's contacts.

Soon after, I met three college guys who were Christians. One of them was Caleb who I met through a Bible study class. I noticed he was very attractive at first glance. He smiled at me and offered to give me a ride. I was not shy about my former employment in the sex industry, which shocked this gentleman. My first assumption was that he would discard me like the other men I have met through my journey of survival. When he mentioned church, I assumed I was going to be "*Bible thumped.*" When I returned the next time, I met his roommate, Brennan. They both offered their friendship to me. Soon after, there were other students from the college that welcomed me with open arms. They were aware of my past experiences and didn't flinch or judge me, instead, they embraced me with love and didn't force religion or their Christian values on me. They used grace to love me unconditionally and the guys wanted to show me love that didn't involve sex at all. This was very unfamiliar to me.

Then, "Jules" broke out again and slapped me in the face, *"What the hell is wrong with you? Are you seriously crazy? You can't live a normal life! Have you forgotten where you came from? Do you seriously believe they actually care about you? Once they find out who you really are, they will toss you aside - just like all your other friends. Remember they are not like you and me. We are the outcast. They are trying to change you, be part of them."*

Not only was Jules getting the best of me, but I was still grieving the loss of my baby. I didn't have anyone to talk to or confide in, and I felt very much isolated and misunderstood. The majority of the people that I was friends with were familiar with the maternity home and congratulated my strength in my choice to place my daughter up for adoption, but I wanted to grieve, cry, feel anger, and resentment. I wanted everyone to stop telling me everything was going to be okay. I didn't want comfort, I wanted to be heard and that was the one thing that was missing out of this *"happy"* life. Deep down I was falling in and out of depression and made multiple attempts of suicide.

I couldn't take that chance. I had to be away from there and start burying myself in a new life unconnected to anything from that hidden one. That included the place where My Angel was born.

So, no more than several months after the birth of my daughter, I was on the road again. There was never a moment I didn't think of my daughter, and I was still missing her terribly. I would find moments alone in a random church or secluded chapel to send forth a few prayers and cry over my loss, and that became my way of releasing the grief that lingered in my heart.

I never felt safe in those days. I was still in Texas, moving around as I could. I couldn't forget my time in Vegas, and my mind was no longer drawn into the simple pleasures of creating a child and living in the safety of a home. I was not naive to how much power Marco wielded. I had witnessed first-hand how far his vengeance could reach when he wanted to, and I could only imagine how much he wanted to hurt me. If he found out I had given his child away to adoption, he wouldn't rest until I was dead. Those were the thoughts that consumed me, so I began to feel and act like a fugitive.

Everywhere I went, I watched my tongue and let no one in close to me. Every person I came in contact with, I gave them a pseudonym and never used my own. I made sure they were never close or the same, ranging from Stacy to Rachel or Kimberly, Amy, May-Hi, or Julie. Trust was a foreign concept to me. I remembered Kat now, and the way she had seemed like a friend. That had been another illusion to fall shattered around me some time ago.

I knew Kat had sold me into slavery, but it had not been until I was fully in Marco's clutches as his concubine that I had uncovered the full truth of it all. When going through his papers, a recruiter was mentioned who I was sure at the time was Keith. Marco used code names and tried to cloak their identities, but I had figured out who he was talking about. He also had Kat listed under his contacts. That wasn't a surprise, considering she had sold me to Marco's team of traffickers. What I hadn't known was how wide that net spread. Keith had been a recruiter for that same team. When he lost track of me after I ran away. He had chalked it up as a loss. I don't know what punishment he had received, but word had spread of my description. Kat had always seemed like she partly recognized me that day on the street when she first saw me. My description had fit her information, and she had picked me up in the net that was trolling to get me back. Kat had been a Madam in her own right and had fought for her right to try and "train" me. Only once I had proven untrainable had she sold me wholesale into Marco's clutches.

The state of Texas, as a whole, was risky given that's where my Angel was. I started to drift into places I had never been before. County to county, state to state, I moved through the Carolinas, Florida, up north into New Hampshire and then back down to Kansas and Colorado. I found reasons to pass through Arizona and California as well. I used every trick I could think of to avoid being found and stayed completely off the grid.

During my first time being on my own, while bouncing back I realized I had to find ways to make some money in order to survive. Even after my stay at the maternity home, I was still back at square one. With no ID or papers to prove my legitimacy, I began to sell myself. I had to start in Texas before I could head out to other states. I would begin by going to a random church asking for cash and disguising myself as a pregnant teen. I was surprised how many of them believed my lie. *"This is not the time to feel remorse if they don't give you the cash you won't find food,"* Jules whispers that reminder. In order to bury my remorse, I ended up getting high to justify my fraud.

Once, I was able to grab some cash and I bought myself a cheap motel for the night and ran in-calls through my room to make more money. Once I made over $1000 in a day. I took the cash, got myself a bus ticket out of Texas and headed back West. By the time I was in Los

Angeles, CA, I was entranced by the Hollywood idolizations from the media. No matter how glamorous it appeared there were rough moments in make money. Some of the customers were brutal also.

One evening, I was in a fancy hotel and there were multiple guys who had a shared hotel suite. Myself and three other ladies were also in the room. As long as they paid me I didn't care who else was in the room. After the session ended, while I was walking to the elevator, I saw two of the girls from the room surrounding around a young black girl.

"My daddy, he takes good care of me. He'll take of you too." One of the girls was bragging.

"I... I don't know." Said the black girl.

The other jumped in, "He doesn't beat on us, he spoils us and he's the nice Pimp."

From where I was standing I could tell the girl felt pressure. I walked between the two and sat next to her.

"Why tha hell you gonna' need a man to sell your pussy?" I flashed my hundreds at her. I saw her pupils widen. "You see all this? It is 100% mine. No more splits and no more him taking care of me. I don't need a man to take care of me." I wanted her to know she didn't *need* anyone to sell her body. I noticed a bruise on her arm. She remained sitting there confused. The other two girls eventually walked away.

"Do you have a ride home?" I asked.

She just nodded.

"Is it your pimp?"

She nodded again.

"I know you don't know me, but I have been beat by a man and you don't need that type of bullshit in your life." I dug out a business card with my pager number and the name "*Kim*" was printed on there, I handed her my card.

"You don't have to decide today, but when you get in a tough spot and you need a place to stay or get out, you can page me, 'kay?" I asked. She was very quiet and hardly said a word. She nodded and accepted my card. My cab pulled up and I had to leave. I didn't think I would ever hear from her again. About a few weeks, she called me from a pay phone in tears. I called a cab and had her picked up. When we got back to the motel where I was staying, we introduced ourselves.

"I'm Kim," I stated as I laid my belongings on the foot of the bed. If you don't mind sharing the room, that bed is yours." I pointed to the other bed.

"I'm Eboni," she smiled. All she had was a backpack and a tiny latch purse. She sat at the table with the chairs.

"Well Eboni, I don't know about you, but I am starving, are you hungry?" I asked, going through the yellow pages. I watched her dig through her bag.

"Whatcha doin? Did you bring groceries with you?" I asked.

She smiled and was looking for her wallet. When she found it, I watched her pull out crumpled bills.

"Girl, put that away, it's on me." I smiled.

From that point on a beautiful kinship formed. Little did I know at that moment, she was my former foster sister in Chanteloup County in Oklahoma.

"Wait, you were in foster care in Oklahoma?" I asked.

"Yeah, I had an Asian sister and a baby foster brother. My foster parents abused all of us since we weren't related to them." She explained. The more she continued, she described elements of my time in foster care. I kept thinking... "No! Could it be?"

"Shamecka?" I asked. When she looked up at me from going through the yellow pages, we looked at each other and immediately cried. The reunion felt like a storybook that only happens in movies. We were so happy to be reunited that we talked as if there was no tomorrow.

We made a promise to have each other's back. We always had respect for each other; between two best friends, that you don't find as common today. We didn't allow anyone—guy or girl—to come between our friendship. It was an unspoken rule of respect. We never dated the same guy we had an interest in. We never pursued any exes.

Now that we were entering a new world of depravity, we had to stay close. Trust was all we had. We started traveling together, and there were moments I would witness how others would treat her differently. I never understood the racism or why she was denied assistance from random churches, but when I would step up to a door there was no hesitation. This angered me, so I decided to swindle church members to give me money by exaggerating my disability. When they bought it, I felt justified in deceiving them. Yet, no matter how I felt, Eboni didn't always agree with my tactics. She was used to this type of prejudice and became tolerant. I was the boisterous one who didn't see remorse in swindling the ignorant.

There were moments where Eboni and I would get lonely and find a guy to be with. This went on in phases and explains why Eboni didn't travel with me full-time. No matter how long it had been when we parted, we always found a way to reunite as if we never parted before.

This was not an easy life, as you can imagine. When Eboni was not traveling with me, I spent the night in the homes of kind strangers, hoping they would not prove to be animals. I slept in bus stations and various churches whenever the watchful keepers of either didn't kick me out. In very few desperate attempts, I even called collect to Caleb and Brennan, begging for financial assistance. I knew how to use them as they were unfamiliar with my manipulation. They weren't equipped to build healthy boundaries around me, so whatever I asked for they gave in. I didn't think twice that that supply would soon run short. I would receive funds via Western Union and once I received it, it would be weeks before they would hear from me again.

I was selfish and didn't care about anyone or anything except survival. And as far as I knew, anyone who was generous without sex or bargaining with me for something, became very suspicious to me. Nonetheless, Brennen and Caleb never saw me as a threat or a burden. They did their best to continue showing me God's grace.

After I received the funds, I would continue along my way in the world of survival. I even admitted myself to a psych ward on a few occasions just to have three meals and a cot to sleep on for a night until they kicked me out as being without need for mental recovery. Ironic, how they were considered experts yet could not figure out my ploy for survival. The facility brought back PTSD of me being the "good girl." Authorities and structured facilities only frightened me, which resulted in me acquiring the status of a *"well behaved"* patient, which was the purpose for my release. That was odd, considering the suffering I was going through. At the time, I hardly argued. I dared not stay too long in one place, anyway.

Finally, the life began to wear at me, and I wanted to find connection to my past. Time was starting to dull my fear, and I had this feeling like I had finally dusted off any pursuit. The emotional trauma was still with me. I started to yearn for a path to resolve that, and for that, I needed people who would care for me. I needed someone to do what Louise had done after I gave away my baby. I needed someone to cradle me and tell me I was still human despite all that had been done to me.

At one point, I was passing through Durham, NC. I decided it was time to settle down for a few weeks. The city had grown stale and part of me felt it was time to move on. My fatigue was growing, and I stayed at each location for as long as I could manage. It was also at that time that I took things up a notch.

During the mid to late 90's, the phone chat line became a trend. Girls got to talk for free while guys had to purchase minutes just to talk to the ladies. I utilized the chat lines to find potential customers with a specific greeting or a certain "word" that would give the customers a clue that I was looking for compensated companionship.

The lack of a companion, eventually, led me to meet a guy through the chat line. I made him believe I wanted a relationship, having used several such hotlines to find shelter with lonely guys. When I corresponded with Todd, we had great conversations and we mutually felt a bond, even though we hadn't met in person. He was so eager to meet me and wanted me to visit him, so he paid for my bus ticket to North Carolina.

When I arrived in North Carolina, Todd was there to pick me up at the bus station. He was tall with red hair, stocky and built like a football player. He made me feel safe, like I had my own bodyguard. The sexual rendezvous began as we headed to his place. We were starting to get hot and events were leading rapidly towards a trigger. He mentioned to me with a bit of delight that he was looking forward to this, partly due to my ethnicity. "I have never had sex with an Oriental girl."

That reminded me too much of all the times I had played the "China Doll" for my customers, and many of the warm feelings I had for him vanished. I still needed shelter, so "Jules" took over and I let her. He worked evening shifts as a prison guard, so I was able to spend a lot of time simply sleeping alone. It was the best of both worlds for the moment.

I woke up the next morning to the sound of animated explosions and Japanese dialogue. I thought I was dreaming until I walked into the next room and saw Todd sitting in his recliner watching anime cartoons. I was never fond of anime. It reminded me of my first rape, and there was something sadistic and pornographic about the plot lines and their characters. So, I went into the kitchen to find something to eat. He stayed where he was, not coming to ask for me. Another part of my fondness for him passed. Sure, I didn't expect all his attention, but this was just the morning after our first night of sex. I was already feeling like I was his private fantasy which he didn't need to entertain during the day.

Despite that, Todd didn't really think I was dangerous or lack trust in me. He would leave me home alone while he ran some errands without a second thought. One day while he was out, I decided to enjoy the pool that belonged to the complex. It didn't take long before I made a few friends who lived within the complex. Wanita was one of them. She was an older black female and mother of three, who lived in another unit. She was in her 40's, and her face appeared very youthful. She had a full-figure build and was absolutely beautiful. I admired her persona and the way she carried herself. Her eldest son was in high school.

That day, we started chatting around the pool. At first, it was just a normal day. I was disappointed, but the "Jules" part of me was trying to calculate how long we could use this place to crash until moving was necessary. I felt solid. I fought off the potential flashbacks of torment at the same time Todd seemed to be using me; even though I was using him, but I managed to treat it all practically.

Then, Wanita mentioned Greensboro.

A shudder rippled over me.

*   *   *

A red light shone at the corners of the ceiling. There was a group of other women nearby, but they didn't look damaged like us. They looked more upbeat as if they were from a more reputable sort of Madame who protected her girls.

They were talking loud and you could hear the bass music coming from the other side of the walls. This was a party house of some sort we had been called to service that evening. We had no idea what this would mean, and all of us were intently curious. We were being ordered about by a blonde who resembled a lingerie-model in a goth outfit. Her hair was up, but the ponytail itself looked like it was pointed out wildly in different directions. She wasn't giving us any plans for the future, just telling us where to go moment to moment.

I was with a group of girls who were all foreigners, and we had no answers. In order to find out where I was, I decided to blend in with the "American" crowd. I walked up to another girl and pulled a Southern Belle accent. "Where am I supposed to go?"

The other girl spoke back, saying with a vague smile, "I didn't hear 'ole girl. I was listening to my Walkman." I was now in her group. No one paid attention. They fell into my trap, and at least I would be able to speak English for the night. I might get in trouble later, but I could always claim I got confused. They hadn't been telling us where to go very well.

The one lady instructed us to head into the next room, following after a set of women who looked like they were the "other" side of the business, the organizers. The line of girls followed after those women and were spaced out so that it felt like we were about to be interrogated by the cops or being identified as a "perp" in a crime. Next thing I knew, the velvet curtains that were laid in front of us, and a white man in his late 30's or early 40's was looking back at us with good humor. He had the opportunity to pick one of us. The ones that didn't get picked were put into a backroom. The room for the "American" girls was quite different from the ones I was usually put in. Their rooms had a couch, a tray of finger foods, make up, lingerie costumes everywhere, and curling irons plugged in. The atmosphere felt more relaxed in comparison. Normally, I lounged on wooden benches in cramped rooms without food or amenities.

We would be summoned, a few at a time, to get dressed and ready for the next clientele. After one appointment, feeling filled with further momentary rebellion, I decided to hold off going back down into the waiting room. I slipped over to one of the doormen and asked if I could swipe a cigarette from him. I used my southern-American accent to sound natural and worth his time, and he fell for it. He took me to the back door and cracked it open to give me a chance to have a breath of fresh air while I puffed away. I was surprised it was night. It hadn't been when we got there. I never seemed to know what time it was.

The doorman casually reached in his pocket, grabbed one of the cigarettes from his full pack of Camel, in the beige looking box with gold trim, and handed me one. It had been awhile since I had an opportunity to smoke one, so I started coughing and trying my best not to look like it had been awhile. The guy held the door open with his back while we both watched other girls running up and down the hall. I remember seeing the street lamp on and in front of me was a bunch of trees. I could see some glistening light from headlights across the way and I could hear the traffic as if it was near the alley.

I remember looking at the wilderness, and wondering what it would be like to run free again, and then yelling at myself for thinking about things that could never, ever happen again…

*   *   *

I blinked away the flashback. Greensboro was like that, but I wasn't trapped. I wasn't there. I fought my way back to clarity and paid attention to what was around me. Very green and mountainous, with beautiful vistas everywhere. Wanita would take me on drives, heading along highways which separated the trees. It was like watching movies when cars would drive through forest highways, and the boughs leaned in over above the road to make a tunnel of trees stretch out in front of you. It was the sort of scene that made you wish for normality. It was the essence of wholesome, southern states living. She was chatting away about her children, and it didn't matter what she was saying. The tone behind her voice spoke of love and approval and concern for their well-being. They could be anywhere, and she would care for them. They could do anything, and she would try and protect them.

I had a pang of desperation at missing my family. I yearned for that sensation. I knew my family and life had never been like that, but I had wanted it often enough. Now, I wanted it again. While Wanita was pulling up to the gas station, I saw the payphone and pondered at the idea of calling my family. It had been years since I heard from them. Our last correspondence didn't end well. I had had on and off again fights with my parents since '94. There were also other incidents that I won't mention here because they are irrelevant. My family wasn't your typical Brady Bunch family (who would welcome you back with open arms no matter how much you wronged them). However, after careful consideration, I decided to take a chance and call them.

I headed to the Shell Gas Station on the corner. I could smell the evergreens on the other side of the road. I found the nearest pay phone and called collect to my parents' home.

"Hello?" I heard my father's tone.

Just the sound of his voice called me away from so much darkness. A tear fell from my eye and I sniffled as I managed to say, "Daddy?"

"Song Ja?" he responded. "What's the matter?" At first, that felt like an odd question. He didn't know where I had been. He only knew that I had distanced myself from the family and been out of touch for years. He must think it was by my own choice. His voice was cold and short, not comforting at all.

A part of me wanted to hang up right then and there. How could I explain? How could he even begin to understand? I kept hoping he would and that he would reach out to me.

"I need your help. I wanna' come home." I sobbed a little and pleaded in the depths of my mind that he would sense this was no longer about old arguments. I needed real help and I was willing to work things out.

He snapped back, wanting nothing to do with hearing about new pain, "Why you wanna' come home? What did you do this time?"

"I just wanna' come home," I answered in a childlike tone.

"No!" His voice was cold and stern as if he didn't want anything to do with me.

"I'm sorry. I'll be good this time. Please, let me come home and I'll try and..." I was begging and tried to hold nothing back, pouring myself out to him and putting all my forgiveness for any past hurts in every word. All he had to do was say "okay," and I could do that.

Once again, there was only stone in his voice, "Song Ja, I say, 'No!' You never listen and you always give hard time, you know that? Bye Song Ja."

"Daddy, I'm sorry." I pleaded and then I heard the dial tone.

I smashed the receiver into the phone as I screamed with frustration and pain. I snarled at the phone, and yelled, "I hate you!" again and again. I tried again an hour later, but he wouldn't pick up the collect call. I tried a different tactic, using what little money I had to buy a phone card so he wouldn't know who was calling, but he hung up on me the moment he heard my voice.

After a while, it became pointless to try. I never managed to speak to my mother or sisters, and my father was deaf to me now. I gave up hope. I was an orphan.

My time with Todd didn't last. He used the excuse that I had to leave because the landlord forbade any *"Chinese"* on the premises. I knew it was pure bullshit, but what could I do? I was not a tenant in the complex, so he offered to drop me off at the nearest bus station. While I was packing up my stuff, I knew where Todd hid his miscellaneous cash, so I stole it as a payback for using me. I felt entitled to be compensated for having sex with a bigot.

I was back at my old stomping ground. I was a ghost in those days, haunting whatever places I could find. Everything reminded me of the past, and none of the past was safe in my mind. If I managed to stay with a family or friend for a couple of days, then I would see the children play in their houses and the pleasant interactions with their grandparents and such, and I would numbly wonder how this could not have been my life? Was I such a terrible a person to warrant the punishment that was my family? I would watch them argue, but violence never surfaced, and they never kicked each other out of the house. I would always leave, chased away by the phantoms of my own past, and never felt like I could ever fit in. It wasn't about overstaying my welcome, but rather my running away from visions that taunted me with their normalcy. I was a stranger to that, and an outsider to normal, family life.

If not tormented by the lives of families and the memories of my own, then it was once again the thought of Vegas that occupied me. No place was my own, and the closest place I had to privacy came when I found secluded spots to lock myself in and lose myself to the unhappy images of the past. I slipped into random gas station bathrooms and would huddle in the corner until I passed out, knowing such dreams were waiting for me.

* * *

"How dare you defy me, you stupid cunt!" One of the handlers screamed at me.

I just stayed on my knees with the cold floor unyielding under the hard caps of my knees. I felt extremely weak, powerless to prevent the results of his fury. "I'm sorry!" I sobbed and pleaded. I didn't even know what I had done wrong in that moment.

"Get down and kiss the fucking floor!" he screamed. He grabbed me by the wrist, pulled it back, and slammed me face-first to the floor. I heard a violent pop and pain flashed into my mind in a hellacious burst.

I started to scream hysterically, writhing about and doing even further damage to the dislocated joint. I tried to get up but the pain blinded me. I just lay there screaming, and he left me to walk out the door in callous disregard.

I called after him as if I actually thought he would help. I didn't, but it was purely instinctive. He was my lifeline, for if he left me I might die there crumpled on the floor. "My arm! I can't move it!" I screamed, "My arm! My arm!" My whole body was washed with a sort of strange heat, and my gasping breath and ragged heartbeats made my chest burn.

"The handler" turned back to me and snorted in derision, saying only, "Maybe, next time you will fucking listen!" He walked out and slammed the door shut.

I would scream and scream...

That wasn't me screaming...

* * *

I came out of the flashback, realizing that it was the next customer for the bathroom who was screaming for me to get out. He was pounding on the door that I had been in there for hours. I tried to clear away the dream, but it clung to me as fiercely as those visions ever did. I knew that this gas station would never let me use the bathroom again. It had happened before. Now, they would know my face, and it wouldn't even matter if I bought something. Another place of "safety" was used up. The place might be filthy, but for a few hours it had been mine, and the world was locked outside.

I slowly got up from the floor. I used my bag as my pillow and my light jacket or a ragged sweater when I had one for blankets. I could hear my stomach rumbling. I needed food, especially after that particularly

155

bad dream. I felt even less rested than when I had fallen asleep. I had to get some food. I opened my bag to count my money, already knowing it was getting short. Ignoring the customer outside, knowing it was already too late to salvage my reputation at this place, I looked over the smeared mirror in the bathroom and tried to groom myself into a rough semblance of order. It was a small act of control when everything else felt out of control. Assembled once more, I slipped out passed the irate customer and the irritated gas station attendant and vanished down the street.

I was so hungry that at times I had to steal to get food. I'd walk into a family-owned gas station where I knew the store manager was working alone. These types of stores made it easy for me to steal. Technology was still sketchy in a lot of those places. I had a few stolen credit cards I had managed to get, and a lot of those places had the old machines where you placed a carbon copy over a swipe-deck. Nothing electronic. It would be days before they knew they had been robbed. I had to move around, and they would only sell me small things at a time, but if I was careful and didn't get greedy, it was easy. I was raised to respect my elders and to say things like, "Yes, ma'am" or "Yes, sir." They never even saw me as a threat.

That same upbringing made me feel terrible each time. I just needed to survive, that was all. I hated living this way, and it tormented me to do it. As my cash began to wane, I tried to save most of it for a night in a cheap motel in case the weather got bad, or in the event, I needed medical care or other miscellaneous. My mother used to teach me to conserve something for the "just-in-case-emergencies." It's funny how at strange moments in your life, lessons from your parents come back to help you even when they certainly never intended the advice for problems like this.

When I was exhausted from selling my body, I would find alternative ways to hustle for money, whether it be selling drugs or stealing credit cards from clients. Winter was a difficult experience and sleeping outside, in truck stops, or random gas stations was risking death when the temperature fell. I held out as long as I could, but I needed a place to sleep. It wasn't even purely for survival. I knew what a real bed felt like, and I was desperate to feel a good mattress, warmth, a clean bath-room, and maybe even a shower. I hung out in country bars and flirted my way into some stranger's bed just so I would have a place to sleep. It may sound petty or ridiculous, but it meant a lot to me in those days. My promiscuity wasn't from loneliness or for fun. I just wanted to sleep in a nice comfortable bed with sheets and a comforter, even if it only lasted two to four hours. I would try to leave before the man would wake up. That allowed me to make off with a little bit of food and some cash. Yes, I was a traveling thief and I hated it. I would sit in a park and cry for hours. My body wasn't the only thing that was tired. My very soul felt tired. I was emotionally and spiritually drained from the constant fight to stay alive.

I learned other tricks for living on the streets and learned to do things that only those who have had to scratch together a homeless living would understand. I learned which restaurants, bakeries, or other food stores threw out the best scraps, and then dug through the dumpsters to find food. You wouldn't believe how much food is wasted. If the crust is broken on a pie, the whole pie is tossed out as unsellable. When someone's not satisfied with their steak or fish, the whole plate was thrown out. This was the golden treasure you could find. It's strange, but when deprived of food, shelter, or care, humans become like animals scrounging for survival.

I remembered as a little girl when I would take the trash out during my family's time in Elmore City. I once recall hearing a plastic bag being wrestled inside one of the cans near our apartment's dumpster. When I looked inside, I found a small dog trying to get out.

At first, I thought he was trapped. I'd said, "Aww, you poor thing. Are you trying to get out?" I grabbed the dog and tried to ease him out. The moment I let go, he was trying to jump back in. It took me awhile to figure out what he was after. I looked in the dumpster and saw the half-empty box of food the dog had been nibbling on. I ran back inside the house and while Momma was in the living room, I went through the 'fridge and got some cold hot dogs.

Returning outside, I called to the dog, waving the package at the little pup. I opened the package up and gave the dog one hot dog after another. Then I ran back inside and got a bowl of water for the dog to drink. After a while, the dog began return to visit me and every day before school, I would lay out sandwich meat near the dumpster for the dog and a small bowl of water. I have never seen such loyalty earned so cheaply as that, for I was the king of all creation to that dog. I was its angel.

Now, here I was living on those same scraps, and thinking kindly of any shop owner who threw it out. They wasted the food, but I loved them for it. I remember crying as I ate the leftover food, knowing I was wretched and lost, and yet unable to stop from eating. I was a slave to my basic needs.

I tried to hold on to some element of my previous self. No matter how hard things became, I knew I needed to not give up entirely. I used what I stole to get cheap motels or used my charm to get into the homes of strange people, and tried to not let myself devolve completely. I took baths as regularly as I could, even if it was with just a wash cloth and a tiny bar of soap. I would steal towels, bottles of shampoo, and lotion from those places and hoard them for when times were lean; then take bird-baths in bathrooms when I had the chance. A washcloth and a small piece of soap could go a long way. If I ever wrote a "How to Survive on the Street," it would be a New York Times Bestseller.

A bitter irony came to me one day, for I was a naturalized citizen. I recalled (in a sort of bizarre melancholy way) the day my parents and I became American citizens. After years of going through the processes demanded by the government, we were finally there in the courtroom. I was in a dress, my hair pulled back in a ponytail with my bangs covering my forehead, the way my mother liked to style my hair. The courtroom was packed with people, and my dad was holding my hand. Everyone was all so serious. My mother and father were exchanging words in Korean, then whispering to my Aunt and Uncle who were also there. I had no idea what was going on and I didn't care. I wanted to go and play, but my dad had summoned me to be still.

I remember seeing the double doors on one side swing open, and the crowd got quiet. I heard a gentleman that resembled a cop calling out our family's name. We all had to get up and walk towards the front. I stood in front with my parents standing behind me. I watched my parents being sworn in, saying formal words that I didn't recognize. I was told to be on my best behavior as I was going to meet someone important. My father guided me to my right, towards a line of people waiting to get their certificates. They had been ahead of us. That line moved to shake the hands of others in this long line of well-wishers that led up to a more formal reception at the end.

I was too young to understand politics, but I remember seeing the President from the TV. I got to meet him, but he appeared older in person. I wasn't sure what to say, but that I wanted to go home. He handed me the small version of the American Flag and held out his hand, "Welcome to America, you are now a citizen of the United States." Although I had no clue what he was talking about, I scooted down to shake his wife's hand and she handed me a lollipop. I smiled and walked away with my parents. That was all I could remember.

Later, I was living a version of the American dream that no one wanted. I wondered what that girl back then would have felt if she had known where that "Welcome to America" could lead. I wanted to love my country, but for the moment I felt utterly shut out of everything that it stood for.

CHAPTER 10

PITTSBURGH

As much as I tried to find safe places to hide away, sleep was typically scarce. Whenever I would awake, it was all too often with a cry and a start, ripping free of a flashback dream of my childhood abuse or my time as a prostitute. One evening, I actually started to drift off to sleep while walking down the street. I blinked, and suddenly realized I had no idea where I was or where I was going. I needed sleep.

I saw a nearby motel and asked for a room. The man barked a laugh at me and stated quite clearly, "No Room!" I begged and pleaded, even asking for a closet or back room to stash away in for a couple hours, but he brushed me away. Fortunately, one of the motel maids heard the conversation and took me aside as I left the office. She said she had a room I could use for a while and wouldn't let the manager know. I promised that if she needed it, I would leave, and she confirmed I had to get out before 7 a.m. in the morning. I was so grateful for her help. I followed her to one of the rooms and she said if she knocked a certain way, I would know it was her. She told me there was food in the small fridge and I was able to take a bath.

The maid's kindness made me remember the maternity home's charity. Brimming with more than gratitude and a rush of peace I hadn't felt in a while, I gave her a huge hug and cried, "Thank you so much!" She smiled back, let me in, and left me to my rest.

I looked at the clock and it was 8:53 p.m. I jumped in the shower and just sat there in the tub, allowing the water to fall on my bare skin. I sat there with my knees close to my chest and just cried. I was over-whelmed with gratitude and with fear of the unknown. I knew this evening would only be one night, but to me it was memorable. It was a rock amidst a swirling pool of my life, and my mind anchored to it and remembered what it was like to have a steady life.

I sat in the tub for a good hour and allowed the hot water to burn my skin. The cleansing ritual felt wonderful. After the shower, I made myself comfortable and slid into bed. The next morning, the hotel maid woke me up and I assisted her in cleaning rooms. Her invitation for me to stay grew from one day to the next. Since I had assisted her in some of the cleaning, she gave me cash. I saved some of the money to get my own room, so I could continue with *"work."* After I got my own room, I took a shower and flipped on the TV. I flickered through the channels and came upon a chat-line advertisement. It was time to raise money again and along with that was a healthy dose of boredom and loneliness. I decided to leap at the chance to connect with someone for a few minutes. The "Jules" in me might have been already thinking ahead to the next night, and where I would spend that night. For the real me, it was more about hearing a real voice for a few minutes.

I picked up the phone and dialed the phone number. While the other callers were looking for phone sex, I wanted real conversation. I was able to get through a caller name Danny. He carried a Jersey accent that I thought sounded sexy. At the time, I was on the outskirts of Greenville, North Carolina, Danny shared with me about Pittsburgh. I had fantasized about being on the East coast. He wasn't affectionate or sensitive, he was blunt and to the point. There was something about his domineering persona that I found attractive in his tone. It's astounding that I found his rudeness to be enduring rather than a *"red flag."* One of the redeeming qualities that caught my heart was the fact he enjoyed hearing me sing or he fooled me into thinking he was interested. That was when he mentioned that he was a music producer and that I should come visit him. To see if he was desperate enough, I challenged him to get me a bus ticket. I was unsure if he would take the bait. Would he be that eager to see me? I was excited and couldn't wait to leave North Carolina. I began to have visions of me singing in front of a mic.

Two more weeks of ongoing phone conversation, my tickets were set, and our rendezvous established. I headed for the Greyhound station. As with every time that I got onto a bus during my fugitive status, I had to use the fake ID that the traffickers had given me. Most times, if they didn't accept it, I would shrug and wander on to the next town and try again there. This time, I needed it to work. I pleaded in silent prayers that she would allow me to get on the bus. She did, and I was off. The drive was only around eight hours, but it started out around noon. I arrived in Pittsburgh around 8 or 9 p.m.

I sat in the lobby waiting for this Danny guy to pick me up. Instead, he sent a friend of his. I didn't know this guy, and I got a little nervous. Then he introduced me as Danny's friend, Larry. During my conversations with Danny previously there were a few times I would hear Larry in the background, so I was familiar with who he was. What surprised me was, Larry appeared older, in his mid-30's. This began to scare me a little, but I was determined to see Danny.

We got to Danny's house to the sounds of a party. I looked around and was stunned to see the people milling around. Most of these guys were around my age. I thought it was odd that Larry was the oldest one in the room. When I first saw Danny, I couldn't believe he was the guy I've been talking to. His appearance was not what I had envisioned. He appeared to be a very tall teenage boy. I wasn't sure if he was even 18. There were so many red flags in this scenario but I brushed it off. I didn't want to feel that my visit was a mistake, so I remained in his home. The music was loud, and I could barely hear. The guys were in the bedroom conversing when I walked in the room and there was Larry along with several other guys.

The music was blaring with mixture of rock and metal music. It was too loud to do much but listen and drink. I was sitting next to Danny amongst the other people in the room. I wanted to be alone with him but didn't want to be rude and ask him to be alone. The next thing I knew, the door was shut and soon after, the lights went out. I felt multiple hands touching me, groping me, and taking my clothes off.

I became frightened and anxious in the dark. The light under the door brought back flashbacks of my childhood when I was locked in the closet; in the storage units where me and the girls were held; and also, in the hotel rooms when I was brutally raped by a buyer. All those flashbacks came rushing into my mind. I was calling out for Danny but he didn't respond. Because of the darkness, I couldn't tell if he was still in the room.

I heard the pounding of the door from the other side, a female's voice demanding for someone to unlock the door.

"What are you doing! Open this door right now!" She demanded. I was being raped by multiple men and I couldn't see their faces. The light under the door distracted me with horrid flashbacks.

*   *   *

I was slammed onto the bed, my wrists restrained to the bed posts, and all eight of them did what they wished, for however long they wished.

"No!" I screamed, again and again, just hoping it would all go away. I screamed at the top of my lungs, but no one could hear me. How could they? I was in a basement or some abandoned warehouse. I remember staring past the men atop me and looking at the cemented ceiling, begging for my mind to go numb. I could feel my body shaking frantically and I could feel each one of them aggressively thrusting themselves back and

forth inside of me. I could feel my insides bleeding and feeling torn from within. The physical pain no longer existed.

That didn't stop them. My tears were a sexual arousal to them. Every moment became agonizing and I couldn't wait till it ended, but each moment they just wanted to make it go on and on until they had proven they could do what they wished with me.

*   *   *

It was hell. My mind had fled, but it had fled into a flashback, and there had been no numb relief. My own mind had betrayed me, and I was doubly shattered as I lay there on the bed.

They were finally done. My body was shaking and I was still lying there, barely moving. I would see the silhouette of the men walking out one at a time. Danny threw my clothes at me and told me to get out.

I slowly got up and grabbed my panties along with my bra and the rest of my clothing. My body was shaking and I couldn't close my legs. My upper thighs were so sore that they felt scraped down to the bone. I didn't know what to do. I checked my bag with a feeling of total loss, knowing what I would find. My meagre money supply and everything I had was all missing. Knowing it was worthless to try and get it back, I walked out with nothing.

I didn't know where to go or where to find help. I went to Pittsburgh for a dream, but it had turned into a nightmare. It was early morning, just past dawn. There was a chill in the air. I didn't watch where my steps took me as I staggered away. I kept thinking over and over how stupid it was to fall for a monster. I berated myself again and again in my mind. It must've been an hour later with the fragments of all that depravity tormenting my mind. Maybe an hour. Trapped like that in your own private hell, you lose track of time. I remember the roads were so hilly that when I'd walk down the street, it felt steep enough that I nearly lost my balance. A ridiculous thought crossed my mind as I looked at the newly risen sun; it was so beautiful yet also horribly depressing. I could've enjoyed the sunrise with Danny if he was human; instead, he was this monster, and I was cut adrift again.

Where was I? Alone, stranded in some city I've never been in before. Depressed didn't begin to match what I felt. All my time as a fugitive, I had felt dirty and on the edge, but I had been the huntress and the manipulator. Suddenly, I was back to being the one torn, hurt, and lost.

Whatever progress I had made suddenly felt cheap and absent. I had nothing.

I was back on the streets, which meant I was at risk to fall back into what I knew best. I struggled and survived like I had done for the past year. My money was gone and I was desperate for work, and I seriously considered my usual mode of survival. I didn't want to use my body, though. Not then. Not ever again, especially that soon after being attacked. The very thought was enough to make me sick. But, I knew how to make people feel good in other ways. I knew about nightclubs and that sort of life. So, I opened the yellow pages and started searching under the "clubs/massage" category.

I found a job working as a masseuse for this guy named Al. Within a few days, I met Marcie. She was one of the girls who worked with me at the massage parlor. Marcie was Puerto Rican with long black hair with spiral curls and bright red lipstick. She was very bubbly, outgoing, and could be aggressive at times. She was a younger version of Kelli without the harsh vindictive edge. We were also the same age, and I felt better equipped to offset her more aggressive tendencies and hold my own in the relationship. I wasn't her lackey. No, instead, we clicked immediately as if we were sisters. It was nice to hang out with someone close to your age and see life in a different perspective. She would let me crash at her apartment which was above a shop, but I didn't become her roommate. Despite how tenuous life could be without a home, I needed and enjoyed the freedom I had at that time.

On one occasion, she asked me to go to a house party. I nearly laughed, but it was a chance to not be alone for an evening, be warm, and have some food.

It was a quiet party, not a blow-out. Marcie was reclining on a couch, "talking smack" about the way girls were treated by guys. I was folded over the top of the other couch, hanging my head into the conversation pit. I had on a pair of Daisy Duke shorts and enjoyed the feel of the material on the back of the couch as I bounced my legs off of it. My butt was up in the air, bouncing a little. I was generally acting a little silly, but it felt good to have a good laugh. I said, "Yeah, I can't stand it when these dudes be treatin' us like we sum' object or sumpin.'" I was using my street accent along with East Coast slang, gladly ignoring all the proper grammar rules I had learned in my English class.

At the party, there was a Latin guy sitting in a recliner. I had noticed him off and on throughout the party. He wore a black leather jacket, a buttoned up white dress shirt, and jeans. His hair was dark-brown with length to his neck line, as it fell onto his face. He wore a goatee that was nicely rough without being ridiculous. He was looking around the room as he held a cup in his hand. He looked unattached. There was something captivating about him. Even as I talked with Marcie, I was shamelessly wiggling what I had in hopes that I might draw his attention. It worked.

Instead of just coming over to chat, he walked behind me and slapped my bottom. It was enough to make me bolt upright. He just stood there, smiling and completely unrepentant. "Wear more clothes Mamasita, and I'll treat you like a lady." He smiled from ear-to-ear.

Not about to take that lying down, I snapped my fingers at him as I waved my neck back and forth, saying, "Do you know who I am? You do *not* come up in here and disrespect me." Real anger was swelling inside me. He might have thought it was a joke, but the wounds in me were too fresh.

Still smiling, he stood there laughing and said softly, "Ok, Ms. Ostrich head," as he leaned closer to my ear. He was passing by me to get to the other side.

I huffed and puffed and told Marcie we were leaving. She laughed and went along. Even though she did not understand, she was willing to support me.

As I headed out the door, he tapped me on the shoulder and asked, "Leaving so soon? I thought we were just starting to have fun!" He was lucky I didn't claw his eyes out. Some part of me knew that he *couldn't* have known why his words made me furious. At that moment, I wasn't all that concerned with being fair to him. He's just lucky I didn't hurt him. I stormed out of the door with Marcie in tow. I believe that was the last party I attended with Marcie.

I didn't know his name, nor did I know how to reach him. Instead, fate decided to play its hand. Once again, the church was involved. I was falling into depression. I had made another hopeless phone call to my parents, and this time my mother had actually picked up. She hadn't said much, but she insisted I return to the church for guidance and any hope of salvation before she turned me away.

I nearly tossed her idea out faster than she had tossed away the idea of inviting me home. I wasn't into God at the time, and in no place mentally to remember the help other Christians had given me in helping with my Angel. I fought the idea for as long as I could, but once again, I found that my family values and connections didn't go away easily. After all this time, I still felt a burning desire to obey my mother.

Somewhere deep inside, I knew how much churches had really helped me. On top of that, I had always admired big, tall cathedrals. So, I bowed to the twisting pressure inside of me and went into a church in the heart of Downtown. I stole a dress from a thrift store so I wouldn't be dressed in a way that was too revealing. I went in and knelt down in front of the row of candles.

A short Latin lady approached me. She revealed to me that her son was a recovering addict and needed a positive friend to attend a meeting with him. She asked me if I would be interested in attending with him. I had no idea what she was referring to and assumed there would be free food. That was all I cared about at the time, so I agreed. She took me home with her.

They lived in a Victorian house, and I was in awe. We walked up to the place and through the large front doors. The decor inside made me feel out of place in my used, baggy, stolen dress. The lady said she would get her son, and called for him to come downstairs.

When I saw him coming down the steps, pausing to stick a cigarette in his mouth, I was shocked. It was the same guy who had slapped my butt! I couldn't believe the coincidence and had no idea how to make a graceful retreat. Instead, I pretended like I had never seen him before. I covered my forehead as if I had a headache as his mother introduced us. I was 4'11" and he stood about 6'2", so it was easy to try and block his view.

It was all for naught. He was sharper than that. When his mother left the room for us to get better acquainted, he leaned over and said, "I almost didn't recognize you with clothes on." He chuckled lightly. I looked up and glared at him. "Let's throw some chairs up in here." I clenched my fist and shook it at him.

He cupped my fist with his big hand and said with another low laugh, "Calm down little Chihuahua. No one is going to hurt you." He stood up and headed for the door, I followed behind him.

We walked outside, and I saw his royal blue Chevy truck. It had a king cab and dark tinted windows with white silhouettes of two hot, shaped ladies on each bottom corner of his window in a sexy pose.

"Nice," I said sarcastically.

He just laughed, chuckling back as good as he received and taking nothing personally, "Do you need help getting in? I don't have a stepstool for little people."

"No, thank you." I opened the door and swallowed hard. The black, leather seat was tall and high and resisted my every attempt to get a hold. Embarrassed, I struggled to get in without much success.

He sat in the driver's seat, lighting up a cigarette while waiting for me to get inside. He looked at me and shook his head with a smile.

"What?" I asked in a frustrated tone.

"Are you sure you don't need my help?" He asked.

"I don't want you to touch me. I can do just fine and besides, what is it with men and leather seats?" I was totally exasperated and defeated.

Manuel remained sitting there smiling and watching me climb in like a toddler climbing into a tall recliner. I stood back down on the ground and gave up. I exhaled hard and stared at him. He just looked back. He wasn't going to make this easy on me. Finally, I asked, "Help?"

He laughed, slid around the truck's hood, walked over behind me, and pushed me up into the truck. He pushed quickly, and I bumped my head on the ceiling. It had hardly been a chivalrous rescue and I squawked, "Hey! You didn't say go."

He shrugged, smiled again, and replied, "Sometimes you just have to prepare quickly." Then he got in his truck and we were on our way to the meeting. While he was driving, I knew there was no way I was going to look like an Asian-version of the "Golden Girls" for this meeting. The dress I had stolen was bulky and not my style. So, I pulled out my duffle bag and picked an outfit for this meeting — Daisy Dukes with a white halter top.

Manuel was bewildered, "Wha... what do you think you're *doing*?" He tried to keep his focus on driving while I made my change. I expected him to be turned on as I stripped down, but he looked more frustrated than anything.

Not about to stop, I shot back, "I'm changing. What does it look like to you?"

"Do you want me to drop you off at a strip club?

"No, why would you say something like that?"

"Look at how you are dressed!"

"So? Just in case there's a hot guy," I said while applying makeup and staring at the visor's vanity mirror.

"Most of the people are sick."

"You mean the triple A?" I sprayed water to dampen my curls and applied mousse.

"You mean Alcoholics Anonymous?"

"They have alcohol there???" I asked excitedly.

"Really?" He took a double take then shook his head and started to laugh. "There is this one location with a bunch of hot guys."

"Yes, take me there!" I answered excitedly.

He took me to a "Seniors" Alcoholics Anonymous (AA) meeting. I never felt so embarrassed in my life. Of course, I had all the eyes on me, but it wasn't the type of attention I was looking for. By the time we approached the door, an elderly man in a walker greeted us.

"Well, you're such a pretty little thing." He smiled amusingly.

"Oh, no! I'm not an Alcoholic! I'm here with him." I answered.

"Oh, honey, we're all in denial." He continued to stare with excitement, while Manuel was snickering. He had won another of our little rounds.

"I think they liked me!" I said as we walked out of the meeting towards his truck.

"I'm sure they liked what was bouncing in front of them." He sneeringly smiled.

As we both jumped into his truck, he offered to buy me a cheap meal through a drive-thru. Shortly after, he asked me if I trusted him. Honestly, I didn't care. He was very handsome and I wanted to get laid, so I answered, "Yes." While he was driving up the mountains, I began to feel regretful. *"Oh, my God! He's going to kill me and chop my body into pieces! No, don't cry. Be strong. Oh, what if he tries to rape me first?"* Anxiety and my thoughts continued to ramble in my head. I sat in the front seat remaining still. By the time he parked, I was anxiously waiting for him to step out of the truck and pull me out, but when he turned on the radio of a love song station, I was perplexed. *"He's going to kill me playing love songs?"* I asked myself.

He parked his truck up on a nice vista overlooking the city, turned on a soft music station, and broke open the food. Once finished, he lit a cigarette, "I love being out here, it's peaceful and helps me think."

Being short, I could hardly see anything. I kept using the seat cushion to help me bounce so I could see over the dashboard. When Manuel noticed, he smiled and shook his head. He began to pull his seat back to make room for me to lean over to capture the view. I could see the river surrounding the downtown area for the first time. It was a beautiful view indeed, and I was in awe. My facial expression made it clear that this was a first time for me and gave away that I was no Pennsylvania native.

"You're not from here, are you?" He asked.

"Nope," I answered, still admiring the view.

"Do you have family here?"

"Nope."

"Friends?"

"Nope."

"Where are you from?"

"Oklahoma."

"How the hell did you get here?"

"I met a guy," I said.

He slapped a hand to his forehead, shaking it in mock pain. "Why am I not surprised? So, where is he now?"

I wasn't about to get into the specifics of that with *him*. Not then and there. I just said, "It didn't work out."

"Figures."

"What is that supposed to mean? You don't know me! You don't know what I've been through." I started to get angry.

He held up a hand to halt my tirade, "You're right." He settled back, not saying anything for a while, trying to calm me down. Silence fell between us. It wasn't uncomfortable. It was just a moment for us both to recover. Then, he looked at his watch and said, "Well it's almost ten o'clock and it's time for me to take you home."

"I'm an adult, you know. I don't have a curfew."

"Well, unlike most men you've run into, I don't want to keep you up late."

"Just drop me off downtown," I said without hesitation.

"I'm not dropping you off downtown. It's late and it's too dangerous."

"*Damn!*" I thought. I don't know why it mattered, but I had no wish for him to know the truth of my homelessness. There was no way I was going to let him know, so I lied to him. I picked out a nice Victorian home. From the moonlight view, it looked white and wholesome. He pulled up to the curb, and I hurried to jump out of the truck, tossing a "Goodbye!" over my shoulder.

As I walked up the pathway to the house, I heard his truck door open and close. I turned around to see him following me. "*Oh shit!*" What is he doing? Why is he making this so *hard?* Trying to brush him off, I stopped and said, "What are you doing?"

"I'm walking you to the door like a gentleman."

"I'm an independent woman. I don't need a man to open doors for me."

"What is it with you women? 'I want a nice romantic guy who's sensitive.' When we become that guy, then you want to be independent."

"Why do you care?" I asked trying to find a way to deter him.

He didn't. He was persistent and completely ignored me with a charming smile. I wondered if he was on to me and trying to catch me in my lie. He continued to walk me to the door. When I opened the screen door, I went to take one of my keys even though I knew that it wouldn't fit. I was going to bluff right to the end. Instead, before I had the chance, he turned me around, held my face, and gently kissed me. I was surprised, but after the initial shock, it started to feel right. It felt different, not perverted but different. From that point on, I knew that a new relationship was starting.

After he left, it dawned on me that I was stuck in a suburban area where payphones were not available as in the urban cities, so I had to find one, which caused me to walk miles away. I kept reminding myself of that sensual kiss, so the walking didn't bother me. I had to get in touch with Marcie so I could stay at her place.

I spent all night there, and the next morning I was on the phone with Manuel. We spoke like two teenagers in love. When I made plans to see Manuel later that night, Marcie had other plans.

While I was in the shower getting ready to see Manuel, Marcie called Al and told him she was sick and insisted he put me to work. By the time I got out of the shower, I saw my pager and it was Al. I was disappointed and didn't want to go into work. I called Manuel and canceled on him. When he asked me what had happened, I lied and told him that I was helping a friend move.

After I went back into the bathroom to change and put my makeup on, Marcie called Manuel and informed him that I was a prostitute and challenged him to come see it for himself. Later that evening, I had my cocktail dress on, makeup done, and my hair up with curls. The doorbell rang, Marcie was on the bed watching TV and rolling up a joint.

"Can you get it, babe?" She asked.

I walked over to the door and when I saw Manuel, I was shocked.

"Wow, you're going to help a friend move in heels?" He responded in disgust, "You know what? I don't want to have anything to do with you."

"Fine!" I slammed the door with a sting of pain in my heart. I couldn't understand why he showed up. It didn't dawn on me that this could be Marcie's doing. I trusted her and didn't assume she would betray me.

That evening, my pager went off and it was Al, instructing me to see an out-call client who fantasizes for an Asian girl. I began to feel nauseous. Oh, how I wanted to be with Manuel instead of being here. When the cab arrived to pick me up, I continued to think about Manuel. When the driver asked me where we should go, I instructed him to drop me off downtown. That evening, I just couldn't go through with it. I never went to meet the client and I didn't care.

Maybe the feelings I had for Manuel sparked an awareness that I didn't have to live this way. I meandered through the downtown area, walking past the strip of nightclubs and pubs that were lined up in a row. I was in my cocktail dress walking around downtown and didn't care about the eyes sizing me up or other girls pointing and whispering among themselves. I knew I fit right in because everyone else attending the clubs I passed by also had on revealing clothes, from bikini tops with short skirts to elegant evening gowns.

After two weeks, I fell sick and was vomiting blood. I checked myself into an emergency room. The nurse assumed I had Tuberculosis, so I was transferred to a closed area. When I was told that the disease I supposedly had would eventually kill me, I didn't want treatment. I didn't care at that moment if I died. I felt I had lost everything that was important to me. I had lost the love of my life. I had been discarded and sold. I had lost my baby and couldn't parent, and now I was homeless and infected by a lung disease. What was the use for me to get treatment, so I could return back to the streets? No way! If there was a blessing in this disease, it was to free me from homelessness and chaos.

During my hospital stay, I met one of the chaplains of the hospital. His name was Brother David. He was a Catholic monk. I made a negative assumption he would judge me when he stepped into my room.

"Hi, I'm Brother David." He introduced himself to me in a cheery voice.

"I know who you are and I don't need anybody. I'm no longer Catholic and I don't care if I die!" I shot back angrily.

"Ok, I will leave you be, but if you just want to talk, there will be no judging or suggestions from me; just someone to listen to you vent, I am here." He smiled.

Right when he was facing the door to head out of my room, I called out to him.

"Wait!" I didn't want to sound like I was pleading, but I felt so alone. Then a nurse scolded the chaplain for not wearing a mask for protection.

"I don't need a mask." He insisted.

"Brother David, this woman is infected and we have to protect you."
She responded back.

"No, she is not infected. Let's not jump to conclusions. You're still
running tests and nothing is conclusive until we know for sure. When
that happens, we'll deal with it head on." He informed her.

She couldn't force him to wear the mask and he was right, nothing
was confirmed about my illness yet, so he wasn't in any danger. He was
standing outside a giant version of Saran Wrap that covered my bed. He
then turned his attention to me. I was stumped because I didn't assume
he would fight for me. When he turned to look at me, he smiled.

"Yes?" He answered, remembering I had called him.

"You said you would listen? You're not going to scold, judge, or
suggest anything to me?" I asked.

"I'm just here to listen, that is all." He reassured.

"I'm not into that Bible stuff either," I announced.

"I'm not going to preach or do anything that makes you
uncomfortable." He reassured again.

From that point on, we formed a bond that I didn't think would be
possible. He kept his word and just listened. He comforted me in my
anger with clergymen and women who abused their authority in the
church, as well as my own personal experience with child sexual abuse.
I felt consoled and validated.

By the time the doctors came into my room, they informed me that
they were wrong. Whatever I was going through, I did not have
Tuberculosis. I was disappointed because I didn't want to leave the
hospital which meant I would be returning to the streets. Brother David
was with me when I was given the news and he didn't jump to the
conclusion that I would be happy. He was aware of my fears and my
agony. He gave me a list of resources for shelters and other outreach
services should I chose to accept help. However, Brother David was not
aware that I had no documents and without any evidence of who I was,
I couldn't receive it.

Before I was discharged, I decided to call Manuel one more time. I
wanted answers and closure. When I called him, I was shocked his tone
was polite. We spoke briefly and he informed me that Marcie had told
him everything about me. I was for sure that phone call to Manuel would
be the end. He had wished me luck on the rest of my journey in
Pittsburgh and we hung up.

Shortly after, I called the hotline again looking for refuge. Now that
my hopes and dreams of finding a man who truly cared was out the

window, *Jules* returned to my conscious and took over. I needed money to start, so I began to call Brennan and asked for help. I explained to him I was in the hospital in Pittsburgh and I was about to be discharged and would be homeless once again. This time I was hoping to receive cash, but instead, they reached out to one of their church friends.

When they arrived at the hospital to check me out, they put me up in a nice hotel. After our initial visit and after they left me alone, I used the room to run my calls to make extra money while I had time left. That evening, I made enough to run away, but before that happened, I met another guy on the phone and told him that I was in a hotel and in need of being "rescued." That same evening, he drove out to Pennsylvania from Ohio and picked me up. I left the hotel in the middle of the night with a couple of guys I didn't know along with Aaron, the guy I had met on the phone earlier that evening.

In the beginning, Aaron was affectionate and would look at me as the *"hot"* girl. I was blushing and didn't care whether it was sincere or not. I moved in with him right away. After about a month with Aaron, he began to get comfortable and started ordering me around. He would call me a *"whore," "bitch,"* or *"slut."* We would fight and scream in each other's face. He would come home drunk. Then one evening I received a page from a (412) area code. I wasn't sure who it was since I didn't keep many friends in Pittsburgh. I asked Aaron if I could use his cell phone to call my family. Aaron had a two-story house with an attic. I climbed up to the attic and called the number back.

"Did someone call me from this number?" I asked.

"Song?" A familiar voice responded.

"Manuel?" I asked.

"I know this is a sudden, but I really need to see you." He said.

My heart began to flush, I wanted so much to be with him, but at the same time, I kept my cool.

"What's going on? I thought you said you didn't want to have anything to do with me?" I asked.

"I know, but . . . I don't know how to explain it. I can't stop thinking about you. I don't know what you did to me, but I can't sleep. I can't eat or even concentrate. I have to see you! Where are you? I'll come pick you up?" He sounded eager.

"Manuel?" My voice sunk. "I'm not in Pittsburgh anymore," I explained.

"Are you back in Oklahoma?" He asked.

"No, I'm in Ohio."

"How the hell did you... Wait, did you run off with some guy?" He knew me!

"Yes," I was embarrassed.

"Well, is he treating you, right?" He asked.

"Yes, I'm doing good. He's been good to me." I lied. *Why did I lie? Was I afraid of failing? I didn't want to add Aaron on the list of assholes I've collected.*

"Well, if you change your mind or he's not treating you right, just call me. I will come and get you." He responded.

"You will?" I was shocked.

"Yes, it's only a three-hour drive, not a big deal." He replied.

Was this my Knight in Shining Armor? Who would drive even an hour to see me? Would he drive further to Oklahoma as well? I was stunned that *Jules* hadn't said otherwise. Usually, at this point she chimes in her two cents. After my phone conversation with Manuel, I knew I had to get back to Pittsburgh, but how?

My harebrained idea got the best of me once again. I called the chat line to see if I could find guys in Pittsburgh to "rescue" me. My original idea was to find a guy to take me from Ohio away from Aaron and return me to Pittsburgh. Then I would leave the guy at some bar and call Manuel to come get me. Everything would work out. Wrong! Instead, I met an older gentleman who was a biker. He was probably in his 50's when he came to pick me up in Columbus, Ohio. As soon as I got in the car, we headed back to Pennsylvania. What I was not aware of, is that he had his own agenda which was Altoona, about 1.5 hours past Pittsburgh.

While we were driving up the mountain, the next thing I knew, the car had tumbled and I blacked out. I woke up in the emergency room in Altoona, and I saw Manuel sitting by my side. He looked like he had been praying. The doctor walked in right as I opened my eyes. I was disorientated when I looked around. I remember the doctor smiled at me and said, "God has a plan for you. He protected you."

"What?" He choked up with words. Of course, Manuel was not happy when he heard about the accident. There were officers there and one officer, in particular, wanted to speak with me.

"Do you know this man?" He asked me.

"Barry?" I asked.

"Are you aware that he has multiple warrants regarding five missing women who had visited his trailer that has no access to phone or electricity?" The officer was concerned. He handed me his card and asked me to testify regarding the current situation. When Manuel returned, he asked the doctor if I was okay.

"She is perfectly fine." He smiled, "She can go home."

"Manuel?" I called to him in a longing tone.

"What the hell is wrong with you!" He scolded. I began to cry.

"What did I tell you? If you want to come back to Pittsburgh, you *call* ME! Where did you find, Barry?" He asked.

"I wanted to surprise you," I said, trying to cheer him up.

"No! Every time you come up with an idea, it gives me an aneurism."

I had no idea what he said nor what that meant, but once we were able to leave, I asked about my clothes. Manuel brought me a pastel pink sweatshirt and pants to match. I wanted my sexy clothes back. When we returned to his big truck, Manuel revealed to me his affection for me. That evening all I thought about was having sex with him. I wanted to be *his* fantasy girl. Whatever he wanted, I would give it to him without hesitation, but instead, he asked to cuddle.

Cuddle? Who cuddles? No intercourse? No heavy petting or oral sex? This was very foreign to me. When we got to the hotel room, I began to take off my clothes. Manuel picked up my clothes and put them back on me.

"You don't want me?" I asked in disappointment. All I ever knew was to be the Asian fantasy doll, and this time I wanted to be *his* fantasy doll. When he clothed me, I accepted it as a denial.

"I do want you in the worst way." He smiled while putting my clothes back on.

"What's wrong?" When he saw the disappointed look in my eyes, he sat on the foot of the bed, pulled me closer to him and pointed at my chest.

"I want this." He pointed.

"Me too, that's why I'm giving you my heart," I explained.

"Do you know what intimacy is?"

"Yes, it's sex."

"No, that's called intercourse. You do know that intimacy doesn't require intercourse or anything sexual, right?"

"Well, that sucks." I was disappointed, hoping I would get laid.

"We are getting to know each other, why would you take your clothes off for me?"

"I thought that's what men wanted?"

"What about what you want?" What *I* wanted? It was the first time anyone had even asked me that and actually, I had never thought about it. At that point, I felt lost and confused. I was so brainwashed into believing that rough sex, orgies, and BDSM was a form of intimacy.

"Have you thought about abstinence?" He asked.

"Oh great! You're a Christian?" I asked.

"No, but what if I was? What's so wrong with waiting?"

"I don't want to wait 'til I get married. I think it's stupid."

"Have you ever thought about getting to know someone outside of the physical element?"

"What's the use of that? That'd be boring."

"If you really want to give a man your body, what is wrong with him working for it. Make him wait and see how much he respects you."

I never imagined making a guy wait, so his lecture didn't help. I began to feel like a slut. Shortly after, Manuel began to teach me about intimacy, love, and respect. He inspired me to demand respect and accept nothing less. He also taught me that an orgy and a threesome is not love nor should any man manipulate the word *"love"* to gain what they want sexually.

After a month of getting to know each other, he saved up some money, and we got an apartment together. Most people would say our relationship was fast, but it felt safe. It felt different from anything I had ever experienced before, and in a good way. We offset each other's sense of humor.

In public places, he would speak Spanish to me and I would speak Korean to him, then we would chuckle at the strange looks we would get. He taught me to enjoy coffee shops and helped me have my first real conversations. We loved each other in a simple, uncomplicated way that few couples seem to find. I never had to ask him if I was beautiful. It shone in his eyes, and I could feel his sincerity when he said the words without me having to ask.

We had so much in common, but the one thing that bonded us closer together was the darkness in our childhoods, and the addictions that resulted from our torment. We had both grown up Catholic and in abusive homes. Our families were both middle to upper class, and in the presence of our church friends, people saw our families as perfect and worthy of admiration. Behind closed doors, there had been violence.

Not only did our childhood traumas bring us closer, but there were also our addictions. He was a recovering addict of alcohol and I was a recovery addict of cocaine and worse. Together, he and I would go to meetings on a regular basis. It was the first time since my Angel was born that I had a real break from substance abuse. That had been for her sake. This time, it was for *my* sake.

We took turns picking which meeting we wanted to go to. This was my first time learning about AA and Narcotics Anonymous (NA), and I wanted to explore what was out there, which groups felt right, and to meet new people who were struggling with the same problem. I loved our rides to and from those meetings. I felt like it helped Manuel and I connect even more deeply as we talked over what we would share and then what we had heard.

I began to develop new, healthier friendships within the meetings. The ladies would remind me how lucky I was to find such love. I felt so happy inside because I knew they were right. Manuel and I weren't your perfect couple. We definitely had flaws and the occasional disagreement. However, it never resulted in violence and he never stooped to name calling or playing games, or anything like that. If we argued, he would walk out before it escalated and came back after he cooled off. We made promises to each other that we didn't want to repeat what our parents had done. We helped each other find counseling we could trust, and tried to work out our own issues privately. This helped our relationship as well.

I recall the first time we made love. He was always gentle with me, and that time was no different. I started to cry. Worried, he asked if he had hurt me. He was above me, rocking me gently in his arms, as I held his body close to mine. "Song," he whispered, as he looked deep into my eyes, "I love you. I don't want to hurt you."

I felt my heart skip a beat, as a rush ran through my body like a waterfall falling over us—washing away whatever lay behind us and making the future fresh and new. I didn't want that moment to end and for the first time in my life, I gave him my heart completely. Others had come close to having that, and fate had ripped them all away. This time, I said the words. "Manuel, I love you, too," I whispered it back to him. Then he leaned his head towards mine, softly pressed his lips against mine and we kissed.

I could feel the warmth surrounding my body as I felt his hands explore my body. He softly touched my skin and admired my body as if he was staring at an exotic painting. I felt beautiful and sexy, and it was a good feeling. That evening we made love from evening until the morning. It was just pure bliss. It wasn't even all that much about sex. It was about closeness and love. He could hold me in his arms and we would both be naked and it just felt right. He would wrap his arms around me and ask me to sing to him.

This became a regular thing for us. I enjoyed singing to him while he laid his head on my chest and I would stroke his hard, brown hair with my fingers. His favorite song was, "Dreaming of You" by Selena. Every time I sang that song to him, he'd fall asleep in my arms. It was romantic and simple, but it was our thing.

For him, his thing was drawing. Manuel loved to draw. When I was not looking, he would sketch me into a picture where the background would be a rose garden of some sort. He would insert me into the foreground and make the colors mesh beautifully around the fringes. Once, I found the picture underneath our bed and I assumed he was having an affair with another woman. It didn't look like me at all! When I confronted him with worry, he smiled and said I was so cute for not recognizing my own beauty. Being near him, I felt loved. I felt beautiful. Most of all, I felt free. I had the world at my feet and it was a feeling I hoped would last forever.

When he assisted me in finding a real job as a store clerk, I was disappointed. I would brag about how call girls would make a decent living. He put that to the test. When he took me downtown he asked me to brag it to the world. When he saw me hesitate, he asked me, "Why?"

"Weren't you the one who said they make a decent living?" He asked.

"Manuel, you don't understand!" I was getting frustrated with him.

"Why do you look embarrassed? You think it's wrong?"

"It's not that."

"If you have to hide what you are doing, don't you think it is wrong?"

He broke it down in a mathematical format. When I explained to him that I didn't want to accept a job that paid minimum wage, he then showed me that selling my body was no different than minimum wage except for dignity. Especially with the way I was able to make money and still couldn't keep a budget.

After six months into the relationship, I remained in the job he offered. Every day, he would call and leave me a message on my pager. He would always leave sweet comments and let me know when he would pick me up. My usual time to get off from work was around 7:00 p.m. Our daily schedule was pretty consistent. Monday through Friday, we'd go out to eat somewhere or go home and have dinner; then we'd head off to an AA or NA meeting. Afterwards, we'd stop at a coffee shop for coffee or grab some fast food to talk over the meeting. Then, we'd head straight home.

Weekends were our time together. We were like a simple couple, and it was glorious. We'd go run errands, grocery or household shop together. Sometimes, we'd just enjoy a park, museum, or just sit and park the truck in the midst of the woods and enjoy the moonlight in the evening while holding each other and listening to romantic love songs on the radio.

One Friday evening, that changed.

Manuel called me up and said he was not going to pick me up after work. He said the night's schedule had to change. At first, I felt worried that something was wrong. Then, he surprised me with a limo. The driver had instructions on where to take me, and he said the next stop was a day spa. I settled in with amazement and could see my co-workers I had just left behind giggling and pointing. I felt like a princess just then. I sat back into the couch-like seats, but no sooner was I fully ensconced when the car phone sitting diagonal from me rang. I wasn't sure how it could be for me, but the driver encouraged me to pick it up.

I did, and asked, "Hello?"

"Hey baby, it's me. How are you doing?" I could hear his voice sounding so warm and tender.

"What's going on?"

"Just wait, baby. You'll see. The driver is going to take you to a day spa. When you get there, a lady will show you the dress I picked out for you to wear for tonight's dinner."

"Tell me what you have planned for the evening! I want to know!" I playfully pouted.

He wasn't telling. "You'll see, honey. I love you." He hung up, and I settled the handle back on the catch and exhaled a long breath. I tried to bribe the driver with fifty dollars to get a hint at where we were headed, but he turned me down with a smile.

With little else to do, I leaned back in the seats and tried to imagine what Manuel had planned for me. When I arrived at the day spa, I told them my name, and it was clear they knew I was coming. I was ushered in, taken to a room with a nice, steamy bath, and then treated with a full body massage and manicure.

Once I was done with the pampering, the lady brought the dress into the room. There it stood: a royal-blue, one-piece Chinese dress with a cut slit on the side. It was beautiful! The ladies did my hair and makeup with chopsticks holding my hair up. I had my bangs over my forehead and a long strand of hair that slightly curled around my face. I looked in the mirror and almost didn't recognize myself. For the first time, I agreed with Manuel's vision of me. I was beautiful.

I felt a rush of excitement come over me. I felt like the Asian Cinderella. When I got back into the limo, the driver did a double take. That reaction made me even happier. I knew I was striking. The driver handed me the car phone again and asked me to call a number on a sheet of paper. I dialed and got my response almost immediately.

Manuel answered, "I see you are done there?" he chuckled.

"Manuel, what are you doing?"

"Ah-ah! What did I say about asking questions? The driver will bring you to the Embassy Suites Hotel. When he drops you off at the carport, you'll see a gentleman that will be waiting for you at the front and will escort you to where you need to be. I will see you soon, My Queen."

"Manuel?" I had hoped he didn't hang up.

"Yes?" he answered.

"I love you."

"I love you, too." And we both hung up.

When the limo pulled up at the carport, I was greeted by the concierge and he offered his elbow to me. "You look very beautiful tonight, Miss." He smiled.

"Thank you." I nodded and smiled.

We then headed to the elevator, and he explained to me that the reserved room was a presidential suite. On arrival at the top floor, he walked me to the double doors and slid the card into the slot. Once the double doors swung open, at my toes was a trail of rose petals all the way to the back bedroom. I saw the fireplace across from me, and candles were scattered liberally through the room, seeming to dance with the soft music in the background. I was beyond amazed, and no longer had any words to describe the welling up of love and warmth that lay in my heart. I hadn't even notice the concierge had backed out of the room and left me to make my way alone towards the bedroom. Out of the corner of my eye, I saw a candle-lit dinner waiting out on the balcony with two chairs around the table.

I moved in towards the bedroom, but Manuel didn't make me wait. He stepped out so I could see him in his three-piece suit, gleaming and polished, and grinning from ear-to-ear. I wanted to laugh and cry at once, and the only emotion I could really pull out of all the flurry that was running through my heart and soul was "serenity." This felt so very, very right.

I walked in to him, and he took me in his arms. "Wow! You are so beautiful!" He began to caress the side of my face. "You're quiet. I hope you're not disappointed?"

"Oh no! I'm speechless! I don't know what to say." I could do nothing but stare at him. I knew at that moment, we were bound together in person and in spirit. I had never loved anyone as much. We slow danced for a time, then followed that with candlelight dinner on the balcony. It was so perfect, I wondered if he had read my journals to know all the right moves for a perfect proposal for me.

That is what it was. Yes, he knelt on one knee and asked me to be his wife! I was crying as I said, "Yes." From that point on, I started to create dreams of the life that I wanted; to cater to one man and to love him with all my heart, and to bring a family into being so that I could be the mother that I wanted to be for my children.

This engagement ended up being only a dream. A month later, he was taken from me.

They said it was officially labeled as "suicide," but there was no way I could believe that.

At one point, I had told Manuel about the people I used to know. I told him of my fear that I would be found, and that it was that fear which had kept me running and using false names. I had told him my fear that now I was with him, using my name, and with our names on a register out there in the world, with a normal life, that it would get us both killed. I remember him bravely telling me that he would protect me.

I believe in my heart that is what happened, but there is no accurate evidence to prove such a thing. Not anymore. He died on November 11, 1998.

*   *   *

The horn of Manuel's car sounded behind me in the rain. I had just stormed out of the car, and now he was trying to get my attention to stop me from stomping off.

I spun on him, and yelled back, "What?"

He got out of the car, gesturing wildly, "Man do I love you in the worst way! But what just happened?"

"What?" I asked.

"I said, 'I love you!'"

"Then why the fuck are you yelling at me?"

"Because you make it so hard for anyone to get close to you! What just happened back there?"

"I'm sorry, Manuel. I can't. It hurts too much!"

"Everything hurts. But we're everything to each other, and that is worth the risk of talking to me. You said you were a risk-taker!"

"No, not this one. I just can't."

There we stood in the rain at the empty parking lot of Chi Chi's Restaurant. We had been in the car only a few minutes ago when I had started talking about my past. I had seen his face twitch. I had lost my cool and demanded that he stop the car or I would literally jump out. He had tried to hold me off, but when I clawed at the handle to the door, he had pulled into the empty parking lot and I had gotten out of the car.

"Why are you doing this?" he asked.

"What? What am I doing?"

"Why are you walking away? Did I hit a nerve?"

"I saw you flinch when I told you about what happened when I got here in Pittsburgh. You pulled back! You never pull back!"

"Dammit, Song. It hurts me when I hear the abuse you've gone through, okay? I don't like hearing about you getting hurt!"

"Do you think I liked it when it happened to me? I didn't ask for abusive parents but damn it, I got 'em! I didn't ask to be a prostitute, but it was my only way for survival. So, here I am, nothing but damaged goods. Why do you want to help me?"

"Did you need money?" he asked.

"Money? What are you talking about?"

"Back then. The prostitution. Did you do it for money?"

"No! I was forced into it. They took me off the streets, cut up my ID, and shoved me in a cell. Everything that I was, was taken from me."

"What happened? Did you tell the police?"

"Ugh! Quit asking me questions! Shut up! Shut up! I can't do this right now. I can't explain to you what happened!" I heaved myself down to sit near the curb of the parking lot and just cried.

He walked over to me and crouched down to my level. He said nothing. He listened to me. He always listened to me. I loved him so much.

"I'm tired, Manuel. I'm tired of explaining, I just want this to be over. I want to die! I can't take this anymore!" I cried in my arms.

"Don't say that! I can't let you do that. I want you here with me too much to let you go. Get angry. Get your life back! If you continue to live your life this way, then you give them more power."

"I didn't choose this life!"

"Whether you were forced into the circumstances or not, you still choose the outcome. Get angry and fight back!" He wrapped his arms around me and held me.

"I don't know how! I want to but I don't know how..."

"Then let me help you."

"No! I can't let you help me. You have no idea what I am up against. Once I tell you, you will run away from me."

"Do you see me running now?" He lifted my head so our eyes could make contact. I saw the water dripping from the ends of his hair as the rain came pouring down.

"I love you, Song. I really do and it hurts like hell. You can't tell me you don't feel the same."

"I love you, too Manuel. I love you, too." I cried into his arms, closing my eyes against the rain.

*   *   *

When I opened my eyes again, the rain was just the pitter-patter on the hospital window. I had been pulled out of the car and had been fixed up. Again.

I tried to sleep. I kept having dreams and reminiscing of Manuel smiling at me and laughing with me, and our times together. I woke up a few too many times screaming, and I was admitted to a residential psychiatric facility where I would learn to cope with loss. Without health insurance, my stay wasn't guaranteed. As soon as a paying customer came along, the goodwill ended and I was back on the street.

There were moments I felt like I couldn't go on living, my heart felt so heavy. I couldn't sleep anymore. In January 1999, my depression got the best of me once again. I grabbed a kitchen knife and headed towards the woods to try again. I found the very place where Manuel and I would sit and listen to love songs as we held each other all through the night. I wrote on a legal pad my name, social security number, and my family's contact number. I was definitely sure that I would die that night. I brought along a blanket and fell to my knees with tears streaming down my face.

Prayer seemed right, even though it had been so long since I had really believed. "Dear Lord, I know you and I haven't been on talking terms and I'm sorry that I've been away from Your presence. I am in so much pain and the love of my life is gone. I want so much to be with him right now. I am asking you to let me die tonight so my spirit could

184

be joined with his. Please? I'm sorry. I just don't want to live anymore."
I laid back on the blanket and raised the knife in the air. Then, I felt
something cold touch my wrist. I opened my eyes.

Manuel was sitting next to me on his knees.

"Don't do it! You'll regret it!" He warned.

"Manuel? Is that you?" I asked.

"You're going to have our baby." He smiled and reached down to
place both hands on my stomach. I felt an unusual warm feeling over
my stomach.

"What are you talking about? I'm not pregnant." I rubbed at my eyes
and struggled to a sitting position. He disappeared and it was as if
nothing had happened. I was in awe of this strange, surreal moment as
I surfaced from a very dark place in which I *knew* I was going to die, yet,
I did not. I felt unsure, strange, and with the hint of being reborn.

The next day, I couldn't resist any longer. I went down to the ER
and asked for the tests. I was told that I would be a mother and I
immediately fell to the floor in shock.

When I woke up, the nurse was caressing my face. "Hello," she
greeted me with a smile. The light was extremely bright and I thought I
was in heaven for a moment. "You gave us quite a fright."

"Where am I?" I asked.

"You're still here at the emergency room. Do you remember coming
in? You'll be okay. You just fainted. I think it was the anxiety."

"The doctor said I'm pregnant. That's not true, is it?" I asked.

The nurse smiled and nodded, "Yes."

I couldn't believe the news. Was I really visited by a ghost? Could
this really happen to people? I would hear about people being visited by
spirits or ghosts on TV, but never did I imagine it could be me.

I laid there thinking about the idea of carrying Manuel's child but it
didn't come with immediate excitement. Look at what had happened to
me without him! Could I be a mother without him by my side? Did I
have the strength? I hadn't had a chance to deal with the grief I felt from
losing him, and now I was going to be a mother.

I called Manuel's mother and notified her of my pregnancy. She
stated to me quite directly and harshly that she didn't want to have
anything to do with me or the unborn child. She made it clear that I was
no longer welcome in their lives. I wasn't even sure I still had that job
after my life fell apart. I suspected I had long ago been fired. I hadn't
even been in to check my schedule in weeks.

So, I did the only thing I could. I called my family again.

Why did he pick up? Why did my father take my call this time? Maybe he was like me. Maybe, sometimes, the hurt finally passes, and the blood that runs in our veins proves stronger. His anger was still there. It was not gone. When I told him I was pregnant, he paused.

Then, he told me to come home.

His anger was not gone. He immediately said that I would have to come up with the funds to get home. But, he said to come home.

CHAPTER 11

MOTHER, MOTHER, MOTHER

Returning home was not as difficult financially as I had feared. Despite my falling out with Manuel's family, I had a good connection with the downtown church which had led me to his family in the first place. Pleading with them to help me reunite with my family, they agreed with my values and were all too happy to put a family back together, especially with a child in the situation.

With their funding and my memories of my old home intact, I returned home in March of 1999, just as my youngest sister was turning 13. She was excited to see me. We were practically strangers, considering how often I had been away in the first years of her life. My other sisters were a little chillier to me, and I knew the interactions with my parents were going to be awkward to start. Despite those issues, I felt this was the smart play. I knew I could receive prenatal care and a roof over my head while I got my life back together.

My time at home wasn't exactly free. As I mentioned before, being around my family took effort. Things were mild compared to my teenage years. Although I hadn't exactly succeeded in building a life for myself, I had been through enough hardship for at least ten other people my age. It showed behind my eyes, and I was now facing my mother as an adult. I could stand up to her now, but that didn't stop her from showing me her resentment. Every time she looked at me, she would shake her head in disappointment. She wouldn't believe half of what I told her, and I didn't even tell her half of what I had been through.

I gave a lot more to my youngest sister. She hung on my every word, and it was impossible not to be drawn in by her enthusiasm. I told her about the romantic stories of the few good-natured boys and men I had met. At one point, our conversation turned to spirits and faith. I had just shared with her that I had found out I was pregnant in Pittsburgh, and she had asked for more details. Instead of holding back, I told her about my final attempt at suicide, how I saw Manuel come to me, touched me with his cool touch, and said I was carrying our child. I recalled how he placed his hands on my stomach, only then did I feel warm. My sister was struck with awe but didn't call me a liar. I knew I had seen him, and she believed me. I loved her for that. She believed me so completely that she would literally pray to be visited by Manuel as well so she could meet my baby's father. I thought it was cute, but didn't speak of it again, knowing my mother wouldn't approve.

In May of 1999, I had a sonogram done and I brought my youngest sister to share in seeing the life growing inside of me. When the nurse asked me if I wanted to know the sex of the baby, I said "Yes." My sister was brimming with excitement. I had sort of felt like I was going to have another girl, and so was shocked when the nurse mentioned the word "penis" as she pointed out different features on the sonogram. My sister dropped her books and giggled outrageously at the word she wasn't allowed to hear, and I had nothing but chills running up my spine. Was Manuel right?

This was going to be the first boy born to our family in two generations. In the Korean tradition, as taught to me by my father, boys were considered a privilege while girls were more of a burden. I had hopes that my bringing a son into the family would earn me a different respect and love from my parents.

That was not to be. I slowly began to understand what my parents' actual intent was. I was merely the vessel to bring forth this child who they could then honor. Every arrangement for the child was made by them. My mother planned a baby shower for me, and her Korean friends from church brought baby gifts. I say they were *her* friends on purpose. I wanted to plan my own baby shower with whatever close friends I had managed to reconnect with since my return, but my parents forbade it. Their control continued to mount. I felt constricted and began to chafe at their control. My mother had no sympathy at all. She simply stated that if I didn't agree with the rules, then I could move out. She made it clear they would fight me for custody of my baby. I didn't know if they could succeed, but as they were established and I would be drifting and homeless, the threat felt very real. After being independent for so long, I was not used to the many restrictions and rules, but the fear of my mother's threats was all-too-familiar.

The summer of my pregnancy was a trying time. The humidity swelled and the temperature often soared above 100-degrees. I had landed a job in early May as a consultant for DirectTV, which was difficult as I continued to work with my ever-increasing belly. I didn't dare stop because I needed to get some money together so I could move out. Struggling through it, I managed to put together enough cash to consider getting my own place. That caused another dilemma. My parents gave me rides to work, but there was no way they would loan me the car to hunt for a new place to live. I had to do this discreetly. In the end, I made little progress and knew it would have to wait until after my son was born.

My delivery date arrived and I underwent a Caesarean-section in August of 1999. The operation was a success, and he was brought him to me soon after. I couldn't believe he was mine to keep. He was so tiny and I instantly loved him with all my heart. I named him Andrew, though his nickname almost immediately became Drew. He was mine, and mine alone.

Soon, I took him home and started to make him a part of my life. Our life. My parents loved Drew despite their often strange and twisted ways of showing it. My sisters doted on him a little, but my youngest sister adored him. He did not lack attention, and I could go back to work and have him looked after during the day.

My father took to Drew instantly. Small things meant so much to me. For example, one morning I woke up to find the crib next to my bed empty. I had my son there so that I could watch over him and hear him if he stirred during the night. Now, he was gone. I immediately panicked and darted through the house looking for him. When I peeked in my parents' room, I saw my dad holding Drew in his arms. My heart melted. Right then, I wished there was a photo of me and my dad that looked like that. I always knew my father wanted a boy. I had heard him say often enough, "Why do I always have daughters?" Many times, in the past, I had felt I had failed having just existed. I wanted so much to hear him say he was proud or at least happy when I was born, even though I feared he would still say he was disappointed.

He did spend time with us when he could. My father was the type that loved to lecture my sisters and me. He would go on for some time about the ancient times of Korea, the philosophy of old Christian religious quotes mixed with Buddhism quotes. He was a very interesting man, but he was a workaholic. When he had days off, he spent them at my aunt's house drinking, gambling, or staying up all hours of the night watching K-Drama. With my son, it was truly an effort of love. He made time for my son whenever possible, and there was no doubt he was a proud grandfather. At times, I suspected he was almost too proud, and wanted to eliminate me from the process so that he could directly parent my son.

After my initial six to eight weeks of healing from the C-section, the loss of Manuel got the best of me. I didn't know how to cope, living with my family I still felt isolated in the loss. I slowly crept back into the life of narcotics. I wanted anything to numb what I was feeling. I was not a responsible parent at the time. My mother would page me to come home, yet I would be laid out in someone else's bed high. I didn't come home for days or even weeks. This angered my parents, especially my father, and it only proved my reckless behavior. I never shared with my family what I was doing. Since my parents weren't familiar with narcotics or the physical symptoms of an addict, they just assumed I was out with various men. I was amazed by the fact that I had turned into a *"functioning"* addict. I would get high every night and still made it into work by morning. Meth and crack were added to my selection of narcotics to play with. My drug habits weren't as frequent as they used to be. When I was at home, I didn't use nor did I abuse my parents' home at all.

With some money to work with, I could start thinking about my plans to move out. I didn't want to do anything terrible to my parents. They really did love my son, and I only wanted to be treated as an adult. I could have lived with them if they had only made some small effort. I felt justified in my effort and did not see my drug abuse an issue. I was in denial, assuming I could handle being a single parent. At that time, I had assumed being with my son would coat the pain I was feeling of losing Manuel. Except, I didn't know how to parent. I was young and determined to view my son as a possession rather than me giving him guidance and protection. I continued with my plan to move out. I gave them a chance. I tried consulting with my father about me moving out and not cramping my parents' home, but my father refused to hear me out. He refused to even consider the idea that I could manage on my own.

His instant rejection brought the argument out into the open. I started to yell, "Why can't I move out? This is stupid! I'm 23 years old and I can't move out?"

"What's wrong with staying here? You don't have to pay rent. You can work and get free babysitting." He insisted, but in his tone, I just heard what he left unsaid. He was implying that I needed the help because I couldn't make it without it.

He made it sound so tempting but left out the strict control they were clamping down on me. When I could go and where. What friends I could see. How I chose to raise my child. They wanted a say in all of it. Worse, they wanted *all* the say in it. I knew that in their minds, that suited proper tradition. I should bend to their wishes, especially given that this was the only boy of the family. To them, he was far too important to leave to me, the failed child. I needed to have my own space. I attempted to argue my case, "I am not going to move far away. I just want my own place!"

"Do you expect us to come to you to babysit? That makes no sense. No, Song Ja."

I tested the limits, knowing what he would say, "Can I bring my friends over when I want?"

He scoffed, "No."

"I assume I can't date, then."

"You have a child to look after. You have to work, then come home, and care for your child," said my father in a commanding tone. My father was old-fashioned that way. In his eyes, a parent devoted his or her life to the betterment of the child. Social life and frivolity and fun were simply time away from that task.

"You gave me a curfew! I have to be home at a specific time, and mother said she didn't want me taking the baby anywhere with me."

"Of course, not. It isn't safe. Your mother can care for the baby when you are out, and we don't have to worry about you getting him into any trouble."

I knew what he actually meant and I exploded, "Control! Too much control! It's not right!"

"You're a mother now. Why do you need such a wild life? You don't need friends or men in your life!" He exclaimed. "In this house, you are expected to stay home and take care of your son. Nothing else matters!"

"Drew's my son, and it's my life!"

"You need your mother's help. You need *all* our help."

"I don't want her help in every part of my life! I want my independence. I can do this! I can be a single mom and take care of my own son! If mom wants to help that's fine, but I don't want to stay here forever."

He slapped me. I blinked, my cheek stinging from the impact. I was shocked. It didn't even hurt all that much, but that sting went right to my heart. The slap was dismissive. He was mad because I dared to defy him. He wasn't even listening to me.

His words followed right on his slap, and they stung just as much, "Don't you dare talk back to me! I am your father. Did I not teach you to never take such a tone with your parents?" He huffed, and shook his head, "You have forgotten all we have done for you, all we do for you now, and I will not have it."

He closed the door on further conversation, and I knew I had to leave. I know some people might think I was being petty to rebel against those rules, but this was beyond just wanting to set my own hours. It started there, but I knew it would only get worse with time. Every decision on how to raise my son would become theirs. I was fighting against this household that gave me constant triggers for my flashbacks, and I was doing it because it was helping me get back on my feet. If I had no hope of ever breaking free when the time came, then the hope and reason for being there ceased to exist. I couldn't breathe while I was there, and now I couldn't breathe because of how angry I was.

I knew this was a form of abuse. It was pressure. It wasn't just the slap. They were trying to destroy my self-worth and self-esteem, and take my child away. They were trying to convince me of how impotent and terrible I really was. Emotional abuse is not something you can wash away, and they had picked up where they had left off in my teenage years and were now doing it in a different way. For some reason, families always find lenience in the courts and in the arena of public opinion, but the abuse in a family can cut far deeper than from a stranger. It gets inside, digs in deep, and can never be removed.

I went to my room and began to cry. I felt suffocated and alone. My only outlet to the outside world became the World Wide Web. I was careful after my experiences with telephone dating, but that is not what I decided to pin my hopes on. I didn't look for a faceless man to shack up with. I hoped that was far behind me. Instead, I sought out real organizations. The Church had helped me before, and I knew what power organizations with a purpose could wield.

I expanded my search as far as I could to develop a plan for my escape and the life that would follow. I had my son to care about, and I had no intention to let myself fail again. I consulted online advocates about family abuse and felt some peace to know that my feelings weren't different from other abuse survivors and victims. By early February of 2000, I found a faith-based community that was willing to rent out an apartment to me in Dallas.

One Sunday morning, I told my parents that I wasn't going to church. I did my best to look pathetic and lonely and kept my son with me to snuggle and feel better. They drove off, not all that concerned considering I had not been making any noise about trying to leave for weeks. As soon as they were gone, I called my church friends and asked them to come get me. They came with a car big enough to load everything that I owned and my baby's items, and I ran off to Dallas.

I moved into a one-bedroom apartment with my son and made a new home for myself. The quiet evenings began to haunt me as my narcotic withdrawals began to surface again. I couldn't prove my parents right, I had to do something. One evening, I failed. I had left my infant son in his room alone, while I went out to get high. When I got home, I began to hate myself for what I had done. I watched my baby lying there, trusting me to protect him and to be there whenever he needed me, yet I had failed.

On February 22, 2000, I came upon a lake. My son was with my parents at that time. I figured while my son was safe and away from me, I would do one more hit and kill myself. The pain of losing Manuel was deeper than I had imagined and I had given up. I just wanted to die. I gave up all hope and played the pity party game as I sat in my car near the lake. In that moment of solace, I heard a song on the car radio, "*That's the Way It Is,*" sung by Celine Dion.

When the lyrics said, "*I can read your mind and I know your story, I see what you're going through. It's an uphill climb and I'm feeling sorry, but I know it will come to you. Don't surrender 'cause you can win in this thing called love.*" Was God reminding me that I was not alone? I could overcome all of this? My eyes just poured like a waterfall. It was the message I needed to hear.

Thoughts came over me of "standing up and dusting myself off." I kept reminding myself what Manuel had said to me. "In order to defeat your oppressors, create a success they cannot imagine." He was right! That day, I threw the drugs in the water and never looked back. I drove to my parents' home and saw my son standing in his crib cooing at me with a huge grin. I held him in my arms and cried out, "Mommy is so sorry!"

My new relationship with my family began to improve. With my sober freedom established, I started to rebuild my life. Along with the apartment, the organization that had been helping me also helped me find a job with enough pay to allow me to afford child care. It was a data entry position and was both solid and regular. I felt like I was truly established. The job I had was through a staffing agency and it was a temp job, so when I was laid off in the early summer, I once again began to look for work.

My job search stretched to three months and I received a notice on my door for possible eviction. This couldn't be happening! I was afraid to ask my parents for assistance as I knew they would mock me for my lack of responsibilities, so I asked the church. When I was denied, I tried other outreach services but to no avail and was unable to receive any rental assistance.

In a desperate attempt to keep my home, I swallowed my pride and dug through the yellow pages once more. Just seeing the label *"Escort Service"* gave me a cold chill, as I hadn't visited this industry in close to two years. I began calling and asking for employment, of course, they were always hiring "Asia" women. I called a friend to come and babysit for me while I went to find work. This time my plan was to go through it once to make enough to cover the upfront cost to avoid eviction.

What I'm about to share with you is going to sound completely odd, but it is my testament. I received a call from the Madame on the phone that a man was requesting an *"Asian"* woman; just hearing that brought nausea upon me. When I arrived at the gentleman's home, I was surprised to see an attractive, young man. He appeared to be in his 20's. When I walked in, he denied me immediately. Typically, a customer can deny a woman simply due to her physical appearance, hair color, not his type, etc. So, I called the Madame and informed her that I had been denied and she told me to keep my pager on for other customers. After hanging up the phone, the guy touched my hand and I immediately jerked my arm away.

"I don't think so!" I scolded.

"God told me to talk to you." He explained.

"You're nuts!" I said as I was making my way to the door.

"God told me you have a son."

I stopped as my heart recognized the painful feeling of truth, but how could it be?

"How do you know? Who are you? Are you following me?" I lunged towards him like a protective mother bear. His expression changed to fear as he did not want me to hurt him.

"God knows you're hurting. He knows you need money for rent and he doesn't want you to do this. You don't have to do this anymore." He continued.

"Why are you doing this?" I began to cry, there was no other emotion, but to cry. Was this even real? He stepped forward towards me and took me by the hand, turned my palm face up and inserted over a thousand dollars in my hand. When I looked at my hand, tears fell like a waterfall once again.

"He knows you are hurting and He wants you to know you are not alone. He does not want you to come back to this life, or otherwise, He can't promise He'll save you the next time." He stated softly as he closed my fist that held the money. "I called a cab for you and it is here," I remember being stunned and as I walked out to the cab, I looked into my hand to see if it had all been a dream. Sure enough! The money was still there. I asked the driver to wait and I ran up the steps and knocked at the door. An older gentleman answered and I asked him about his son. The man had no idea who I was talking about and explained to me that he lived alone. I looked back at my palm and the money was still there. That was the last time I ever opened the Yellow Pages for an escort service.

My life continued with a new job prospect. I was also dating and everything in my life was fine. I was happy and living life again. I had met a new guy who had stolen my heart. I wanted to spend my life with him until one evening, I received a call from an anonymous source.

"Hello?" I answered.

"You need to leave and take your baby with you. Kat knows you are back in Dallas, and they are going to come after you."

"How does Kat know I'm back? I haven't told anyone!"

"Your friend told her."

"Who is this?"

"I have to go, but leave now!" I heard a click shortly after. Part of me wanted to believe this was nothing but a prank call, but she knew "Kat." She knew I had a son. This was a specific warning, and I felt in my gut it was real.

I had not fled from a place in a while, but I hadn't forgotten how. The only difference this time was that I had to take a bag for my baby as well.

I went to Mark's place to stay. He was my boyfriend at the time. I felt a little secure in staying with him for a couple of days. I needed a plan. The only downfall in this circumstance was that my relationship with Mark was going to end abruptly, and without him knowing. I couldn't risk telling him anything.

I had met Mark through work, and we had been dating for a good three to six months. I feelings for him were starting to grow, but I had been far more cautious than I had been with Manuel. He didn't have the same background of abuse, and I had no idea if he could deal with it. As such, he had no clue about my past and I couldn't just yet bring myself to tell him anything.

After staying with him a few nights to strengthen my plan of relocation, I was ready. Mark was totally unaware of my scheme. It was hard, but I just couldn't tell him. I couldn't bring myself to risk his getting hurt. After losing Manuel, I wanted Mark to still have a life even if it meant without me. Every ounce of affection, every kiss, and every time he held me in his arms made it hard for me to pretend everything was the same.

I would need his help. I needed a ride to the train station. He would wonder why, so I made up a story about visiting a friend in New York. One lie compounded on another, but I kept him in the dark.

That evening, he held me in his arms and our fingers intertwined. "Song?" he softly called my name, assuming I was asleep.

I wasn't, my mind racing with thoughts of my plan. "Yes?"

"I'm falling in love with you."

I didn't know what to say after hearing that. I just squeezed his fingers with mine and scooted closer to him. My tears began to fall as I knew this would break his heart. We later heard Drew whining in the next room. Mark had the door open so we could hear him. Drew was about 10 months old, but not quite sleeping through the night. Mark got up and held him in his arms as if he was his very own. He talked to him and cooed at him. I started to melt.

Then, "Jules" erupted in my conscious. "You're not going to tell him. You can't. Remember Manuel? Even if you start to love him, they might kill him for being near you."

"I can't do this to him. It'll hurt him."

"You'll hurt him even more if they know you were with him. It is safer this way. You can't afford to be with him right now." The inner me backed off because I knew "Jules" was right. I sat there watching, my heart aching, yet I continued with my escape plan.

Using the local library to find resources on the internet, I found an organization called "Escaping Prostitution." They had a 1-800 number for me to call, and I followed through on that. A female advocate told me that I could find help, but that it would move fast given my circumstances. I had to make a quick decision, and I was going to have to leave everything behind. I had no time to notify anyone. It was almost as if I was in a witness protection program.

I needed to clear my stuff out. I asked Mark to let me visit my apartment. We drove up and went in. When I saw that the door was unlocked, I snuck in carefully. Papers were scattered everywhere as if someone was looking for something.

I didn't realize Mark had followed me in. "Song, what happened to your place?" he asked in shock.

In the pit of my stomach, I felt it had to be *them* rummaging through my stuff. I had no idea what they were looking for. I guessed they were trying to find some trace of where I had gone. If that was the case, then I was glad I found resources at the public library rather than my home. Nothing had been stolen. The large TV was still on the stand; the computer and everything was still in its place. It was just papers and things that were dumped out of the drawers in both rooms. I turned to look at Mark, and said, "Please, go back. The baby is in the car." With a look of apology, he ran back to the car. I unplugged the computer and the printer and brought it out with me.

"Song, what was that?" he asked.

"I'm rearranging some things," I explained as I turned around and looked at Drew. He smiled back at me. I put the computer and printer in Mark's trunk.

I got back into the car and we drove back to Mark's place.

"What's going on?" he asked.

"Nothing. I had some things to work on."

"Your place is a mess. We need to go back and clean it. I'll help you," he insisted.

"No!" I yelled, a little too hard. Mark became more concerned.

I had to calm down or he would know something was up. "Everything is fine. I'm going to New York to visit a friend. There might be an opportunity to do big things for me out there. I was just going through some papers that she needed, but I couldn't find them right away. Then I got caught up being at your place, so I left it for later. It's no big deal."

Drew and I were scheduled to leave that evening, so I got Mark to drive us downtown. We sat and waited for the train. Mark was under the impression that I was only going to be gone for a week.

"What do you want me to do with the computer?" he asked.

"You can keep it. It's yours," I said without hesitation. I could tell from his demeanor he was shocked. I didn't really catch on as to why that was surprising. Items never bothered me, no matter the value or cost. I was used to giving free expensive gifts without ulterior motives, but that was just me. With the announcement of the train's arrival, we held each other one last time, all three of us. Drew smiled up and said, "Bye" for the first time. We looked at each other like proud parents, but this ending was piercing my heart. The train arrived and Drew and I boarded. I saw Mark waving at me and smiling. Once the train moved on, I cried uncontrollably in my seat while Drew was asleep in my lap.

Mark was a good man, and I didn't want to hurt him. The decision was painful for me and extremely difficult. When it came down to it, the safety of my son was all that mattered.

I moved to Minnesota. I was placed in a battered women's shelter for safety. I got ahold of my friend through the church, and she confirmed that my apartment had been torn apart. I thought for sure they would be searching after me every way they could, so I didn't call anyone else.

Finally, after a month, I knew I had to call Mark. I needed to explain, and I needed to know he was all right. I had a small fear that the traffickers had found him as well and questioned him. I called with some nervousness.

"Hello?" a voice answered.

"Mark, it's me. Song."

"Song, where are you? You haven't called. You said you'd be back in a week. When I didn't hear from you, I was worried."

"Mark, I'm not coming back. I'm not in New York."

"What? I don't understand!"

"I'm sorry, but it's over."

"Why? What did I do? Tell me and I'll change. Did I hurt you?" He was demanding answers that I couldn't give him.

"I'm sorry, but something has come up and I don't know how to explain this to you."

"Where are you at? I'll come get you."

"I'm... in Minnesota." I shouldn't have told him, but I did. "Jules" hissed at me in the corners of my mind not to give him reason to come looking, or know anything that he might be able to give away.

"Why are you there? Where are you staying?"

I was even more vague as I listened to "Jules." "I'm staying with some friends and I think it's best that we just go our separate ways."

"What? Wait, what? I thought we had something! I don't know what the problem is, but can't we at least try and work it out?" Without breath, he continued to ramble on and on, trying to say the right thing to get me to open to him.

I just couldn't tell him about my past. I felt I was already in too deep and I knew my heart would always wonder about him. I was fond of him, but that wasn't enough to overcome my fear and suspicion. My vulnerability got the best of me, and I began to have doubts of this escape. I wanted to be close to him, but then I had to think of my son.

Listening to him ramble as he tried to figure out what was going on reminded me of the time James had shut me out without a reason. I knew his reason was not the same. I had to find a way to ease the hurt on my end.

"Mark, I cheated on you, that is why this can't work." I lied. I had hoped with this statement he would let me go.

"Fuck you! Song! Fuck you!" He cried angrily. I knew for sure he would let me go.

"I'm sorry, it is my fault." As I was about to hang up.

"Damn it Song! You owe me an explanation. What did I do? I'll change, whatever it takes to make it work." Why was he still hanging on?

"I have to go."

"I hate you Song," he began to sob on the phone. "I love you so much and I told you I didn't want to fall in love again." He had said that. I recalled him saying he had been betrayed by a lover once before. That only made this worse.

"I'm sorry, I have to go now. Bye." I knew I was driving a knife into his heart. It didn't matter. I had already decided.

"Song!" he screamed out on the phone.

I hung up, unable to hear any more. I sank to the ground with the cordless phone still in my hands and cried on the floor.

I had my own life, but this wasn't how I had wanted it to start. I wanted to know when Vegas and all I had been through there would finally stop haunting me.

CHAPTER 12

SHATTERED VESSEL

After years of suffering abuse and trying simply to avoid it, I had reached somewhat of a crossroad. When you have been crushed for so many years, how easy would it be to surrender and end up in a mental institution? I had come closer to even worse, such as my very close brush with suicide. Then, came the fantasies of revenge. The concept of revenge had long been my ally and misery, both wanting it and fearing it at the same time. I have gone through the checklist in my mind of the people with whom I would want to even the score, and to think of all the ways I could be most harmful to their lives.

I have learned the hard way that revenge truly does not equal justice, nor does it bring any real peace of mind. If all my fantasies were to come true, what would that leave me? Would I then be just a used-up husk, with all my energy expended to see others destroyed, only to find that I had nothing left within me? That was my fear. As my journey through survival continued, I recognized the revolving door of emotional pain. I didn't want this pain anymore. I finally got sick and tired of being sick and tired. An adage I learned from NA. Being in Minnesota gave me new hope, new insight, and a new life.

I had never resided in the Midwest, and the change was tangible. I felt full of potential again. Even the weight of the air felt different. With heady optimism, I became a "client" of a nonprofit organization who advertised a philosophy of rescuing and rehabilitating women who had lived a lifestyle of prostitution. I was not scared, but rather excited to be a part of the program. I wanted to share my story and be a part of the fight against exploitation even as I tried to heal the wounds from my own experiences.

Once again, I was to be vastly disappointed. The positive impression given by the organization on the surface soon began to show cracks.

I was living in their housing quarters at the time. The first indication that all was not right were the discrepancies between their own standards and the actual conditions of the housing. No one seemed particularly eager to fix any issues. Most of the occupants were underage women, and as an adult, I felt somewhat responsible to act on their behalf. This was not always easy. The staff refused to categorize me as an adult, generally lumping me in with younger girls. I was never able to fully integrate with the younger girls nor with the more senior staff.

I was beginning to feel confused and a little isolated. I had truly thought that a worthy program like this would be immune to typical system abuses, but I was proven wrong. I approached the executive director of the facility on more than one occasion to discuss the issues. I was not only ignored but told to keep silent and to even pretend to be younger than I was for funding purposes. I felt like I was being pimped again, but this time by the very institution that was recognized to rescue and rehabilitate me.

Shortly afterwards, there was a visit from the program founders. Now I was really confused. Would they not see the terrible conditions? Shouldn't the executive director care about the issues I had pointed out which would certainly raise the anger of the people who had founded this charitable organization? The visit came and they left without comment. There was a general feeling of satisfaction in the group if I had to describe their reaction. They were financial backers, and to them, it remained an investment that was not losing money and earning them charitable tax breaks. They were blind to anything else. After that, I was completely ignored, and the executive director would no longer accept my calls or visits.

The problems continued to intensify. I suspect they were always there, but I began to really notice them. Women who had come to escape the life of prostitution were continuing it under that roof. Using the cheap housing as a base, they brought johns back to the quarters. The girls would often discuss better business practices for their sales rather than discussing how to escape the lifestyle altogether. Despite the house rules against drugs and alcohol, the other girls would return high or intoxicated on a regular basis without chastisement or attempts at counseling.

I was by no means fully healed, and was still fighting my own addictions. I had hoped to find an environment of safety, and instead was living in a world of temptation. Perhaps still naive, I again tried to discuss this with the executive director as well as my personal case manager. On the few occasions, I got through to either of them, they would simply encourage me to take it up with the director, both passing the blame and responsibility further up the chain of command. Of course, the director was never present. Knowing I would get no support, I saw there was a contact listed around the house for a sort of ombudsman who could take complaints should they arise. The help line promised confidentiality from an outside agent.

I made the connection and sent in the issues I had noticed. Within a short span of time, a letter was returned to the directing team for the house. The letter stated that I was using narcotics on the premises and that I was using my residence as a prostitution hideaway. The very same complaints I had sought to be corrected were being cast back at me as accusations!

I was devastated. I was trying to help, and instead was being attacked. It made no sense to me. I contacted a legal service with a Human Rights division. Their first question was to ask which charity was I referring to. Upon hearing of them, they refused to assist me any further. That stunned me to think of the chain of power and control that had to have been in place. They were either cooperating with each other to keep this systemic abuse in place, or utterly willing to fight against what they perceived was too big of an enemy. Either way, I felt betrayed and without recourse. I was at a loss and had only 30 days left before I would be homeless again. I kept journals and diaries of what I had done there and the circumstances around me, but I was alone. The eviction date came around, and with nowhere else to go, I returned to Texas and to my parents.

Like a moth to a flame, my family drew me back in. Perhaps, the distance away from them dulled the memory of the pain their presence always caused me. I wanted to have a loving home life so very badly. When this new life was spoiled in front of my eyes and I was betrayed by those who should have helped me, my first thought was to return to the safe shelter of home. Most would consider this a normal reaction, for this is where I should have instant acceptance and love.

It did not take long for me to remember why I had left. My mother and I returned to our pattern of arguments almost immediately. Once again, my stature and confidence made any threat of physical violence less likely, but that didn't prevent the blistering condemnation in my mother's eyes and in her words. She would trigger flashbacks in me constantly, and those pummeled me nearly as badly as her actual fists. What hurt most was that I knew they loved Drew intensely and wanted to be a part of my son's life, but I continued to be the daughter they could not accept. I wanted to give them that chance, and yet they betrayed my trust over and over again while under their care.

One day, I was protesting against my mother's control when I saw my son watching us, uncertain and not sure what to do. I had no wish to place him at the center of our confrontation. He was young, and unconditionally loved both of us. I saw it in his eyes, and couldn't be the one that destroyed his view of his grandmother. Not right then. Without thinking much on it, I was overwhelmed and just fled.

I was not sure where I was going to go, but I returned to Dallas and stayed at a friend's place. I didn't stay in Dallas very long. One of the county caseworkers in Minnesota had called my pager to inform me that my case was coming up and the caseworker was not aware that I was not in Minnesota. I wanted to fight that fight. I wanted to craft a reputation for myself that would be one of respect, and for my child to look at me with pride. In that moment, I didn't think I could do that with him beside me. I also knew that my parents could take care of him and forge a real relationship with him, but not as long as I was there. I was the oil to their water and threw gasoline on the fire of my family's life every time I arrived. So, I left Drew in their care while I went back north to Minnesota.

Once there, I joined another program and started to get myself situated. I engaged a new agency for legal support and even found one willing to stand against those who had been taking advantage of the other program and residence. Circumstances were looking more and more positive. Unfortunately, those efforts were only in the initial stages when my life was once more thrown into turmoil. Only a month away from the house, I had a strange feeling that something wasn't right. Maybe it was in my mother's tone of voice, or simply my own instincts as a mother. I dug a little harder and found out my parents had filed guardianship and custody of my son as if I had fully abandoned him.

There was no time to be stricken with shock over this. I had to act fast. At that time, I had less than 48 hours to show up and lay claim to him. Engaging the help of the agency assisting me as well as an advocate in Texas to be with me for my court appearance, I managed to make the trip South.

My family was shocked that I made it to court, and didn't try to hide their disappointment. They spoke about me as negatively and condescendingly as they would have if I had not been there, not softening the blows at all. I felt depression inch its way into my heart. I had no one to speak on my behalf. I did what I could to speak for myself.

The judge heard both sides, and he granted me custody of my son.

Victorious, my feelings were still mixed. I wanted to be a mother for my son, but I didn't want to tear him away from his grandparents. He loved them. I wanted Drew to love them and have them in his life. Sure enough, after I won the case, my parents wanted nothing to do with me. They blamed me for the whole affair and for causing a rift by using the court system to take away their right to be with Drew even though they had started the whole process. That wasn't fair or right, but it didn't matter. They cut me off completely.

Now, I was really on the clock. Returning to Minnesota with my son, I was still living in the battered women's shelter. Most shelters only allowed you to stay for a fixed time, and it took exceptional circumstances to be granted an extension. After that, you needed to look for your own housing. I started to look for another residence, having had no time to gain any sort of grounding while I was fighting for custody of my son.

I found a third such residence, and this one had a longer period of occupancy. I began to build my support network slowly but surely. I sought additional resources for mental health, including finding a doctor who could help with my mental illness and flashbacks.

I was rather taken aback when the program director and his staff produced a letter which demanded I see one of their therapists as part of the program guidelines. I had already found a counselor that I trusted and didn't have a desire to see anyone else. I asked the coordinator if this was necessary. She took this to be a refusal to participate in the program and said my only alternative was to seek housing elsewhere.

I didn't want to cast myself and my son into the streets due to a simple technicality. I was upset that this was yet another shelter for hurting women that seemed more concerned with following draconian laws than actually listening and helping the women who were under its roof. The housing complex was comfortable; however, I decided to try and play at their game. They were not openly ignoring flagrant violations. They kept the residence in good repair. I didn't want to raise any big waves. More disappointed and frustrated rather than truly hurt or angry, I decided to comply with their regulations.

The counselor was a male intern, and I wasn't convinced of his methods right from the start. He didn't work at creating any sort of atmosphere of trust. Right away, he locked onto the part of my file that indicated I was a former prostitute. He pushed to hear my stories of that time, saying it would help to speak the words out loud. I didn't feel comfortable with that and instead tried to get into the issues of my family, my child abuse, the resulting flashbacks and other mental problems I was experiencing. Despite my best efforts, he kept concentrating on my periods of prostitution.

His questions grew more and more unprofessional. At first, he began to ask emotional questions that made little sense, like "Did you ever enjoy any of your calls?" He would seem almost disappointed when I recounted how I had to suffer through them, and disliked when I again shied away. This devolved into his questions on "How much it would cost to have me cum on your face?" and even further into asking what type of man I preferred. When he began to insinuate that I was into him and that those like me never changed, I grew incensed. Furious anger set in when he actually said, "Once a whore, always a whore."

When I tried to leave his office, he cornered me in one of his chairs and assaulted me, fondling me without my consent. Immediately, I sent my complaint to the director whose response was less than encouraging.

She asked with mock concern and much disbelief, "Are you sure he said that?"

It was an old line, and one I had heard so many times. This was the question asked by those who were in power and didn't want to admit there was anything broken. They didn't want their neat world to be mussed and refused to believe anything could be wrong. I called up attorneys in the area and asked questions on my options, and those answers were always the same. I could do nothing without physical evidence. I was appalled. I would have to be raped for them to help me? I was under a physician's care while he probed my most intimate secrets, and he took advantage of me, crossing my physical boundaries. I already felt like I had been violated! Still, they would do nothing.

I knew what would follow. I was living in this residence, and the same thing would happen as had happened before. I was living under their roof, and so they would tolerate none of my rocking of the metaphorical boat. The coordinator ordered me to a meeting and wanted me to sign an affidavit that my previous accusations were false. They wanted to say I was delirious or having hallucinations caused by my previous trauma. If I didn't comply, the results were predictable enough: I would be kicked out.

I was horrified. What could I do? I was trapped between having a place for me and my son to live, and seeking any sort of justice or protection for any other woman who might go into the room with that man! I couldn't do it. I felt for sure I had failed as a mother, but I also couldn't sign that paper or submit to that sort of abuse. So, in the middle of the holiday season, I was evicted along with my son.

I had nothing left to do. I couldn't live with my son on the streets. That wasn't fair to him. I felt beaten down but didn't want to admit defeat. I had nothing else to do, so I went to Child Protection Services. I didn't know where that would lead, but they were supposed to be there to help children in trouble. When I first arrived, they counseled me that because I had voluntarily sought help, this could be resolved without the court system. I was self-identifying that I was in trouble, so they would help me. Once again, I was deceived by the very system I thought was supposed to protect me. After a year-long evaluation from CPS, I found myself in another situation in which I was falsely accused of the said date and time. At the alleged time of my relapse, I just so happened to be in a counseling group. I shared my frustration with my counselors but none offered to testify on my behalf.

I felt so stupid. Almost immediately, even as they led my child away, I knew I was in trouble. I was required to attend several evaluation sessions to ascertain my fitness as a mother. Then, I was brought in front of a judge. There was no help, but only a strict application of two choices which left me aghast. First, to place my son for adoption, which would surrender him forever to another family and I would be unable to regain custody in the foreseeable future. Second, to allow my family full custody of my son and wait two years to attempt to regain custody once again.

It was a terrible choice, yet also an easy one. I could never give up any right to see him again, and despite all of my issues, I knew Drew loved my parents. I could only hope he would be okay under their roof.

Of course, it couldn't be that simple. There was one further sacrifice I would be called upon to make. As part of my interviews, before I had any thought that my parents would be considered as an option, I had told the caseworker for CPS that I had been abused by my parents. To allow Drew into their custody, I had to write a letter stating that all the accusations I made about my parents were untrue. Writing that letter caused me deep pain. It felt like at the time I was turning over the right to ever again tell anyone about it. Dealing with that was central to any healing I could ever do, and now it was being torn away from me. If it wasn't for thinking of my son, I couldn't have done it.

It was extremely hard all the same. I cried so much. I felt as if my life could not succeed or improve. I felt as if my life couldn't get any better. My son departed, and I lost so much hope.

I found a friend who allowed me to stay with him until I was back on my own. His belief in me helped me pull myself together a little bit.

In 2003, I started the process to receive a housing voucher through a program for the disabled, and that allowed me to get my own place in 2004. I moved out on my own and had my own place in 2004.

My son had been with my parents since September 2002. I never stopped thinking about him. There were nights I would dream about him and would hear his laughter or his voice. There were nights I held onto my pillow crying, wondering if I would be able to see him again. Financially, I couldn't afford to travel back and forth to see him. I missed out on his birthdays, holidays, and Christmas, but I tried to keep in touch with him by phone each month. My parents and family made this difficult. I was kept isolated. I wasn't receiving pictures, and neither my parents nor siblings contacted me unless it was about money or custody issues.

The longer this went on, the more my frustration and sadness turned to anger and a rising determination. I knew in my heart that if I gave up believing in myself, I would never see my son again. Only I could salvage my life and return him to my own arms.

With that belief firmly entrenched in my heart, I returned to therapy. It was not easy going. After years of ongoing medication and one-on-one counseling, I was not making any progress. The methods they were trying didn't stop the nightmares or the flashbacks.

One day, I walked into my psychologist's office with a new determination to find a new way forward.

He sat there calmly in his chair, and asked, "Yes, Song how can I help you?"

I stood across his desk, trying to find the right words. Finally, I lost my cool. I had brought all the medications that he had prescribed to me and wanted to discuss. Instead, I took a handful of them, placed them in my mouth and started spitting them at him. I swept my arms and cleared his desk with one wave. "This isn't working!"

Dr. Zeffer didn't budge, nor seem overly surprised by my violent tantrum. He sat there and started to applaud.

Puzzled and half ready to strangle him, I demanded, "Why are you clapping?"

"I have been waiting for you to take control of your therapy."

"You knew this stuff wouldn't work and you gave it to me anyway?"

"No, but I knew you were articulate enough to tell me what would and what wouldn't work when you were finally sure. So far, the feedback you've given me has been to mollify me or placate me. It wasn't really what you felt. You were just being nice. Now, you're telling the truth.

Now, we can really get into depth of what is wrong. So, I'm congratulating you."

I was still confused, but the way he was being patient calmed me immensely. I asked him what could possibly be next if the medications and other techniques had failed.

He suggested an alternative option called Dialectic Behavioral Therapy (DBT) started by Marsha Lanahan. I was intrigued enough to learn more and give it a shot. I attended group once a week, then saw my one-on-one counselor to learn about new coping skills.

This type of therapy was unlike anything I had ever learned or experienced. I loved the outcome. Once I was able to recognize "Jules" as an alter ego, I was able to control her from coming out. I felt empowered into integrating myself as one. This took me years to control, but the skills and steps of DBT definitely helped. When I was diagnosed with Borderline Personality Disassociation, PTSD, and Bipolar Disorder and discovered that the results in successful therapy were slim, I was angry.

I began to reinvent myself. Not everyone believed that I could, nor that I was making any progress. This all took time, and I had retreated from my circle of friends and acquaintances to focus on this effort. I heard several rumors that I had fallen on the wayside and relapsed back into prostitution as I laid low from the public. I began to seek out agencies that I believed in, researched them to ensure they were legitimate, and gained knowledge in the areas of advocacy for former victims like me.

In 2003, I was accepted as a Legal Advocate in training, advocating for crime victims in the area of battered women. When I would appear in court in a three-piece suit, I knew I had changed when I saw the shock on the face of the very judge who once took my son from my arms and made me give him up to my parents. His shock was my vindication, and I was on cloud nine. It felt great to bounce back and to show those who underestimated my strength, resilience, and determination that I could be more and put to rest all of their gossip.

After a few months of working as an advocate, we were instructed to attend a training regarding "Human Trafficking." My first thought was that it was about traffic tickets. I didn't think I was about to get a real education of my own past. The training was at a local university. In one of the rooms, I saw a victim on one end and three women who were known as "experts" on the other end. They had the victim share her story. She was from Russia and had a thick accent as she shared her testimony. As she shared details, flashbacks of the abuse I endured came forward. When she mentioned being bound, I immediately thought about the storage units, and I sympathized with her pain. I began to cry uncontrollably. One of my coworkers looked at me and asked me if I was okay, but I could only wave her off. What could I say?

By the time the initial education was over and we were on to Questions and Answers, one of the students raised her hand and asked if this episode could happen to an American person. When one of the so called "experts" replied, "No, that sort of enterprise doesn't happen here," I knew my moment had come. I had not intended to break my silence, but the level of naivety and lack of understanding by this so-called "expert" was staggering. I couldn't let these other legal experts be misled by that sort of ignorance, not when I knew so many others were still suffering what I had experienced.

I got up and explained myself. "I'm sorry, but I don't agree with you."

The "expert" scoffed, "Who are you? What's your expertise?"

"It happened to me!" I said boldly. Now, everyone was looking at me. I hadn't expected that all their eyes on me, and I began to shut down. My insecurities got the best of me and I was immediately embarrassed, so I quickly left.

A few days later, I had not shown up at work. I was visited by two advocates from the Immigration Office. When they knocked on my door to introduce themselves, I became instantly afraid that they might deport me. My papers and ID had been an ongoing source of uncertainty. Too many times, I had been hurt by a system when I couldn't prove who I was.

Nervously, I asked, "Can I help you?"

One of the officers asked mildly, "We heard you were trafficked and we'd like to talk to you about your case."

"What do you need to know?" I was still standing behind the door, not allowing them to come in.

"We can assist you and you will qualify for a visa," they explained.

My thought immediately went to Visa credit cards. I wondered how much I get for that sort of pain, and why they would give me a card for having been tormented? Since I was raised here in the United States, I didn't understand immigration. Even when I shook the President's hand, I was only eight. My parents never sat down and explained to me about their journey of being naturalized and what a T or U visa meant.

I opened the door, assuming I was being awarded a credit card in exchange for my testimony.

Once we were downtown and got into the interview process, I quickly learned that not only was the visa, not a credit card but that I didn't qualify for the actual visa program they had meant to give me. According to Trafficking Victim Protection Act (TVPA) 1993/2000, visas were only sent to foreign victims. Americans didn't need such things, and as an American, I didn't qualify for any of the benefits. I asked what recourse I had, and the officers said there simply wasn't any. I was an American and was not afforded those benefits that a foreign victim would be granted such as shelter, legal services, social services, etc. American victims, especially minors, were considered "Child Prostitutes." Given that title only further damaged American victims. The victims who were lucky enough to avoid conviction didn't have social programs available to them as there was very little education and resources regarding Domestic Trafficking at that time. I had participated in the few there were in the form of the shelters of which I had resided, and I knew how poor they were.

This lack encouraged me to fight and go to Congress to start a bill for American victims of human sex trafficking. After ongoing research, attending classes, and learning the legislation side of trafficking, I became fully educated about the concepts that lay behind "Human Trafficking" and what it entailed. I befriended an immigration attorney who explained to me how the dark system worked, and that my exposure to it as a slave and then as a Madame were not isolated incidents. In fact, it was far too common and protected by powerful elements of the American society. From that point on, my passion for helping those affected by this phenomenon took full hold of me. I knew it would take years, and I had no idea what form my fight would take, but I vowed to fight for victim rights, either in Congress or in any forum I could.

I had experienced my own share of helplessness when various programs and nonprofits had ignored or taken advantage of me. I started to see other women and children in poverty who were caught in those same snares of bureaucracy and systemic abuse. I saw unyielding procedures being applied with cruel indifference, and the heartless way assistance programs would cast out victims of brutality and abuse into the streets as if they did not follow the program protocols verbatim, even when those protocols did more harm than good. How do you tell a sick woman to get healthy without any resources or referrals? It's like throwing a child in the water filled with sharks and say, "Survive!" I knew there had to be a better way.

I resolved to forge myself into being that missing link. The system had advocates, case workers, psychiatrists, and attorneys, but none of those were designed to give life skills or guidance to the victims. They were intended to process the victims and enforce the rules upon them. In the case of legal advice, they were there to navigate the court system. This did not translate into any type of emotional or spiritual help. They didn't teach life skills. They had timelines to meet and would discard cases after six months without progress.

After ongoing abuse, I found it incredible that a hard six-month window would even be considered. These programs set high expectations for vulnerable people and made goals almost impossible to reach. They would take their charitable campaign documents, file their taxes, and believe good work had been done.

As I began to study and research local philanthropy, I discovered this issue was not so rare after all. There were many organizations that created opportunities to draw clients in, obtained financial backers who could use those organizations as charitable tax shelters, and then disavowed any care or desire to know about problems within those organizations. They were nonprofit outfits, and as long as the books balanced and they remained a deduction on the tax sheet, no one uttered a word.

I decided to do something about it. I resolved to create an organization that was unlike any other. Instead of going through the philanthropic loopholes to gain corporate backing, I based my funding on faith, empowerment, and spirituality. I have been considered naive, ill-advised, and doomed to failure with this approach. However, I knew my intentions were right. I didn't want to just give temporary shelter to victims. I wanted to empower them. I wanted to give them back their lives. I knew this might limit me to being smaller than I otherwise might be able to achieve, but I didn't care. I'd rather be a poor, small nonprofit and empower the people who trusted me without imposing senseless limitations rather than systematically pimp the constituents of a faceless business to my financial backers.

From 2003 through 2006, everything came running at me so fast. My biggest mistake was in thinking I could handle it all smoothly. After the announcement that I was a survivor of Human Trafficking, I found myself on the front cover of local magazines, newspapers, and speaking behind podiums and such. I became a poster child for America to tell my story so that nonprofits could gain funding and profits for my pain. I thought I was gaining experience in the field of charitable organizations to aid in my own efforts to become an actor on that particular stage. This is where I wanted to be, but I felt like I was being used and pushed around to suit the needs of all these other organizations.

I learned that through all this, I could've been compensated. I had no knowledge of "honorarium" and I assumed you had to be a college graduate to even ask for compensation. Little did I realize, I was being re-exploited in a different way. It was a complicated emotion, because I wanted to help and not appear ungrateful for the lessons I was learning on how to present myself, but it was terribly trying and I earned no income for all my effort. Still, I did gain exposure. I began to appear on local news, then to national sectors and East coast local news like CN8 Washington (DC), New York, New Jersey, and Pennsylvania, along with Montel, CNBC and so many more.

The lessons I learned were not taught by anyone: they were lessons I learned through hard experience. No one taught me how to speak, what to share or what not to share. All this came through my own mistakes and surviving them. When I told studios that I didn't want to delve into my family's life, they lied and said I could share but they wouldn't post it. Later, I would learn my story was still being used and even sensationalized for the public. Others would wonder why I hadn't shared more of my story with them and assumed I was holding back for some other purpose.

One evening I received a call from Los Angeles from a screenwriter who was interested in turning my life story into a film. I wasn't sure at first, but after several phone interviews that lasted for hours, he had me convinced this could be of value. Next thing I knew, we were swapping documents back and forth. Events started to happen very quickly.

During that time, came the terrible news that my father fell ill while visiting South Korea. I was frustrated with my family for keeping secrets from me. In 2005-2006, I was juggling the launch of a nonprofit, keeping up with public appearances to share my story, dealing with the film process, and also the worry of my father's illness. In 2006, I learned my father had been diagnosed with stomach cancer and I became very afraid.

One can understand why the focus on my nonprofit was difficult to achieve. I was trying to establish an organization called MAISE (Minorities and Survivors Improving Empowerment). I had little idea about the effort this would entail. I didn't appreciate how this was not just a charity organization, but had to be treated as a business, needed fundraising, strategic planning and most of all, gathering the support of those I could trust. Starting up a business isn't just black and white. I hadn't thought about needing to decide on who funds could be entrusted to, and I realized too late that not everyone could be trusted with them.

I met a fellow survivor, and we instantly became friends. She noticed my determination in developing the nonprofit and offered to financially assist me. My hypervigilance in trusting others made me immune to other survivors, not believing a fellow survivor would deceive me. She had donated $10,000 and I didn't accept her as a donor. Instead, I invited her to be a partner in the charity I had founded. What I was not aware of at the time was that she was still recovering. A few weeks later after a violent tantrum, she demanded her funds back of which had already been spent on the organization. She had been with me and helped me pick out expensive technical equipment. While handling my father's illness and the responsibilities of the organization, it all began to fall apart. I stayed clear of my former friend, hoping she would find recovery.

Somewhat heartbroken at seeing my effort come to nothing, I finally accepted the truth and called it to an end. I closed out the nonprofit and decided to take a couple years off to truly find myself. While I was making my transition to return to Texas to be closer to my father, the screenwriter was still working on the screenplay of my story. Lost in grief and misery over my failed enterprise, it was my mistake to just glance over the script. I just wanted the project to be over with and didn't expect for the producer to distort what had been started.

CHAPTER 13

REFLECTIONS

Anyone who has been through any sort of traumatic experience or addiction recovery knows that the status of "survivor" or "in recovery" is an ongoing process. It is *not* a steady state, and can never really be considered fully complete. It is an ongoing struggle. One of the key lessons I learned in the period following my decision to strive towards the betterment of victim care was that in spite of that, life had to move on. It couldn't just be about surviving, but it had to also be about moving on no matter the ongoing struggles; whether within me or outside chaos. I had to realize I had value, and that I deserved a life of my own despite all I had endured.

Since my return to Dallas, Texas, in 2008; I discovered there was a warrant for my arrest from Minnesota so I was extradited from Texas to Minnesota. I attended my arraignment without knowledge of what my arrest was for. While dealing with my father, as well as my transition and move to Texas; I had completely forgotten about my former business partner. During the arraignment, the prosecutor addressed me as a thief of the $10,000 that was donated to our organization. I was appalled at the accusation and refused to accept a plea deal. I was not guilty and asked my fiancé at the time to financially assist me.

Sometime during 2008 and 2009, my finances dried up as a result of traveling back and forth. I had hired a private attorney to represent me, but then funds completely ran out. Around that same time, I regained custody of my son and he needed me. I couldn't risk losing him again. I plead guilty due to lack of financial backing for my attorney and to return home. It was the most difficult decision I had to make. Since I had a private attorney he made a bargain with the court that I would only serve probation with no time served.

When I finally returned home, my full concentration was on my son, being a mom, and cherishing every moment that I could. Making up for lost years without him was all that mattered to me to me then. Of course, I was angry, and what was ironic was that out of all the manipulative games I had played in the past, along with stolen money and credit cards, I was never indicted for any of that but instead indicted for something I did *not* do.

One of my biggest breakthroughs came when I learned to accept my own imperfection. Indeed, I learned the beauty of seeing the tapestry of my own life as a unique thing which *could* result in much good being done, and only because of the hardships I had first endured and then overcome. It became a challenge for me to stay ahead of those challenges, and not falter in my recovery. After all, to make my mark, I needed to stay clear of falling back into that darker side of life. It became an incentive even as it was a hazard.

In this constant struggle, one truth is that the recovery is never finished. The "Jules" part of me will always be looking to rise to the surface and invoke her style of cruel practicality on my life. Such struggle can never be easy. I had to find a way to appreciate that way of life. I refused to accept all I had been through as mere misery, and this would be one of the greatest lessons I could teach. I wrote this book with hope of inspiring my readers to rise beyond the simple act of surviving. We, as survivors, deserve better than that. We deserve happiness. We deserve respect (including self-respect). We deserve peace in our lives and our hearts.

One of my greatest challenges has been my romantic life. I have told you through this work about my upbringing, including the romantic idealism I held at an early age. This became tarnished during my struggles, but what never changed was an inner desire to have a healthy marriage with a man I could love and respect. I have been asked several times how, after all, I had endured, I could possibly stand to be married to a man. The answer is wrapped up in all that I have already said. This is not just about surviving. It is about living. I still wanted a happy marriage. It was a true desire for me, and that it lay at the core of who I was. I deserved that, and I could not let my past overwhelm that fact.

Before I could ever love another, I first had to learn to love myself. Whether you are gay, bi, transgender, or straight, that is where it all must start. Some people asked me if I had stopped wanting men because of this. That was never the issue. My sexual orientation had not changed: the damage was done to my ability to trust another as intimately as you must trust a partner in marriage. That was the key. I understood that I had to trust myself, believe in my own strength, and be prepared to work at a relationship when the storms invariably came.

I was married in 2008. It wasn't an easy ride and we both had so much to learn. Everyone knows that in a typical marriage, it takes a lot of work, but when you add two damaged people in one mix, it's one hell of a ride. We had to learn about each one of our triggers. We had to learn how to communicate and adjust to what helped us compromise. We knew each other's skeletons from our respective closets and didn't shy away from them. We did our best to find peace and even humor in all of it.

To explain that, I will look back at the moment he proposed to me. My engagement was a poignant portrait of this very struggle, and the way we chose to overcome it. It was after about five months of knowing him that he proposed to me at a Kobie Steakhouse. It was New Year's Eve of 2007, and I asked him while dining on the delicious food if he had any New Year's Eve resolutions. As an answer, he turned to me with an open box and a ring. He wrapped one arm around me and smiled, and said, "To marry you."

What was my reaction? Without hesitation, I replied passionately, "If you ever try to control me, beat me, abuse me or belittle me, I will be that crazy Asian woman that will chase you down the street with a cast iron skillet in my hand. I refuse to be a victim to anyone. I demand a man to respect me, treat me with equality and love me with tenderness, do you understand?"

His response? A smile, and the words, "So, does that mean... Yes?"

Looking back at that scenario, you might laugh and think of me as ridiculous. He knew I was reacting not from a place of love, and not a place of resolve. I needed to say the words. I needed to demand it as part of who I was, not for any fear that he would not give me that respect. I was absolutely serious, and I believed for any relationship to succeed, both people involved must know what you will or will not tolerate. He understood that. In that moment, he knew what I meant, and he didn't dismiss what I was trying to say. He was simply telling me in his own way that I need not worry, he would not fail me. He is a military man and I was his wife. As a result, so he brought his own set of unique trials to the relationship. He included me in decisions and changes required by his military lifestyle, and I chose to walk that life with an open understanding of the circumstances it would entail. He accepted my charity work, and the struggles I would have to go through to make it succeed.

I think he finally truly understood how much this work meant to me when he saw me speak for the first time at a speaking engagement in Davenport, Iowa. It was an emotional experience I never imagined. The event was, "Take Back the Night" in April 2010. Normally, it was an outdoor event rally, but the rain had forced it indoors with a live music band. I was the keynote speaker for the event. Days before, my husband had seen me practice my speech, and I had become rather shy with him watching me standing there. He was so worried that I would flop on stage, but I wouldn't hear anything regarding him not being there. I wanted him to see and hear what I had to say. I wanted to make him proud of me.

When my time in the spotlight came, I didn't succeed in spite of his presence, but rather because of it. I wanted to make him proud, and seeing him sitting out in that audience gave me strength. I spoke with truth and honesty for the awareness of my cause. My emotions as a mother and wife inspired an empowering poem that I wrote and recited. The crowd stood up and cheered. I remember feeling my heart palpitating with excitement and looking out at my husband's face as he smiled. That was the greatest accomplishment of my life.

When anyone asks me how I could be married to a man, this is the story I told. He did not stand between me and happiness. He was one of the reasons for it, one of my pillars of strength, and proof that survivors of such terrible things *can* have what they deserve: a life with the one that they truly love, while being true to themselves.

Now don't get me wrong. I still have my insecure moments and mood swings, but the life I live now is nothing I ever imagined. One of the toughest lessons I realized after three or four years of marriage, was that I had gone from being a victim to a predator. I was not aware that my violent tantrums and fear of betrayal resulted in me being predatory towards my husband. I discovered that in order to develop a healthy relationship, I could not perceive a thought pattern of "I will not allow you to hurt me *again*, so I will remain in control." Meaning, I had assumed my partner would fail me, and instantly I would sabotage the relationship to prevent becoming a victim; unaware I was abusing myself and my husband.

I had to learn to set healthy boundaries even in my marriage. If my husband had upset me or I felt my needs weren't met, instead of assuming failure I would substitute the thought to: "*If you continue to watch a film that causes triggers, I will not be present in the same room. Please respect my request.*" Something to that nature. I also had to take anger management classes, as the triggers and pain never goes away no matter who you are connected to.

Since my marriage in 2008, I have lived a very fulfilling life. My story was made into an independent film, and it was well-received. My story has also been publicized in reputable magazines, and national talk shows. I have had the opportunity to travel all over the world, educate, and share my testimony to over 200 universities, organizations, and law enforcement training.

In 2013, my father passed away after battling stomach cancer for eight years. He wasn't perfect and he had his own faults. Looking back at all the things my father went through from a handsome young man, who was my dad, to a cancer victim. I am so proud of the man he was in my life. He planted seeds of love and open mindedness.

My father taught me so much. He came to the United States to find a better life. The downfall was that he struggled with wanting more, and that was the disease that killed him in the end. He was a gambler and was constantly trying to portray living a lavish life while living a frugal life at home. I love and miss him so much. He was the Asian redneck dad. He collected broke down cars on cement blocks around his seven acres of land, He ate anything he caught in the creek behind our house. He loved Kenny Rogers and Alabama, and he truly enjoyed fishing every summer at Lake Murray in Oklahoma.

After my father's passing, I began to reflect over my life, starting with my earliest childhood memory. I know in reading this, you have heard many horror stories, yet, there is so much more to me than my trauma. In 2016, I began to learn that my mental diagnoses do not define who I am today. They just explain my trauma and how I react to my triggers. For the first time, I no longer refer to my actions as "Jules," "Kim," or "Chong." I have begun to address them as me. I have learned to integrate myself as one person.

I have become more than a statistic. I remember reading an article about people with severe psychological disorder due to trauma who were damaged and less likely to live a normal, happy life. At first, I began to feel hopeless, but something in me said, "NO!" If there was ever any retribution in being *"defiant,"* I believe it was this! My escape route from any trauma growing up was to pretend. I would pretend I was Cinderella when I was commanded to do chores. I would pretend to be in a musical when I had to hang the clothes on the clothes line. I pretended to be a comedian at school while I was being bullied so they could laugh under my control.

From losing people that are close to me, moving away, ending relationships, and even facing death, I have discovered that life waits for no one. Every moment should always be cherished. I have been a public speaker for more than 10 years and recently, someone asked me how can I be so vibrant and bubbly when I approach the stage. The accurate question was, "How can you be so happy?" Then I realized, "Why not?"

Don't allow your past circumstances to prevent you from leaving a legacy of strength, resilience, and hope.

CHAPTER 14

NEW SEASON

This book is not an easy read. I am aware of that. But I want to thank you as a reader for making it this far. There are many others who are like me—caught up in this sort of terrible series of events, and they live through as much or more daily. By knowing my story, you can know theirs; you can believe they exist and understand the tragic idea that this transpires near you, not halfway around the world. As terrible as that is, being close means that if you know about it, you can do something about it. That knowledge has driven me for years. That I can do something. I *must* do something.

When I people say to me like, "I couldn't go through what you did," or "You are so strong to have come out of that," I can't help but think that I don't know what part of me allowed me to survive. As a little girl, I admired superheroes as much as anyone, but I didn't possess the magical powers of Wonder Woman or Supergirl. I may have fantasized about being them, but I never predicted or dreamed about the danger they faced. I would never have wanted to suffer through all I did for the chance to prove myself. In the end, I don't feel like a hero should feel, so I suspect that I am not one. I am simply doing what I can, because I know I must.

Where did my strength come from? It wasn't from anything like a survival book, or a psychology self-help guide. Dialectic Behavioral Therapy gave me the path that led to my sobriety, but what gave me the strength to stay on it? In the end, I can only attribute that to my faith and determination.

I told you at the beginning that this was not a Christian book. Over the past 10 years that I've been writing this memoir, I have come to terms that this book is actually a Christian story of triumph. It is my testimony about my faith through which I share my beliefs and what led to my successes. Who says Christian books can't involve violence, sex, and abuse of power? Heck, the Bible has more violence in their pages then I do in mine!

I had my moments in which my faith was severely challenged, and at times when it set me free. As I enter into the next stage of my life and the new challenges that await me, I realize that this is how I am still able to still smile, even when people anger, test, or betray me. Everyone needs something to lean on other than ourselves when going through a crisis, traumatic experiences, or facing our own demons. We can't handle the world on our own.

For me, being a believer in Jesus Christ and His Father is what I chose, but there are other paths. Buddhism, Yoga... who am I to know or judge? But I would encourage anyone to explore and find what speaks to them. For me, I was raised Catholic and have experienced other faith-based denominations. I have found reason to feel gratitude for all of it, as my religious beliefs continue to protect and strengthen me.

A pastor I met long ago surprised me when he said it was okay to be angry with God: to yell at him and storm at him. God can take it. His mercy and forgiveness are infinite, after all. I went through my fights with Him, and now I can't stop being amazed at how my life has transformed, and how positive I can still be.

Filled with a sense of purpose, I wrote this personal experience. Not to hurt or exploit anyone in this book, but to speak to those who are feeling lost and in despair. Perhaps even, to speak to those who wonder if these troubles really exist, and wonder what they can do about it. I want these people to know they are not alone. I don't know how to write a "How-to guide," but I can share what I have learned from the mistakes I've made.

My healing is far from over, but it is a continuum. My family is a large part of that pattern of life. I have two beautiful children who have become amazing adults, now living their own lives.

My father passed after battling with cancer for eight years. He died a week before Christmas in 2013 and the holidays haven't been the same. My siblings all live in Texas. We are within driving distance from one another. One of my younger siblings moved in with my mother, so she wouldn't be alone.

My relationship with my mother is perhaps the most complicated part of my story. How can I explain how I feel about her? How could I hope to make anyone understand us after all we have been through? Only recently, I was challenged to figure it out myself.

My mother had the opportunity to return to Korea without my father. Of course, my sisters and I were extremely anxious about her safety. I heard my mother would be visiting Korea without any of her family; she'd be traveling with one of her friends. It fell on me to organize her trip.

I spent most of my time finding travel accommodations and things she would need during her trip. Why did I work so hard to see her safely taken care of after all the pain she caused me? With my father gone, the feeling only intensified. I admit, the thought of losing my mom scared me more than when I lost my dad. How was that possible? But there it was—truth staring me right in the face. As my sisters and I took my mother out for a Sushi Buffet as our one last meal before she flew out, the thought of not being able to reach my mother anytime I wanted brought me to tears.

So, have we reconciled? How does one define reconciliation? For me, it was about letting go and setting boundaries. It's like living with an addict in the family. You still love them but have to ensure they can't hurt you. At the same time, you have to be cautious about hurting them. My mother was capable of finding my triggers even when she didn't mean it. We are closer now, but not as close as I wish we could be. We still have a lot of healing to do, so much so that it might not even be possible to fully recover. But we have found a balance, and that is all I can do for now.

Why am I sharing this? Because family can be as powerful as religion in helping you survive and go on to live a real life. I mentioned how complicated my relationship is with God. Well, the connection to my mother is no less. When I was in the middle of my journey from homelessness, being on the street in another state, or even during the times I was trafficked or going through the agony of survival, the memory of her was there. Warm thoughts of her filled me.

I remember one time I was homeless and I was sleeping on a bench at a cemetery and I thought I heard my mom's voice, so soft and endearing. "Song ja, it's time to eat. It's your favorite, mixed cold noodles with eggs." I would remember that, and my stomach would growl. Whenever I was lonely or scared, I would think of my mom and yearn for her to comfort me. I would imagine her holding me in her arms and singing to me like she used to when I was really young. I have so very few memories like that, but I cherish them and in spite of everything else, how can I let those things go? They helped save me. If I lose her, I will have lost those good things as well.

Yes, she can be difficult. She is in constant concern about my disability. She fears I can't handle the world on my own. My mother prays the rosary faithfully, but always in sadness when she does it while thinking of me. I pray she would have faith that everything will be alright. I wait for that day. I want it. That hope gives me strength. The lesson I take from it, and offer to you: There is value even in the difficult relationships, especially in the family.

We need every weapon at our disposal, and what a powerful weapon a mother's love can be! That is worth fighting for. Even when it seems lost, even when the relationship seems forever damaged, it can save your life. There is power there that never fades. I don't view my mother as a monster, rather I see her as troubled, lost and lonely, but she is still my hero.

So, what then is my path going forward? I can truly say that I have hope for this new season of my life that I can share with you. Embracing my faith and safeguarding the family and friendships that continue to give me strength.

It is amazing to me all that has been possible. I remember that my ambitions earlier in life involved being a singer, working in law enforcement, and finding justice for children by being a lawyer. That was my passion. Perhaps, I will never be a singer, but I can write beautiful, thought-provoking poems. I also assist young talent in finding their potential by giving them opportunities they might not have had otherwise.

Being a manager to amazing new artists is like being a singer to me. I may not work in law enforcement, but I work alongside with cops, FBI agents, and attorneys who have a passion for real justice. I give them insight into my own experiences, assist them with various cases, and even provide free workshops to those who are interested in learning from a survivor's point of view. I may not be an attorney fighting justice through court procedures, but having the opportunity to work alongside attorneys for seven years in Minnesota, I've learned much about Criminal, Family and Domestic Violence Law. Through my experience, I also assist victims or my friends in finding the right attorney for their cases so that they can receive the justice they need. I have found my way.

Last, but not least, I have my own family. Whatever I might feel about my mother, I have been blessed to have the chance to bring a boy and a girl into this world, even though I only got to parent one of them. Even that adoption has given me perspective when helping others facing that difficult decision of abortion or adoption. These decisions impact both the unborn child and also the mother who is carrying the fetus. Anyone who thinks it is simple has never experienced it themselves.

I would love to meet my daughter and try to explain that to her. To let her know that bringing her into the world was an effort of love, and that trying to give her a home that would love her as much as I was also that act of love. I believe that, and I will cherish that knowledge until the day I can hopefully share it with her. Until then, I will love and raise my son, and try to give him a life with love he will never have cause to doubt.

I'm slowly growing and that's okay. I don't have to be perfect. As the saying from Narcotics Anonymous puts it, "Easy does it."

I've embraced my imperfections. My next agenda is to write a workbook for Christian survivors. That book will feature more of my faith. For now, the journey for this chapter has come to an end. I hope you have not only empathized with the hurt and pain from my personal experiences, but also have hope that a future is possible. Reconciliation is possible. Healing is possible. Set boundaries, find your inspiration, and most of all—never be afraid to find your true purpose.

Undefeated

Bound by restraints, you thrashed me to shame.
Down on my knees, I had forgotten my name.
My blood was spilled on the damp dark floor,
You perused my body and made me your whore.
My existence suppressed; you controlled me through fear,
Imprisoned underground, where no one could hear.
Precious freedom appeared far away;
Caged like an animal, enslaved every day.
Favored by destiny I finally escaped:
A pursued fugitive, beaten and raped.
Ten years have passed now, I stand proud and tall,
The healing was painful, no intervention at all.
Because of my plight, I learned to stay strong,
The survivor within became my true song.
Recanting my life, I look back on your face,
You tried to break me in guilt and disgrace.
Your still small voice pierced the inflicted silence,
I shattered your bonds through faith and defiance.
Presuming my identity was crushed and deleted,
I triumphed your arrogance, I'm now undefeated.

November 17, 2005

Copyright © Chong N. Kim, aka: Song, 2005

83244511R00139

Made in the USA
Middletown, DE
09 August 2018